THE LAURELS
AND THE TIARA

THE LAURELS
AND THE TIARA

Pope Pius II 1458–1464

R. J. MITCHELL

DOUBLEDAY & COMPANY, INC.

GARDEN CITY, NEW YORK

Nihil obstat: James A. Reynolds, Ph.D.
Censor Deputatus

Imprimatur: ✠ Francis Cardinal Spellman
Archbishop of New York

February 20, 1963

The nihil obstat and imprimatur are official decla-
rations that a book or pamphlet is free of doctrinal
or moral error. No implication is contained therein
that those who have granted the nihil obstat and
imprimatur agree with the contents, opinions or
statements expressed.

TO FLORA GRIERSON

FOREWORD

Without the generous help given me by the Leverhulme Foundation, the Pilgrim Trust, and the British Federation of University
women, that made possible prolonged study in Italian libraries and
archives, it would have been impossible to write this book. My
warmest gratitude is due to all these institutions. The idea of this
biography is to present Aeneas Sylvius as a person rather than to
harp upon political activities that have already been exhaustively
described by Voigt, Weiss, and Pastor. The notes are sparse, full
references being given only in the first instance; it may be necessary
to refer to the bibliography for exact references concerning sources.
An introductory chapter is included for readers who are not particularly familiar with the background: otherwise the material is
drawn mainly from the writings of Aeneas himself and of his friends
and contemporaries.

I owe a great debt to Miss Flora Grierson, who has translated a
number of these writings, above all for her generosity in allowing
me full use of her unpublished translation of the *Commentaries*.*
Thanks are due also to the Marchesa Iris Origo for her sympathy
and help, to Canon Aldo Franci of Pienza who generously offered
me his notes on chronology and other matters, to Dr R. Hunt and
Professor Roberto Weiss for constant help and encouragement, to
Mr Esmond de Beer, and to Dom Aelred Watkin, o.s.b., and Mr
John Hale of Jesus College, Oxford, who both read the book in
manuscript and gave most valuable advice and criticism. I also wish
to thank Dr Elisabeth Pellegrin of Paris, Cavaliere Luigi d'Aurizio
of Bologna, the Direttore of the R. Biblioteca Palatina at Parma,
and all the officials of the Bodleian and other libraries in England
and Italy who have helped me to find material for the text. And I

* Now deposited in the Bodleian Library at Oxford. See Bibliographies.

must acknowledge with gratitude the inspiration of the late Dr C. M. Ady, my tutor and friend, who first kindled my enthusiasm and whose book on Pius II was the starting point of my studies.

Lyme Regis, 1962

CONTENTS

INTRODUCTION

Now that his *Commentaries* have become available in their entirety it seems that the time has come to make a fresh appraisal of the career and personality of this rightly famous Pope, taking into account the other new material that has become available in the last forty years. Certain of his works have been printed for the first time, there has been careful study of his buildings in Pienza, contemporary records and letters have thrown light on obscure questions and have corroborated many of his remarks. Above all, a new and more realistic approach has been made to the problems of Renaissance study. A fresh examination of the sources has led to some modifications of the nineteenth-century opinion of Aeneas as man and as Pope; in both England and Italy he is now seen as an individual and no longer as a type, a figurehead, or a target for vituperation.

The sequence of events in Italy and in Europe during the first half of the fifteenth century is as elaborate and complicated as the design of a Persian carpet. Although the idea of this biography is to present Aeneas Sylvius Piccolomini primarily as a person, in order to understand the significance of his career it is necessary to try to trace some of the main threads running through the pattern.

Those who are familiar with this period will not need to be reminded that the early years of the century saw a great transformation in the social scene, with the metamorphosis of the old feudal régime into a new society governed by capital and highly conscious of the arts of diplomacy and military skill.[1] This is particularly easy to discern in Italy, where new families rose to power almost overnight and assumed control of the towns or cities where their fortunes had been made. The great fascination of the history of this era is its sparkling kaleidoscopic quality. The new rulers might come from the ranks of the gentry, winning themselves power and position by their military technique. On the other hand, they could be merchants or bankers who had reached prominence by their business acumen, or indeed they might rise from almost any rank of society. Their origins mattered very little so long as they had the personal qualities to hold the position they had won—some ruled by sheer strength of character, some through the affection and respect of their fellow citizens, some by brute force, a few through the terror they inspired. Not only was it an age of political and economic change and ferment, it was also a time of great achievements in literature and the arts, of violence and unnatural crime, of zealous reformers like St Bernardino, of bloodshed and of elegance. Black and white, vice and virtue, were placed in startling juxtaposition: at no time was the effect one of greyness or uniformity.

At the beginning of the fifteenth century the death in 1402 of the Lord of Milan, Gian Galeazzo Visconti, had thrown northern Italy into confusion that had repercussions spreading not only to the south but also northwards across the Alps. Fifty-two years later the position was stabilized by the Peace of Lodi. This gave a respite of several decades, when the principal city states were able to turn their attention away from private warfare to their own affairs at home, to commerce and communications abroad, and to the heightened civilization that this made possible. Between these two dates lay half a century of strife and bickering, of shifting loyalties and mutations of allegiance. Feuds between families were transformed by marriages into brittle alliance, quarrels flared up and as quickly died away; reconciliations were as ephemeral as the disputes that gave rise to them. The lesser towns lived in constant terror of absorption by their powerful neighbours: often this led to political intrigue and sometimes to savage faction fighting within the city walls. It was an uneasy time; to be fully aware of the political position at any given date needed diplomacy and flair that amounted almost to witchcraft. Miniature wars raged intermittently, although more often as demonstrations or manoeuvres than as a systematic extension of frontiers, such as the determined encroachments by Venice into Milanese territory that had so alarmed her neighbours in the first decades of the century.

Filippo Maria, the younger son of Gian Galeazzo Visconti, gradually gathered together the Milanese dominions that had fallen apart in the 'free-for-all' struggle that had followed his father's death. With patient cunning he bided his time until the insane cruelty and debauchery of his elder brother had provoked his assassination.

Filippo Maria was then able to exchange his patrimony of Pavia for the Lordship of Milan and, by marrying the widow of one of his father's generals*, to restore to his dominion a number of cities that had been lost to this soldier of fortune. Gradually he restored the frontier line, but when Filippo Maria died in 1447 without leaving a male heir the Visconti rule ended and again there came a crisis in Milanese affairs. This time, however, the Lordship passed with scarcely a struggle to Francesco Sforza—ablest of generals and one of the most notable characters of early Renaissance Italy. He had already secured something of a claim if not a title to the succession by marrying Filippo Maria's illegitimate daughter Bianca. At the time of the Duke's death Sforza was actually intriguing with Milan's enemies, Venice and Florence—although he was still in Milanese service—to renew the war. In the face of such a threat the Milanese were forced to rely upon Sforza for their defence. With the utmost skill and smoothness Sforza brought his army into the city; although they had hopefully declared a Republic, before they realized what was afoot, the Milanese were compelled to recognize the general as their new Duke. This was an act of treachery that did in fact bring Milan a good and stable government, for Francesco Sforza (he was acknowledged Duke in 1450 and died in 1466) proved an excellent ruler throughout the sixteen years he was in power. In one of the most charming of his pen portraits Aeneas Sylvius described Sforza after ten years of his reign had passed[2]. '. . . he rode his horse like a young man. Tall of stature, most dignified of body, and of a serious expression, his speech was gentle, his conversation kindly, and all his manners worthy of a prince. He seemed to be the one man of our age whom fortune loved, for he excelled in gifts of mind and body, was unconquered in war, rose to a throne from lowly rank, married a wife distinguished by beauty, birth and virtue, by whom he had very lovely offspring[3]. He rarely suffered from bad health and obtained everything on which he set his heart . . . All judged him worthy of his power.' That Sforza had gained his Dukedom by force and cunning counted for little to Aeneas Sylvius and his contemporaries: that he was successful and magnanimous seemed adequate reason for their praise.

---

* Facino Cane. The widow was twenty years older than Filippo Maria; after his position was secure he did not hesitate to rid himself of her.

While Milan was settling down under this firm and capable administration, Venice began to realize that it was not in her true interest to commit herself too deeply as a land power. Her most valuable qualities were commercial and maritime, therefore—as in past centuries—she concentrated her attention on the problem of her Levantine trade. It was useful to have a certain hold upon the mainland and to control at least some of the passes across the Alps, but her main concern was with her trading stations on the shores of the Adriatic and the eastern Mediterranean. When Constantinople was sacked by the Turks in 1453, under their brilliant leader Mahomet II, Venice rightly feared that her trade would be disrupted. The Venetian galleys, officered by members of her most patrician families, could take as much as two hundred tons of merchandise below deck[4]; they carried their precious cargoes of silk and spices to Flanders and to London as well as to nearer Mediterranean ports. The ships were specially built for each purpose, from the long low vessels bound for Constantinople or Alexandria to the 'great galleys' that could make the voyage from Southampton to Otranto in thirty-one days[5]. The Republic of Venice was proud, secretive, and self-centred. The Venetians had no wish for close relationship with other Italian states; although their dominion over subject territories was comparatively benign.

From time to time during the lifetime of Filippo Maria Visconti Venice sought an alliance with Florence against Milan. This was in many ways an unnatural union, for the states had practically nothing in common beyond their antipathy to their powerful neighbour. Florence like Venice was a commercial centre, but her prosperity was built less upon overseas trade than upon banking interests and the work of her own skilled craftsmen. It is worth noting that when a Venetian noble was rich enough to build himself a house in which to spend his declining years, he chose a villa with a garden sloping down to the river Brenta, or on the outskirts of Padua, on the far side of the lagoon, whereas leading Florentines rejected country houses in expensive suburbs in favour of town houses close to their business premises or even continued to live over their shops. It would be hard to over-emphasize the importance of the piazza and market-place as social centres for the exchange of gossip and ideas. As Professor Hay has pointed out[6], it was not the castle on the hill-top that was the nucleus of political life, but the open spaces in the towns where citizens forgathered for business and pleasure.

In the general confusion that followed Gian Galeazzo's death in 1402 Florence had successfully snatched the city of Pisa, situated at the mouth of her own river, the Arno, and some years later she was able to secure a second port—this time by purchase from Genoa, Venice's ancient rival. Pisa did not finally surrender until 1406. Livorno was bought in 1421. These possessions greatly strengthened the position of Florence territorially and commercially, but the Florentines' passion for democratic equality led them to evolve a system of government so complicated and rickety that it was only one step removed from chaos. In actual fact Florence was ruled by a close oligarchy that manipulated the constitution while acquiescing in the system of appointment to offices by lot. First the Albizzi family and then the Medici dominated the city without ever adopting a despot's title: with the banishment of Cosimo dei Medici to Padua in 1433 it seemed that the Albizzi had triumphed, but within a year Cosimo had returned to Florence and his rivals had been driven out. For more than thirty years Cosimo dei Medici was first citizen in Florence; his power was the stronger because he wielded it so unobtrusively. When he died, in 1464, his son and then his more famous grandson—Lorenzo 'the Magnificent'—succeeded to his position without disturbing the prejudices of the Florentines or seriously rousing their resentment.

Although Florence had a strong claim to be considered the intellectual centre of the world of scholarship, as well as the chief arbiter of taste, she never at this time was the home of a university in the ordinary sense. Her citizens studied at Pisa and took their degrees there, just as the Milanese did at Pavia and the Venetians at Padua. It is remarkable that none of these capitals was genuinely a university city, and with them at this time must be ranked Naples and even Rome. The most famous of all Italian universities was Bologna which, in spite of its size and relative importance, at this time was no more than a second-rate power in Italian politics. It must be noted, however, that 'university' is one of those words that have changed their meaning since medieval times; if it is taken to cover the whole body of professors, doctors and scholars together with their officials and specially appointed booksellers, it is better to render it as 'Studio'[7]. This is the term employed throughout this book to signify 'university' in its broadest modern sense. The word *universitas* really meant no more than 'guild' or 'body': thus 'the Jurist university' referred only to the faculty of Law, and even the students divided themselves into the two 'universities' of foreigners (*ultramontanes*) and southerners (*citramontanes*), each organized under its own Rector. Something of the working of this system will be seen in Chapter II, where the Studio of Siena is under consideration.

The tangled affairs of southern Italy, where the French house of Anjou contended with the kings of Aragon for the kingship of Naples and Sicily, were closely interwoven with papal policy: the capricious support of successive Popes could mean the difference between failure and success. When Queen Joanna II died without direct heirs in 1435 civil war was inevitable. She herself had preferred Alfonso of Aragon (who had been King of Sicily since 1409) to her distant kinsman Louis of Anjou and had adopted him as her heir, but just before her death she made a fresh will bequeathing Naples to Louis's younger brother, René of Provence. At first René, having secured the Pope's* favour and flushed with victory by a naval battle fought on his behalf by the Genoese fleet, seemed likely to succeed. Before long, however, the astute diplomacy of Alfonso had won him the backing of Filippo Maria Visconti; with the strength of Milan behind him the scales tipped in Alfonso's favour, though he was not formally recognized as King till 1442. From then until his death in 1458, the year Aeneas Sylvius was elected to the Papacy, Alfonso ruled admirably and made his court a centre of learning and culture; Aeneas greatly enjoyed the time he spent there as an envoy and his references to Alfonso in the *Commentaries* are for the most part highly appreciative.

A great opportunity came for René of Anjou to claim the Kingdom of Naples on Alfonso's death, and he was not slow to recognize it. The only heir was an illegitimate son named Ferrante who had incurred the enmity of the first Borgia Pope, Calixtus III. This Pope only outlived Alfonso by a few months, but he spent the time in strong efforts to prevent Ferrante's accession, for, being himself a Spaniard, he wanted to find lands in the south for his three nephews—two of whom he had already created Cardinal. They were sons

---

* Pope Eugenius IV. He later transferred his support to Alfonso.

of one Lenzuoli who had married the Pope's sister; they took the family name of their mother. The most famous was Rodrigo Borgia, who afterwards (in 1492) became Pope as Alexander VI. When Aeneas Sylvius succeeded Calixtus III, as Pope Pius II, he promptly reversed his policy; in so doing he made an enemy of the King of France who naturally supported René, his kinsman. By his recognition of Ferrante—who did, in fact, have the better claim—the new Pope made a good friend, but the strained relations between France and the Papacy resulted in a resentful coolness when Pius sought French help to provide men and munitions for his crusade.

The beginning of the fifteenth century had seen the Papacy at a very low ebb. During the 'Babylonish Captivity' the Pope had resided at Avignon, leaving Rome to be administered by petty officials, scheming clerics, or adventurous soldiers of fortune like Braccio da Montone—all intent upon self-interest. Even deeper degradation came with the Schism when a miscellany of rival Popes fulminated against one another for forty turbulent years. At last the scandal became so great that the whole Church was over-shadowed by this monstrous heresy; the idea of calling a General Council to discuss these matters began to be widely canvassed and to gain the support of intellectual leaders.

The incidence of schism, with Popes and anti-popes thundering or shrilling execrations at one another, was by no means new. From time to time during the dark and middle ages there had been rival popes just as there had been rival emperors, but it was not till the third quarter of the fourteenth century and the first half of the fifteenth that Christians were outraged and shamed by the spectacle of a profusion of anti-popes created by the stroke of a pen. Nor was it edifying that such unworthy candidates should be chosen—men who at best were careerists and at worst unprincipled adventurers. The position rapidly became as ludicrous as it was deplorable.

The first, rather tentative, council met at Pisa and dissolved without coming to any conclusion beyond creating three claimants by deposing the two rivals and electing their own (singularly unsuitable) candidate where before there had been two. The German Sigismund* then put himself at the head of the reforming movement

* He was afterwards crowned Emperor (1433) in Rome. At this time his title was King of the Romans.

and, largely through his ambition and initiative, a Council was summoned to meet at Constance on 1st November 1414. The two main problems for discussion were different aspects of the same malady. The restoration of unity had to come first, then there was the matter of reform. The important question of the Hussite movement in Bohemia, the arguments put before the Council and the condemnation of John Hus also had far-reaching effects but these were yet to be discerned. The immediate issue was the ending of the Schism and, as the Council dragged on through four tedious years, this was brought to a head by the death of one and the flight of another of the three rival claimants: 'Gregory XII' died and 'John XXIII' (more distinguished for military ability than for piety) only outlived him by a few months, after escaping from Constance disguised as a groom. Only 'Benedict XIII' remained, but he had already been deposed by the Council of Pisa and was practically powerless. Just four years after it had first met, the Council of Constance elected a new Pope, who took the name of Martin V and exercised his authority by dissolving the Council that had given him his position. At first the Pope resided in Florence, but as soon as he was able to do so he brought the Curia back to Rome and began to rebuild the power and the position of the Papacy.

It was so huge a task that it is not surprising Pope Martin V found it difficult and daunting. Shortly before he died he was obliged to summon a further Council—this time at Basel. During the early spring of 1431 delegates were making their way thither from all the countries of Europe. The Council of Basel became something of a rhetorical sounding board; it was here that the young Aeneas Sylvius made his mark as a notable orator. He was then a layman: after he took Holy Orders and finally was elected Pope his whole attitude changed so that he became the Council's bitterest opponent. In these early years however, before the Conciliar movement had lost its impetus, it seemed to him the best hope of very necessary reform.

Pope Eugenius IV (1431–1447) had been unanimously elected to succeed Martin V, but his was a difficult and troubled reign. It was his successor, Nicholas V, who tried to identify the Papacy with the new intellectual movement and who made a bold effort to lift it to higher authority and prestige. Nicholas V, as Tommaso Parentucelli, had been a colleague of Aeneas Sylvius when they were both members of the household of Cardinal Albergati. He was a scholar of an austere type; as long as he concerned himself with the collection and arrangement of rare manuscripts for the Vatican library, that he founded with such loving care, all was well. Like Achille Ratti (Pope Pius XI) in this century he was a born librarian, but unlike the latter he could not adjust himself to the needs and policies of his time. His biographer Vespasiano da Bisticci said of him that he brought 'some fresh improvement into his government every day of his reign', but also that he spoke of himself as 'wretched and unhappy' although most people looked on him as the most fortunate Pope that there had been for many years[8].

There was a subtle danger in the too close identification of the Papacy with the mood of the Renaissance. The spirit of criticism was, in fact, a two-edged weapon that could as well wound as protect. Recognition of this fact may have been at the root of Nicholas's despondency; in Pius II it stimulated a desire to give the Papacy a positive and militant policy. This found clear expression in his plans for the crusade. Doubts have sometimes been cast upon the sincerity of his project, but there is strong evidence that Aeneas Sylvius from an early age was interested in repelling the Turkish advance and that the fall of Constantinople crystallized his resolve to do everything that lay in his power to recover that city for Christendom. It will be seen that Aeneas grew from an intelligent boy into an ambitious youth who won fame—if not fortune—by fluency in speech and writing. Finally, his shrewd and successful diplomacy led the Cardinals to see in him a worthy successor to the Papacy; they elected him Supreme Pontiff at a time of particular stress and crisis.

Through all his disappointment and adversity, whether these were brought by poverty, bodily suffering, or ill fortune, Aeneas Sylvius retained his humour and his love of beauty, and that most characteristic of all his qualities, his lively curiosity. This brief sketch of the background of the Italy of his time must necessarily be oversimplified, but the fact that the book is broken abruptly into two halves should serve to emphasize the difference between the secular world of Aeneas Sylvius and that other into which he passed when he ascended the Papal throne. Like Thomas Becket who, three centuries earlier, had bridged this gulf between layman and cleric and yet remained essentially the same person, Aeneas became a deeper and stronger character without losing any of his individual traits. To himself he murmured the words 'Reject Aeneas, accept Pius,'[9] but there is no inconsistency between the two parts of his life: each of them he lived to the full and it would be as foolish to believe that Aeneas changed fundamentally in character on becoming Pope as to deny that the human contacts and passions of his younger days helped his deep understanding of human frailty. To the end of his life, clouded as it was by bitter grief, he never lost his sense of proportion nor his appreciation of the arts and of the beauty of all living things. Yet to say that he was a connoisseur of the pleasures of life does not mean that he lacked spirituality. Some of his admirers have lately claimed Pius II as the greatest of all the Renaissance Popes[10]: perhaps the pendulum has swung back rather too far from the denigration of his character by nineteenth-century historians, for most students of the period would think that he fell short of the statesmanship and majesty of Julius II. Nor could he be compared either as patron or scholar with Nicholas V. Even his zeal for the crusade was no greater than that of Calixtus III, who not only raised money by the sale of works of art laboriously collected by his predecessor, but actually pawned his mitre to secure funds for this project[11]. Nevertheless Pius II was indeed a great churchman and a true Christian: he was also a man of singular resolution and courage. Of one thing there can be no doubt at all: he was easily the most delightful conversationalist of his time and the most amusing of its writers.

PART ONE

AENEAS SYLVIUS
1405–1458

CHAPTER I

The Piccolomini

. . . the Pope went to Corsignano. A lofty hill rises out of the valley of the River Orcia, and on its summit there is a plain one mile long and much narrower. At the corner of this plain that faces the rising sun in winter the town is situated, a place of small repute but with a healthy atmosphere and the best of wine and everything that appertains to nourishment . . . The best part of this town once belonged to the Piccolomini, and Pius's father Silvius had here his ancestral possessions. Here Pius was born, and here he spent his early boyhood. – AENEAS SYLVIUS PICCOLOMINI, *Commentaries*

In the Tuscan village of Corsignano, at the first light of dawn on St Luke's Day, October 18th in the year 1405, a son was born to Vittoria, the wife of Silvius Posthumus Piccolomini. There was nothing to suggest that the fortunes of this infant would differ greatly from those of his seventeen brothers and sisters—except the vision that had vexed and troubled his mother when she was pregnant. Vittoria dreamed most vividly that she brought forth a boy with a mitre on his head, a symbol that filled her mind with a deep misgiving. It did not occur to her that this might foretell the great honour that would come to her child; in her practical way she thought only of the shame and misery associated with the 'pena della Mitre'. This was part of the punishment inflicted on felonious clerics: while they suffered torture or execution they were made to wear a paper mitre on their heads and the emblem thus became associated with pain, degradation, and infamy. Sometimes the felon was paraded through the city, mounted on an ass and wearing the mitre on his head, so that he excited contempt and ridicule. The word 'miterino', meaning 'worthy of being mitred', was coined as an abusive term[1] and applied to those whose misdeeds were particularly shameful. Just fifty years earlier the podestà of Siena had ordered one Giovanni dell'Acqua to be beheaded 'colla mitara in capo'—the mitre set derisively on his head before execution[2]—and it is not impossible that eye-witnesses had described the event to Vittoria in her childhood. Such devices as the mitre were used quite commonly to heighten the mortification of a sinner: when one famous humanist, Galeotto Marzio da Narni, had to make public recantation of his heresy on the Piazza at Venice he was obliged to do so sporting a crown of paper devils on his head. The mitre, then, was a very sinister emblem; the terror and misgiving suffered by Vittoria is easily understood. According to Battista Platina, the papal historian, she was never able to conquer her fear until news came that her son had been made Bishop of Trieste. Then, at last, she was able to accept a more cheerful interpretation of her dream, although she could hardly have foreseen that the Bishop's mitre would one day be exchanged for the triple tiara of the Papacy.

Vittoria died while her son was still Bishop of Siena—having been translated there from Trieste—so she never saw Aeneas's final triumph. She outlived her husband by four years; she was buried where she died, at Crevola in Sienese territory, while Silvio's simple tomb was in Corsignano. After he became Pope, Aeneas had his parents' bones reinterred at St Francesco in Siena; he composed for them a Latin epitaph* that was inscribed upon the white marble of their tomb.

Although during the opening years of the fifteenth century the Piccolomini lived in great poverty in the village of Corsignano, only two generations earlier the family had been wealthy and important. Probably, as Aeneas himself claimed, they came to Siena originally from Rome, but this is far from certain. By the thirteenth century the Piccolomini had become one of the leading families in Siena, their estate at Corsignano being only one among the family properties. As soldiers the Piccolomini had a fine record in defence

---

* 'Silvius hic iaceo: coniunx Victoria mecum est;
   Filius hoc clausit marmore Papa Pius.'

This may be rendered:

'Here lie I Silvio with my wife Vittoria;
   Our son Pope Pius enclosed us in this marble.'

of their city; in peace-time they traded there as merchants and shared in her prosperity. Like other noble families they took part in government of the city as long as they were allowed to do so. When, however, the Sienese drove out the nobles in 1385 the Piccolomini not only lost their property in the city but wasted most of what resources they had left in futile skirmishing. Soon, their wide possessions round the city had dwindled to one estate; Enea Silvio was obliged to retire southwards to Corsignano where he still owned lands and the remains of the castle that had dominated the village in earlier times. He died while still a young man and his child Silvio was born posthumously. Silvio, or Silvius Posthumus Piccolomini, was educated and brought up traditionally as though a noble inheritance still awaited him. He was sent to the court of Gian Galeazzo Visconti, Duke of Milan, where he learned something of letters and much of knightly conduct and elegant manners. It would have been more useful to him to have studied agriculture, for when he came of age and gathered together the tattered shreds of his fortune he found the only course open to him was to retire to Corsignano, to do his best there to lead a modest honourable life tending his own vines and olives and bringing up his family as best he might.

Had Silvio married a country girl, born and bred to thrifty ways and accustomed to long hours of manual work, it would have been to his material good and the family might have lived more comfortably. His bride, however, belonged to a family as aristocratic as his own. Vittoria Fortiguerri was nobly born, a woman of great refinement and sensibility, and she came from a family as suddenly and disastrously poor as were the Piccolomini[3]. Vittoria was brave and spirited, but the situation was too much for her; soon she was engulfed in the bearing and rearing of sickly children. On several occasions she had to cope with twins[4]. Of the eighteen children born to this couple at Corsignano there were never more than ten alive at the same time, and in the end only one boy and two girls survived. This boy was the child whose birth had caused his mother such foreboding. As soon as he was born it was decided that he should be named after his grandfather and that the name of Bartholomew should be added in honour of the apostle to whom his parents had a great devotion. Aeneas Sylvius was carried therefore down the steep hillside by stony paths to the gaunt little church outside the walls. This was the Pieve of SS. Vito and Modesto, stark and austere, with no treasures beyond a very moving fourteenth-century carved wood crucifix, and the rough stone font in which two Popes were baptized*.

There was plenty of companionship for Aeneas as a boy; he played with all the 'bimbi' of the neighbourhood as well as with his own large family. Laudomia and Caterina were the two sisters to whom he was always greatly attached; when they grew up and married Aeneas extended his strong affection to their husbands and children. After a man has reached great fame and dignity there are always those who can repeat anecdotes of childhood days that foretell his bright future. Aeneas was no exception. His biographer Campano describes his games with the children of Corsignano, how they chose him for their leader and rendered homage, crowning him Pope and prostrating themselves before him to kiss his toe.[5] An authentic account of his early life is given by Aeneas in the early pages of his *Commentaries*, but he makes no mention of any such activities. He is more concerned with two nearly fatal accidents that punctuated his childhood. At three years old Aeneas had the misfortune to fall from a high wall down the rocky hillside, hitting his head and sustaining a very severe wound. Aeneas afterwards maintained that he owed his life entirely to the skill and devotion of his godfather, Niccolò Monticuli, who came swiftly to his help. Niccolò was no academically trained doctor, indeed he had no medical qualifications at all, but for many years he had used his natural wisdom and skill to help his fellow villagers. The people of Corsignano had the utmost faith in his powers. With the resilience of a small boy Aeneas soon recovered, the wound healing without any noticeable scar. For the next five years he lived an uneventful life. At eight years old, however, he was tossed by a charging bull: this time he escaped death very narrowly indeed. In his own words, 'it was more by the help of Heaven than through any human aid'[6], but again he made a good recovery.

The harshness and austerity of his upbringing undoubtedly fashioned many of the traits in Aeneas's character. As a child he must often have suffered hunger, and the extremes of cold and heat. All his life he remained an early riser, able to live with little sleep and to keep up his dynamic energy on a very slender diet. He mixed

---

* Popes Pius II and III: Aeneas Sylvius and his nephew Francesco.

easily with men of all conditions, a quality that greatly helped him
in later life. It was clear at a very early age that Aeneas had unusual
mental gifts, so his father Silvio determined to do all that he could
to encourage the boy to study. Pietro, parish priest of the Pieve, was
glad to instruct so apt and willing a pupil; he strove to teach Aeneas
everything he knew. Many years later when Aeneas returned to
Corsignano, in all the glory and dignity of the Papacy, Pietro—now
'vecchio e podagroso'—knelt before the Pope to kiss his feet and recalled with tears of joy their earlier association.

In his anxiety to help the boy, and to fit him for a fuller and freer
life, Silvio recounted to his son all that he remembered of life in the
ducal court at Milan where he himself had learned so many hard
lessons. Perhaps Aeneas owed more to his father's experiences than
is usually supposed. When later he wrote his *epistola de curialium
miseriis*[7] he may well have drawn upon these early impressions as
well as from his own observations at the Imperial court. Aeneas
was extremely quick to recognize the hollowness of courtly life and
the futility of seeking there honour, fame, or power. Even those few
who 'really hope to acquire merit or gain their own souls', he wrote,
are doomed to failure; what then of those whose one thought is the
pursuit of riches? Aeneas's perception would seem to owe as much
to Silvio's personal experience, gained a generation earlier, as to
his own acumen in distinguishing between false and real values.

The grinding poverty of his early years, the frustration of trying
to learn without books or adequate teachers, the exhaustion of out-
door work in difficult country—none of these things daunted Aeneas
or gave him any grudge against life. Instead, he wrote charmingly
of his family circle, he was passionately fond of his native village,
and he retained all his life the strongest affection for his family and
old friends. A quarter of a century after he had left Corsignano
Aeneas returned there on a visit, hoping to pick up the old threads
of friendship and to renew his youthful contacts. 'He hoped to find
some pleasure,' Aeneas said, 'speaking to those with whom he had
been young.' All through these years he had treasured his childhood memories of the village and its people. It was a shock to find
how greatly all was changed . . . 'Most of his contemporaries were
dead, and those who still breathed stayed at home, heavy with years
and sickness. And if any showed themselves their faces were so
changed that they were barely recognizable, drained of their

strength, unsightly, like messengers of death . . . he found that the
sons of those he had left as children were already middle-aged. The
town [however] was marvellously decorated, the people rejoicing
and intensely delighted at the presence of the Pope who they could
boast was born among themselves. They could not look on him nor
welcome him enough.'8

Working with his hands and helping his father to cultivate their
fields and groves gave Aeneas a deep knowledge of the processes of
nature. As he grew in mental stature his love of beauty, style, and
elegance developed until they seemed the ruling passion of his life,
yet he still retained a countryman's love of growing things. In the
end it was the Tuscan countryside—symbolized for him by Monte
Amiata—that gave Aeneas the purest pleasure. From his boyhood
days he had roamed these wolf-haunted slopes, wandering through
glades of asphodel, looking down on the river Orcia as it trickled
over its stony bed in high summer, or rushed in spate when swollen
with the winter snows. As he scrambled up the reddish, shaly cliffs,
he noticed the swallows nesting on ledges of the rocks. Aeneas was
always attracted by birds* and made some interesting notes on the
migratory habits of quails; his account of the legendary battle of the
hawks and the ravens is obviously based on his own observation,
and he was naturalist enough to remark that thrushes have a strong
preference for ilex woods9.

All wild life interested Aeneas; he describes the netting of rabbits on the mountainside, when they cunningly hid in briars so that
the hunters' nets became torn and useless. He writes, too, of the
strawberries growing beneath the chestnut trees, and of the cherries
near the summit of Monte Amiata that were not yet ripe in late July,
so fresh and chilly was the air on this high mountain, the highest
peak in the southern Apennines—some 5,800 feet. Aeneas could appreciate other beauties too; he writes feelingly of the dark shade of
chestnut trees on Monte Cimino, their trunks dappled with flecks
of sunlight, of sombre pines, of the grottoes and cascades at Tivoli,
of the cerulean blue of the flax fields at Viterbo10. These he saw
when he was staying there for his health: 'And almost every day at
early dawn he went out into the country to get the pleasant air be-

---

* Like Dante, Aeneas noted the dipping flight of the swallow and the soaring
of the kite.

fore it grew hot, and to see the green fields and the flax in flower which just then was the colour of the blue sky and filled with great pleasure all who looked at it. Nowhere are there bigger or more numerous fields of flax than at Viterbo. For, whether from the nature of the soil or the water in which the flax is steeped, it is of an excellent quality there and is the chief source of that city's wealth. The Pope explored everything, both meadow and sown land, being carried in a different direction every day.'

Throughout his life Aeneas remained insatiably curious; his mind was always alert and tuned to catch every fleeting impression. His love for exploring the countryside by difficult and dangerous paths often brought more mortification than pleasure to the Cardinals who had to accompany him. No anecdote of Aeneas's travels is more typical than the one he tells himself of an encounter near Santa Fiora, on the southern slope of his beloved mountain. It was a hot day and everyone but the Pope himself was thinking wistfully of Tuscan wines to be drunk reposefully in shady arbours. The party met an ancient cowherd; soon the Pope was talking to him as one country-man to another. The old man offered Aeneas a drink of cow's milk from his own wooden bowl, encrusted as it was with mud and filth, 'for he assumed the heat would have made the Pope thirsty. Pope Pius smiled, remembering him who offered water in his two hands to Artaxerxes, King of the Persians, when he was on the march[11]; and was not too proud to put his lips . . . to the black and greasy bowl.'[12] Aeneas then passed it on to the Cardinals to taste. He valued this gift more highly than the 'precious wines, white loaves, fat lambs . . . and such fruit as was in season' that were set before him that evening in his lodging. He could not forbear, however, to dramatize his action; the allusion to Plutarch, too, is apt and neat. Aeneas's delight in his own courtesy and kindliness is so honest that it disarms criticism: vain he may have been, but never smug. He had, too, the rare gift of feeling perfectly at home in any company, for condescension was as alien to his character as was sycophancy. Few men have ever been so consistently themselves.

CHAPTER II

The Studio of Siena

When he was eighteen years old he [Aeneas] went to Siena . . . here he wholly gave himself up to the study of letters . . . with such diligence that he scarcely allowed himself food or sleep . . . He was up long before dawn, and when he went to bed he took with him his books, lest he should lose any time between waking and sleeping . . . Aeneas had a disciplined mind, as keen as it was versatile. – *Letter of Gregorio Lolli to the Cardinal of Pavia*[1]

As he laboured in his father's fields breaking up the clods of whitish earth into a fine tilth and scratching with his hoe to encourage the growing crops, the mind of Aeneas was full of dreams. He worked, however, with a will and as strenuously as his frail physique allowed. When he was fifteen years old something happened that was to turn the whole course of his life. In the late summer of 1420 the authorities of the Studio of Siena decided to transfer the doctors and scholars from the plague-ridden city to some town or village in the hills where they could carry on their studies in healthier surroundings. This had happened before and would occur many times again, but in this year, for the first and only time, their choice fell upon Corsignano. As soon as arrangements could be made, the cavalcade of doctors and students left Siena, went swinging out of the southern gate, and headed towards the Val d'Orcia.

Nothing more deeply disturbed the normal life of Italian cities than the frequent epidemics of plague that ravaged whole districts and brought normal life practically to a standstill. Nobles retreated to their villas and castles outside the city walls, shopkeepers put up their shutters and went away to stay with relatives or friends. The poorest citizens had to choose between braving the infection

by remaining at home or fleeing in panic to the hills. Special difficulties faced civic authorities in towns where there was a Studio
for, as soon as the pestilence appeared in the city or its environs,
they had to plan not only the well-being of their own citizens but
undertake also the responsibility for all the members of the Studio.
The best plan was to allow them to visit some healthier place where
they could stay until the plague had abated, or until cooler weather
brought relief. Citramontane students whose homes were close at
hand could take a holiday, or do some temporary work elsewhere.
Those from a distance—and of course all the ultramontanes—had to
be found quarters where they could live in safety and if possible
carry on their studies. This could be a major problem and was often
very troublesome to the city fathers. There was the danger, too,
that these migrations might result in the formation of a rival Studio.
In practice this did sometimes happen, although the new foundations generally wilted after a few years and doctors and scholars returned to their old allegiance. Migrations forced upon the Studio
by plague were usually looked upon as a delightful holiday, dis-
rupting to one's studies but an agreeable break in the monotony of
intensive book-work.

The people of Corsignano, secluded as they were in a small agri-
cultural community with few outside interests, were more deeply
affected by the invasion than a more sophisticated township might
have been. As the newcomers approached from the direction of
San Quirico the villagers gathered wondering in the fields while the
doctors and scholars rode by with their servants, and their pack-
horses laden with clothes and household gear, and—strange sight
to the men of Corsignano—bales and chests of books. The visitation was not likely to last for more than a few weeks or months, but
during that time the villagers, as they quickly realized, could hope
to reap a golden harvest. Every room in the village was on offer as a
lodging, and it was obvious that food supplies would bring un-
dreamed-of prices. It was now September and the crops had nearly
all been gathered; in the stony and arid fields pale stubble marked
the scene of the recent harvest. Only the olives still hung darkly on
the trees.

Even today few travellers turn aside from the road to Rome to
pass through this windswept landscape; in the fifteenth century
there were fewer still. The young and fresh-faced students brought

with them a lively enthusiasm that delighted the people of Corsignano. Every villager, and dwellers too in the outlying farms and hamlets, welcomed the visitors. Such excitement was rare indeed. To the peasants there seemed every prospect of securing good payment for their produce without having to drag grain and oil and vegetables to be sold cheaply in distant towns. Here was the food, and here too were a number of hungry men: what could be simpler than to supply their needs? At first these countrymen did not realize that water and food sufficient for their own people could not possibly be stretched to provide also for the newcomers. Difficulties became apparent within a very few days. Scarcely a week after the students' arrival their master Giovanni di Mariano had to write an urgent letter[2] to the Sienese authorities, in which he pointed out the shortage of supplies, and begged that grain might be sent immediately to Corsignano.

Nor was this the only trouble experienced by Giovanni di Mariano. Four days after sending his first letter he had to write to the Signoria again. This time he complained of the behaviour of his charges. They were, he said, dissatisfied and intransigent—especially some Spaniards who suffered from 'troppo superbia'. Many of the students were young boys used to strict supervision; in Corsignano there was little for them to do and their accustomed discipline was completely disorganized. It was only natural for them to complain of their surroundings, to play high-spirited tricks, and to mock and tease the villagers. Some of the Sienese students seem to have behaved so intolerably that Pietro, the village priest, was moved to write a letter of protest[3]. Like di Mariano he objected to the 'proud Spaniards' who had acted, he said, in a most arrogant manner and had caused their servants to ill-treat one of his parishioners.

By this time the weather was growing cooler and the danger from plague had diminished. The Signoria therefore felt justified in recalling the Studio to Siena after a sojourn in Corsignano of about five weeks. A letter dated 9th October suggested that the return might be made within the next week or ten days. The doctors and scholars, however, were enjoying the fresh mountain air and the change of scene. By now they had settled down comfortably in their quarters and had made friends with their hosts: they were far from anxious to leave. They found that the quietness of the countryside was conducive to study; the vintage also was approaching with its attendant festivity. Both lecturers and students were inclined to prefer the pleasures of a country life until the shades and rigours of winter should send them hastening back to the city lights. Their letter to the Signoria is a masterpiece of its kind; its respectful tone is balanced by the insolence of its content. In the politest possible way the students refused categorically to return[4].

In the end the members of the Studio, having made their gesture of defiance, found that enthusiasm for prolonging their stay in Corsignano began to fade as the weather deteriorated. Students and doctors were all back in Siena, and hard at work, long before Christmas. In Corsignano the excitement and the temporary prosperity subsided as this exotic visitation became a memory. To the young Aeneas, however, a new prospect was beginning to appear. The idea of a university career had now taken a firm hold upon his imagination. Perhaps it had always been in his father's mind, when he made such strenuous efforts to help and instruct the boy and to fit him for some life other than a husbandman's. Although Silvio himself had not studied in any Studio, there was a tradition of academic learning in his family, for he was related to the famous jurist Paolo da Castro 'who for many years held a chair in Padua and filled all Italy with his judgements'[5]. The parish priest had given Aeneas the rudiments of Latin, though he was not able to ground him in Greek, for in this Pietro—like most of his kind—was completely ignorant. Nor could he lead Aeneas through the works of classical authors because no books were to be found in the vineyards and olive groves of Corsignano. At this time Aeneas had no intention at all of entering Holy Orders; he did not as yet know in what direction his talents would lead him. He meant, however, to learn everything he could of every subject until he should be qualified to make a career, perhaps in medicine or law.

Three years after the students had left his village Aeneas, now eighteen years old, packed his few belongings into a bundle, took leave of his family and friends, and set out for Siena. Poor as he was, Aeneas was in a much better position than many of his fellow students, for arrangements had been made for him to stay with his aunt and uncle in Siena while he studied for his degree. In this way he was saved the expense of hiring lodgings and furniture, a serious problem for students coming from a distance who had no friends or family connections to help them find what they needed. Most students were content to bring with them only their clothes and easily portable belongings—perhaps a skillet for cooking, and whatever books they happened to own. Sometimes it was necessary to secure a licence to bring books into a town where there was a Studio, with its accompaniment of booksellers and copyists ready to sell or hire out the prescribed text-books. In all university towns there was a flourishing second-hand trade in books; there were also *stationarii* or agents ready to supply texts and writing materials. Other dealers offered second-hand furniture; during the fifteenth century there was a tendency for the hostels and colleges to take over this business and pass on or lend for a small charge the essential room-furniture for generations of students. The Englishman John Free wrote miserably from Ferrara to his patron that he had been forced to pawn all his clothes and books and other belongings in order to keep alive[6]: he should have gone to Siena where, in the Collegio della Sapienza, there was a *camerarius* appointed to look after the needs of 'young students' and to provide them with bedding and other *mobili*. A typical inventory is that written out by a foreign student[7] in the latter half of the century. In it he described his couch with its palliasse surmounted by a feather bed, the two feather pillows, the blanket edged and newly lined with white, and a yellow coverlet that had evidently seen better days for he noted that it was 'tristem et cattivum'. At the foot of his bed there stood a chest, a bench, a round stool, and two small cupboards: 'one for bread, the other for his books'.

Life in the Studio might range from great austerity to comparative comfort; to Aeneas his aunt's house must have seemed luxurious compared with his quarters in Corsignano, although in actual fact the Lolli family did live in comparative poverty among the lesser citizens. Bartolomea Lolli was half-sister to Silvio Piccolomini on his mother's side. Her father had been a member of the once-illustrious family of Tolomei who claimed apocryphal descent from the Ptolemies of Egypt; although they were very poor the Tolomei were still held in honour in Siena. Bartolomea's husband was Niccolò Lolli; they had one son named Gregorio, or Goro, who was much the same age as Aeneas and a fellow student. He and Aeneas quickly formed a friendship that was to prove lifelong; from their first meeting they became the closest of companions and in later

years Goro served Aeneas most loyally as his secretary. After Aeneas's death he kept his memory alive, and in a letter written to the
Cardinal of Pavia[8] Goro gave a much fuller account of this phase
of his life than can be gathered from the terse sentences in the *Commentaries*.

Here, Aeneas summarizes his career with the utmost brevity.
'When he had for many years fulfilled various country duties on
his father's farm,' he wrote, '[Aeneas] removed to the city . . . and
began to attend the grammarians. Next he studied eagerly the poets
and orators. Finally he turned to civil law.'[9] Goro Lolli fills out the
picture with some homely details of their daily life. Aeneas at once
showed himself to be ambitious and immensely hard-working. He
recognized that extra effort would be needed to make up his arrears
of reading, so he worked very long hours, denying himself both
food and sleep. Nevertheless he was neither owlish nor a priggish
bookworm, but ready to take his part in picnics or snowballing or
any other activities practised by his fellows. (That he was popular
and greatly respected is clear from the testimony of a fellow student
named Aliotti who described him as the ablest of all the scholars in
the faculty of Civil Law[10].)

Aeneas was customarily at work before daybreak, and when bed-
time came he was still reading as he undressed and made ready
for the night. He used to read in bed, a habit that he never lost, and
Goro recalls that once Aeneas fell asleep over his books and awoke
to find that the little oil lamp had flared up and had set the bedclothes on fire. Fortunately, Goro had not yet gone to bed: he was
talking in his room with some student friends when they heard
Aeneas's anguished cries for help. Rushing to his rescue, between
them all they beat out the flames and found that no great damage
had been done. The adventure ended in laughter and much chaffing
of Aeneas, who took it, said Goro, in excellent part[11].

Although he was highly susceptible to most forms of pleasure,
throughout his life Aeneas was careless and indifferent concerning
food. At a later stage it will be necessary to notice his passion for
picnic and *al fresco* meals, a taste that was not shared by the College of Cardinals. Always he ate and drank most sparingly: when
his interest was deeply engaged he would often forget to eat, and
in his student days he made a practice of forgoing his supper three
evenings a week in order to save money for buying books. This was

the greatest of all his difficulties—as indeed of all poor students: to
secure possession of his texts. At a time when their costliness caused
them to be mentioned in wills on a level with plate and jewels,
books were treasured and treated with reverence. One cannot fail
to note, however, the marginal comments, scribbled verses, and
caricatures that give these ancient text-books a special interest for
posterity. Manuscript copies of legal texts were given marginal
glosses by successive generations of students; these glosses became
almost as important as the text itself and were often incorporated
into later copies. Even second-hand text-books were beyond the
means of such students as Goro and Aeneas, unless they shared
them with several friends. Some young men made their own books;
an Englishman who wanted his own copy of Seneca's *Tragedies*
wrote it out while he was studying at Ferrara under the famous
Guarino da Verona[12], and the same year another English student
found leisure to copy MSS of Sallust's *Catiline* and *Jugurtha*[13]. Time
was very precious to Aeneas; he had to borrow volumes from his
friends and satisfy himself by making notes and extracts. Often he
would sit up all night, copying out long passages, so that he would
not cause inconvenience to the owners of the books by keeping
them too long. From his earliest years he was singularly courteous
and considerate in such ways—a characteristic that partly accounts
for the deep affection and loyalty accorded him by his friends.

Passionately as he worked, however, Aeneas could never quite
make up the groundwork that he lacked. If he had had the opportunity of attending some such school as that of Vittorino da Feltre
in Mantua he might have reached the greatest heights of classical
scholarship. He might, indeed, have been as famous a poet as he
was to become an orator. Brilliant intelligence he had, and taste,
and humour, and a natural gift of style, but for all his appreciation
of the classics Aeneas could not write really pure Latin, and his
knowledge of Greek was never more than superficial. Talent was
there, in abundance: technique was the missing quality.

At the time Aeneas enrolled as a student, the Studio of Siena
had largely emerged from the precarious stage when it was still
uncertain whether it would become a permanent institution. The
schools of Siena had been known since the middle years of the thirteenth century, and had received vague recognition by Pope Inno-
cent IV in 1252. It was not, however, until two successive migrations

there of dissatisfied scholars from Bologna had built up the numbers and the status of students and doctors, that Siena was able to secure a Bull in 1357 that conferred upon the Studio the recognized privileges of a Studium generale[14]. This Bull was obtained not from the Pope but from the Emperor Charles IV, and this perhaps accounts for the peculiar character of its provisions, and also for the very strong German element that persisted for more than a century among the ultramontane students. In assessing the proportion of 'Theutonici' it must, however, be remembered that practically any northern European was likely to be described in this way, and the obituary of San Domenico (where any students from foreign nations who died in the course of their studies were buried) certainly includes Scandinavians, as well as Scots and Englishmen, under this heading[15].

It was not until 1408, little more than a decade before Aeneas and his cousin began their studies, that the Studio of Siena received official recognition—with a further grant of privileges—from Pope Gregory XII. From this time onwards the Studio held a respected position and degrees conferred there gained in value and esteem. It could not, however, be compared with the venerable foundations of Bologna and Pavia, nor with the new and brilliant Ferrara where, almost alone among Italian Studii, the New Learning found a home. The strongest of all the characteristics of the Sienese Studio was its complete dependence upon the City government. The paternal outlook of the civic authorities was shown not only in the control that they exercised over the activities of doctors and scholars, but also in the fact that they chose the professors, paid their stipends, and even leased to them the houses in which they dwelt and taught their pupils[16]. Natives of Siena were not, however, in any privileged position—they were simply classed with other Italians as citramontanes and if they were elected to hold office in the Studio it was by merit of their strength of character or popularity among their fellows.

As Aeneas himself tells us, his earliest studies were of grammar. This was taught him by Antonio da Arezzo. Rhetoric he learned from two masters, Mattia Lupi from San Gimignano and Giovanni da Spoleto[17]. All three were competent teachers and sound scholars, but totally lacking in fire and in that enthusiasm that alone can make pupils give of their best. It was to the great civil and canon lawyer, Mariano Sozzini, that Aeneas had to look for inspiration.

This is interesting because, of all the subjects Aeneas studied, civil law was the one he found most dreary and uncongenial. Mariano Sozzini was, however, far more than a professor of law and the author of technical studies in that subject. He was also a man of great versatility and an ardent humanist. Nearly twenty years after he first met this great man Aeneas wrote a description of him to his friend Kaspar Schlick[18]. Sozzini had every quality and talent that could be desired, Aeneas said, except that he was a little man and so should have belonged to Aeneas's own family, the Piccolomini. (Aeneas had a fondness for puns playing upon his surname.) 'Sometimes the elements of small bodies are the more precious,' he pointed out to Schlick, 'as gems and jewels testify.' Sozzini's great knowledge of law was matched by his eloquence; his skill as a poet in both Latin and the vernacular was rivalled only by his gift for music. 'He is as learned as Plato in philosophy, in geometry he is as wise as Boetius, and in arithmetic he is to be compared with Macrobius.' Aeneas admired too his knowledge of agriculture, his physical skill in athletics and boxing, and above all his delightful conversation and manners. 'If the gods had endowed him with stature and immortality he would himself have been a god.'

The effect of the personality, example, and teaching of Sozzini upon so impressionable a young man as Aeneas was certain to be profound. There existed also a very strong bond of affection between master and student. Aeneas valued Sozzini's judgement and was guided by it in all important affairs; he also enjoyed the ready hospitality shown him by the older man: '. . . my friend is all generosity. His house is ever full of honest company. He is no man's enemy, but protects his pupils, comforts the sick, helps the poor, consoles the widow, nor ever fails the needy . . . In adversity he maintains a brave heart, and no good fortune can puff him up. He has some experience of guile, not in practising but in shunning it. Dear to its towns-folk, beloved by travellers; none hate him, none resent him.' Aeneas ends his letter to Schlick with the words: 'All the time I was in Siena I loved [Sozzini] above all others, and separation from him has in no way lessened my affection.'

One of the qualities that particularly impressed Aeneas was Sozzini's immaculate scholarship, illustrated by the perfection of the handwriting in which he copied manuscripts. He always aimed at the best possible style not only in literature, conversation, and public speaking, but also in such everyday matters as exactitude of dress, the ordering of his household, and not least in physical exercise. He was a man of the world, too, and he balanced his scholarly interests by occupying himself with public affairs and social matters of all kinds. Aeneas found Sozzini witty and delightful and admirable in every way; he took him for his model in the widest possible sense, imitating his sophistication and pursuit of pleasure as well as his deep learning.

Aeneas was influenced also at this impressionable age by a man of a very different kind. This was Bernardino degli Albizzeschi—S. Bernardino—who came to Siena in May 1425, when Aeneas was in his second year of study. An altar and a pulpit were set up for S. Bernardino in the Campo and he preached there in the vernacular to great crowds of townspeople and members of the Studio[19]. Bernardino was himself a Sienese, who had attended the Studio and who had received his friar's habit in the church of S. Francesco in the city.

Sano di Pietro painted a picture of him preaching before this church, the Piazza S. Francesco, filled with men and women listening to the sermon with rapt attention. S. Bernardino knew just how to speak to his fellow townsmen and to play upon their feelings. In recalling the effect that the saint's eloquence had had upon him Aeneas said: 'He could move men to tears in the most marvellous manner; he denounced vices in such a way that he made everyone feel a horror of them, and when he praised virtues he made all men love them.'[20] Aeneas felt an admiration for S. Bernardino that was deep and sincere; indeed, he was so carried away by the saint's eloquence that he seriously considered joining the Franciscan Order. His friends all realized that Aeneas had no vocation for this life, for which he was singularly unfitted both by nature and temperament. With some difficulty they persuaded him that he was being swayed only by his emotions and that the friar's habit would ill become a young humanist with such strong tastes for sensual pleasure. With realistic good sense Aeneas acknowledged that he would indeed make a poor friar, and changed his purpose. He had, however, much deeper religious feeling than has sometimes been supposed[21], and he was greatly troubled by a precept laid down by one of Bernardino's followers: that a man was bound to accomplish a good deal that he had willed. His conscience would not let him rest, and a year or two after Bernardino had left Siena Aeneas walked all the way to Rome to consult him on this matter. After some earnest discussion Aeneas was reassured by the saint and told that his scruples were groundless; he left this interview with his mind at rest and his respect and veneration for S. Bernardino greatly increased[22]. Thereafter he always spoke of Bernardino degli Albizzeschi with deep admiration: in his famous *Letter to Mahomet* written thirty-five years later Aeneas recalled that he had heard the saint preaching 'like a new St Paul'[23].

When Aeneas composed his book *De Viris Illustribus,* brief notices of the great men of his time, he wrote delightful thumbnail studies of S. Bernardino and Mariano Sozzini. They are placed together, between two other teachers who influenced Aeneas's early years[24]; there can be no doubt that association with these notable men had a profound and lasting effect upon Aeneas Sylvius's prospects and career.

CHAPTER III

The Tale of the Two Lovers

Because you have been many times in love, nor yet lack fire, you wish me to weave for you the story of two lovers . . . You will not hear the loves of Troy or Babylon, but of our own city, though, of the lovers, one was born under a northern sky. – AENEAS SYLVIUS PICCOLOMINI: *De Duobus Amantibus,* 1444*

The Tale of the Two Lovers was composed many years after Aeneas had left the Studio of Siena, but it commemorates events that occurred only a year or two after his departure, and the background of student life is obviously drawn from his own experiences. This slight, unedifying, amusing *novella* was written at the suggestion of Mariano Sozzini, as Aeneas pointed out in his dedication. It has been suggested[1], and accepted with far too little consideration, that Sozzini himself was the model for the cuckolded husband of the exquisitely beautiful and desirable heroine, Lucretia. If this were true, it would mean that Aeneas had ridiculed in the basest way and in the worst possible taste the man who had so greatly befriended him and whom he admired beyond all others. The idea seems entirely out of keeping with the nature of Aeneas and his fastidious manners.

It is of course a common mistake to apply present-day standards to an earlier age: many of today's usages would have been rejected with aversion by our forefathers, and the fact that a man was esteemed by his contemporaries as the very flower of chivalry—or of virtue, or of piety—does not necessarily mean that their verdict has been endorsed by posterity[2]. History is full of examples of

* Translated by Flora Grierson, London, 1929.

heroes of their own time whose actions would seem caddish in the twentieth century; Renaissance Italy is particularly rich in instances of liberal-minded thinkers whose behaviour was petty in the extreme. Humanists with great works of scholarship to their credit were moved to denigrate their fellows and attributed to them the basest motives; indeed the greater part of their output consisted of backbiting criticism and invective. This carping attitude meant little more than did the extravagant praises lavished upon patrons who might—or might not—reward the writer with gifts and pensions. No one could compose a more graceful dedication than could Aeneas Sylvius himself, for his flattery was so delicate and so surely phrased that it seemed he was carried away by his own eloquence and convinced by his own arguments. He could also be a stern critic and was easily moved to anger by conceited utterances or vainglorious behaviour. His pen might—and sometimes did—run away with him. Often Aeneas was impetuous and indiscreet but never at any time was he capable of the cold-blooded cynicism implicit in the wounding of an old friend and benefactor. The idea that Aeneas deliberately portrayed Sozzini in his *novella* is, therefore, quite unacceptable. Nor is there any evidence to support it, beyond the fact that Sozzini—after some amorous adventures in his youth—was married to a woman many years younger than himself.

The hero of the book, however, is admittedly a portrait drawn from life. Aeneas intended to please and flatter the Imperial Chancellor Kaspar Schlick by identifying him with Euryalus, who is presented as a gallant and dashing soldier-statesman-courtier from the north. Like Schlick, Euryalus is a close friend of his Emperor, 'like Maecenas with Octavian'. Aeneas describes Euryalus as he rode about the streets of Siena in company with Sigismund. The Emperor himself had an eye for feminine charm and soon espied Lucretia 'displaying herself at an upper window'; he called the attention of Euryalus to this lovely lady. Lucretia had already noticed the handsome German, who 'in beauty as in wealth was well fitted for love', when he first came to Siena with Sigismund. Euryalus was thirty-two years old, 'not tall but of gay and graceful carriage, with bright eyes, cheeks of a pleasant ruddiness and, for his other limbs, enjoying a certain majesty in proportion to his stature'. Better still, he had cleverly preserved his fortune instead of dissipating it in loose living, so that he was able to display his splendour clad in

Chinese silks and robes woven of Tyrian purple stamped with gold.

Euryalus was followed by a long train of servants mounted on the most splendid horses. Aeneas Sylvius was exceedingly fond of horses, as he showed in the treatise on their nature and care[3] that he composed at about this time. His description of Euryalus's mount is as eloquent as anything he ever wrote. 'Now Euryalus rode a chestnut horse, with arching neck and narrow head. Short-bellied and broad-backed, high spirited and rippling with muscles, it was well worth looking at; and when the trumpet sounded, it could not keep still, but twitched its ears and trembled, snorting fire down its nostrils. Its thick mane lay tossing on its right shoulder, and its strong hooves pawed the ground . . . And when Euryalus saw Lucretia, he became as nervous as his horse.'[4]

Lucretia herself had qualities of mind and dignity in addition to her great beauty. She was tall and slender, twenty years old, well-bred and elegant. Her long hair, the colour of beaten gold, was swathed round her head with ropes of gold and precious stones so that her lofty forehead and arched eyebrows looked higher than ever. Her eyes were wide apart and sparkling; her rose and white complexion, her coral lips, and the dimples in her cheeks, made all long to kiss her, so that everyone envied her elderly husband Menelaus. In conversation Lucretia was witty and amusing; she was erudite without being a blue-stocking. 'She did not, like so many, display her virtue in a sour face, but, with joyful countenance, her honesty. Neither fearful nor bold, she bore within her woman's heart, tempered by modesty, the spirit of a man.'[5]

The Emperor Sigismund incited his companion to declare his love with courage and directness. Euryalus was determined so to do, but he started the affair badly, for he could think of no way of sending Lucretia his first love-letter except by the hands of a notorious bawd. Lucretia took—or pretended to take—great offence at this unhappy choice of messenger. Later, she was persuaded to relent and was gracious enough to accept the presents that Euryalus offered her. In return she sent him a golden cross set with pearls. 'It is small,' she wrote, 'but not without value.' In this letter Lucretia had included some elegant classical references that excited the admiration of Euryalus and inspired him to reply: 'For my part, while I read, I love you the more, perceiving that to your great beauty and honour was added learning. Those are but words, with which you ask me

to stop loving you. Ask the hills to flatten themselves out, or the
rivers to flow back to their springs. It is as impossible for me not to
love you, as for Phoebus to leave his course. When the mountains of
Scythia can lose their snows, the oceans their fishes, and the woods
their wild beasts, then only will Euryalus be able to forget you.'[6]

The affair was now moving to its climax. Once, an arrangement for
the lovers' meeting was thwarted by Lucretia's mother, who did
not, as was expected, go complaisantly to church at the time of the
lovers' tryst. Then there came two months' delay when Euryalus
was sent to Rome to make arrangements for the Emperor's coronation. 'And all that time Lucretia stayed at home, with her window
shut, wearing sad clothes, and never would go out.' As soon as
Euryalus returned to Siena a new expedient was tried. Immediately
behind Menelaus's house there was a tavern that overlooked the
back of Lucretia's apartments, and a convenient culvert or gutter,
where Euryalus could hide until his lady was ready for him. This
time they were able to talk and make their plans. Euryalus was to
disguise himself as a farm-hand helping to bring corn into Menelaus's granary, then he planned to slip away to Lucretia's chamber
while Menelaus was busy counting and checking the stores. All
went well until Menelaus came unexpectedly with a friend to his
wife's room in search of a missing paper. Euryalus hid himself in a
safe that was kept under the bed, and trembled for his dignity no
less than for his safety when Menelaus proposed to look in the safe
for the document[7]. Lucretia, however, was equal to the occasion.
'"Look, my dear," said she. "There is a little chest here, under the
window, where I remember you have hidden several documents.
Let us see if the papers are in there."

'And going quickly over as though to open the chest, she cunningly pushed it out of the window, as if it had fallen by accident.

'"Heavens, my dear," cried she, "come quickly, or we may suffer
for it. The chest has fallen out of the window. Oh hurry, both of you!
Why do you stand there? I'll watch from here, in case someone tries
to steal it."'

The house was high, the jewels and papers that had been in the
chest were now scattered on the pavement. While Menelaus and
his friend went hot-foot down the stairs to recover the treasures,
Euryalus was able to retreat to a safer hiding-place. The document
was duly found—in the safe where Euryalus had so lately hidden:

at last the lovers were alone and able to indulge their passion. Lucretia's charms are described in voluptuous detail: they exceeded everything that Euryalus could have imagined, and she too found delight in his manhood.

As long as the Emperor stayed in Siena Euryalus attended him and the lovers were able to meet occasionally. They were helped in their deception, though unwittingly, by another courtier in the Emperor's household. This was a Polish knight named Pacorus who also had designs upon Lucretia's virtue and fancied she had encouraged his hopes—'being handsome, he was quite sure she returned his love and that only her woman's modesty stood in his way. While she, as is the custom of our ladies, looked on all men with a kindly eye.' One day, while Lucretia was out walking with two girl friends towards the Chapel of Our Lady, a mile outside the city gates, Pacorus came to her and offered her a violet with gilded petals: into its stalk he had twined a love-letter written on fine parchment. Lucretia took the violet, but passed it on to one of the young girls. She, in her turn, gave it to a couple of students who had joined the party and they discovered and read the letter intended for Lucretia. The students as a whole were inclined to be jealous of the Emperor's courtiers; they complained that the ladies of Siena now had eyes only for the military, and 'the clatter of arms pleased our women more than the elegance of learning. Hence arose much malice and great rivalry, and the gown did all it could to damage the sword.'[8] In this instance the students were only too ready to stir up trouble, since Pacorus had given them so good an opportunity. Before long the letter was in the hands of Menelaus and the house was in an uproar. It was some time before Lucretia was able to calm her husband by telling him how matters had fallen out and bringing her friends to bear witness to the truth.

This infatuation of Pacorus was very useful to the lovers, for it distracted attention from their own illicit love-affair. When, however, Pacorus followed up his first missive with one that was even less discreet, Menelaus complained to the Emperor and the Pole had to leave the city in great haste in order to escape infamy and retribution. The second letter was as ingeniously delivered as the first; it was wrapped in wax and hidden in the middle of a snowball tossed in at Lucretia's window. In Siena it was winter time and 'the whole town was given over to mirth, and the ladies threw snowballs out into the streets, while the youths threw them in at the windows.' Unfortunately for Pacorus, his snowball rolled towards Menelaus as he sat by the fireside. First the snow melted, and then the wax, 'and the letter was disclosed'. Now indeed Menelaus was moved to suspicion and anger. He watched every movement his wife made, and at last the lovers' meetings became impossible. As soon as the snows melted, Sigismund decided to set off for Rome; Euryalus had to accompany him. Despite his promises to return Euryalus was only able to come back to Siena for three days during which he could catch no glimpse of his Lucretia. The affair was at an end. Euryalus duly married a wife chosen for him by the Emperor: Lucretia languished and died. So ended Aeneas's *novella* which he told Sozzini was 'a true story and an unhappy one'. It became, nevertheless, immensely popular, and by the end of the century no fewer than thirty-five editions had appeared: the first English version was published in 1560 and described as 'verye pleasaunt and delectable unto the reader'[9].

The little book is still delectable to modern readers; it is hard to see why it should have shocked some of Aeneas's biographers. Indeed, it is difficult to guess why Voigt ever turned his erudite and scholarly mind to the composition of his three-volume life of Aeneas Sylvius Piccolomini, since he disliked and deeply disapproved his subject[10]. Aeneas himself at a later date, after he had become Pope, felt that the *Tale* was not altogether seemly for his new position. Like many other writers he regretted an early work dashed off without full consideration of its possible effects, and he did everything that he could to suppress it. The trouble was that *The Tale of the Two Lovers* was too good a story and too well told to pass quickly into oblivion; had it been less well done Aeneas's critics would have had weaker grounds for their complaints. It is incomparably better than the coarse anecdotes that passed as *Facetiae* when written by Poggio or Lodovico Carbone, or the threadbare *Jests of the Widow Edith* that convulsed several generations of English readers. It is small wonder that sophisticated people read and re-read the attractive little book.

It cannot be emphasized too strongly that Aeneas was a layman when he wrote his *Tale*: at that time he had no intention of entering the service of the Church—he was a free-lance journalist, and one of the best who ever set pen to paper. A hundred years have passed since Voigt uttered his harsh judgements, but there are still people today who tend to assess the stature of this mid-fifteenth century character by much later puritanical measurements that do not and could not fit Aeneas's frame. The moral of his story is there for all to see: that illicit love can end only in sorrow, parting, and death. 'The cup of love,' he wrote, 'holds far more of bitter than of sweet.' It is true that this emerges only in the last pages of the book; the general impression carried away is of love's delight. That is due to the artistry with which the characters are presented. Lucretia in particular, with her quick wits to support her in embarrassing situations, is no stock figure of romance. Certainly she was neither chaste nor truthful, but she is a character drawn in three dimensions. Aeneas skilfully, in a few lines, robs the wronged husband of the reader's sympathy by attributing to him the unattractive vices of meanness and gluttony. 'Have you not noticed,' says Menelaus's butler, 'how he ill-treats our stomachs with his unfair measure, always stuffing himself and starving us; it's not enough for him that we must eat mouldy crusts of black bread, but yesterday's mince is served up at table, the salt fish and eels of one meal are carried over to the next, and he counts the sprigs of chives and marks them and locks them up, in case we get anything . . . what could be stupider than to live like a pauper that you may die like a Croesus? How different is our lady, who not only feeds us on veal and young kids, but even gives us chickens and trout, and any amount of the best wine.'[11]

Nothing could be further removed from the character of Mariano Sozzini than that of Menelaus—'ill-natured, turbulent, miserly, and hard to please'. Most of the material used in the *Tale* must, however, have been gathered during frequent visits to Sozzini's house, for the poverty-stricken student from Corsignano can have known little of middle-class home comfort and still less of rich provincial society. Aeneas was not himself in Siena at the time of the Emperor's sojourn; this took place in 1432 whereas Aeneas had left the city a full year earlier. By the time he wrote his *novella*[12] he had to draw on his memory for local colour, but by then he had acquired much first-hand experience of the Imperial court and the ways of courtiers. As he pointed out in his preface to Sozzini, Aeneas was nearly forty when he wrote the book. It can hardly be claimed as a youthful indiscretion. Aeneas was a man of the world—as was Sozzini himself—and declared that love had sent him into a thousand perils: he

seems to have sired at least two bastards[13] before his whole attitude and manner of life was altered by his decision to enter the
service of the Church. During his student days Aeneas had cultivated a devotion to a lady called Angela, wife to a Sienese citizen
named Francesco Acherisi, but it does not seem to have carried him
very far for she scorned him for his poverty and mocked his shabby
clothes[14]. Angela was, however, the inspiration of Aeneas's first
book of love poems, *Cinthia.* Aeneas was encouraged by his cousin
Goro to write poems in Latin and in Tuscan, and Goro later told
Ammanati that he had 'innumerable examples' of them. One of the
most ambitious of these was the two-thousand-line *Nymphilexis*
that he wrote for a Ferrarese friend[15] in praise of his mistress
Battista.

Only a few of these early poems[16] have survived; it is likely that
at this time Aeneas was a writer more prolific than skilful, though
it is clear that he had a considerable reputation among his fellows.
There can be no doubt that his love-poems were the fruit of his own
experience: they are far removed from academic exercises. Indeed,
as Aeneas wrote in his dedication to Kaspar Schlick: '. . . do not be
ashamed to recollect, if ever anything of this kind happened to you;
for you too were a man. He who has never truly felt the flames of
love is but a stone, or a beast. It is no secret that into the very
marrow-bones of the Gods has crept the fiery particle.'

CHAPTER IV

Travels and Impressions

They went on to Basel over the Alps called after Saint Gotthard, stiff with snow and ice, and across steep mountains that almost touched the sky. – AENEAS SYLVIUS PICCOLOMINI, *Commentaries*

Aeneas was twenty-six years old when he left Siena[1]. He had won considerable distinction there but he was feeling the need to spread his wings. Like his contemporary Antonio Astesano, a medical student at Pavia, Aeneas was better known for his poems—both amorous and witty—than for academic studies. Astesano, no less than Aeneas, was drawn to classical literature and shared his love of antiquity. He, too, sported with local maidens to all of whom he wrote a poem with a composite dedication[2]. He was a brilliant and attractive youth, destined to become a friend of such humanists as Filelfo and Panormita, but he never reached the stature of Aeneas Sylvius. This may have been from lack of opportunity; more probably he had neither Aeneas's strength of will nor his power of concentration. Versatility, by itself, was not enough to guarantee success as a humanist.

Aeneas shared with Astesano a profound admiration for Francesco Filelfo and, about the year 1429, he seems to have gone to Florence to study Greek under this great master. The chronology of this part of his life is obscure, and Filelfo himself confused the issue in a letter written to Leodrisio Crivelli shortly after Aeneas's death[3]. In his later years Filelfo chose to feel that he had been slighted and neglected when the young scholar he had befriended in Florence reached fame and fortune on becoming Pope. He told Crivelli that he had taken the youth into his own house and treated him as one of

the family. Filelfo said he had also found him a position in the
household of a Sicilian nobleman, with a stipend of forty ducats a
year so that he could attend Filelfo's private seminar as well as all
the public classes. Filelfo further asserted that Aeneas went to
Milan as secretary to the Bishop of Novara on his recommendation
and, indeed, that Aeneas owed his whole start in life to Filelfo's
backing. Very few, if any, of these statements are corroborated by
Aeneas's own testimony and Goro Lolli flatly denied the whole
thing[4]. Certainly Aeneas did not accompany the Bishop of Novara
to Milan: he went there with Cardinal Capranica. Nor is it likely
that he spent two years studying under Filelfo's guidance—could so
diligent a scholar in that time have learned so little Greek? Yet
Filelfo repeated his claim in a letter of introduction that he wrote
for Aeneas to carry to Niccolò Arcimboldo of Milan. 'The bearer,'
said Filelfo, 'is most dear to me, not only because he has been my
pupil for two years, but also on account of his keen intelligence and
graceful style. His manners are polished and refined . . . I commend
him to you with the utmost goodwill.'[5]

The most probable supposition is that Aeneas for the two years
1429–1431 visited Florence from time to time, studied there desul-
torily, and wandered through the university towns of northern Italy
in true medieval fashion. Aeneas had no difficulty in making friends
wherever he went and was readily accepted on his own terms. At
Bologna he was deeply impressed by the massive intelligence of
the great lawyer Giovanni da Imola[6], and he later wrote a biography of him—as he also did of Sozzini—in his *De Viris Illustribus*.
While in Ferrara Aeneas consorted with the Sicilian poet Giovanni
Aurispa and the most famous of all humanistic teachers, Guarino
da Verona. Some thirty years later, when Guarino died at the age of
eighty, Aeneas included in the *Commentaries* an obituary notice
that shows his sincere veneration for the great scholar, as well as
his gift for turning phrases. '. . . The death was announced to Pope
Pius,' he wrote, 'of that famous man Guarino da Verona, who duly
settled all his affairs in Christian fashion and fell asleep in God.
Wise men mourned his passing, especially his disciples who had
flocked to him from all over Europe. For he taught the Greek and
Latin languages and translated several books out of Greek into
Latin, and it is through his toil that we read Strabo[7]. He left learned
sons. Many epitaphs were written on him, none of the scholars of our

day left a better reputation. His body lies at Ferrara.'[8] Aeneas seems to have made only a short stay in Ferrara, breaking the journey there when he was returning to Siena from Padua: he sent a graceful 'Collins' to Aurispa after he reached home. 'I found in you so much courtesy,' the letter ran, 'and so much charity and kindliness even in the smallest matters, that I do not think anyone in the world could have been more considerate or more gracious: moreover you were willing to include me among your close friends.'[9]

Although Aeneas was beginning to make a name for himself and to find acceptance among writers and scholars, he still had no commissioned work, no patron, and no settled position. At this time—early in 1431—it was obviously the most prudent course for him to return to his home town and take up his career within the city walls. War had already broken out between Siena and Florence: as a nobly born Sienese he might well be suspected of conspiracy if he chose to stay on longer in Florence, whereas with the backing of his old tutor Mariano Sozzini, Aeneas would be able to practise as a lawyer in Siena or perhaps lecture in the Studio. Neither prospect attracted him at all: his whole being revolted against the idea of dull security. Now that Aeneas had had a glimpse of wider horizons and had developed a taste for humanistic society he could not bear to take root in Siena for the rest of his life. He did, however, return there for the time being.

For some months Aeneas stayed on in Siena, nervous and unhappy. Then, in the autumn of 1431, there came to him his great opportunity. 'By good luck,' Aeneas tells us in his *Commentaries,* 'Domenico Capranica was then at Siena, a man of lofty spirit and understanding . . . by him Aeneas was engaged as secretary and went with him to Piombino.' Capranica, who was Bishop of Fermo, had been made Cardinal by Martin V but Eugenius IV had repudiated him: since he was rejected at Rome he now resolved to defend his position before the Council of Basel. A generation later Pinturicchio painted the finest and most delightful of all his ten frescoes in the Piccolomini Library[10]. It is a representation of the young Aeneas setting out with Capranica for the Council of Basel, riding on a spirited white horse towards the seashore, with a backward glance at the city of his ancestors. The ground is carpeted with spring flowers (here there is more imagery than truth, for it was November when the cavalcade passed through the city gate). The landscape glows with colour in the light of an approaching storm. A great black cloud stretches over the horizon; already the sea is troubled but in the foreground all is bright and gay. The Cardinal's scarlet robe, the horses' trappings, the hint of thunder in the air, the carefree attitudes of the travellers and their well-wishers, all are symbolic of the adventurous career unfolding before Aeneas.

At this stage, Aeneas could refuse nothing that life had to offer him. He would go everywhere, see everything, and sample every experience that came his way. As well as the qualities of observation and receptiveness he had, however, a very keen critical sense and an excellent idea of proportion. This saved him from being a mere recorder of fact and experience: it is this selective quality that gives artistry to his impressions, enlivened as they are by shafts of wit that never quite become malicious. As he grew older Aeneas naturally became more mellow, but his vision was never blurred and he retained almost to the end of his life the zest and wonder that characterized the young man setting out to seek his fortune.

Since Capranica was strongly out of favour with Pope Eugenius IV, and the Council of Basel that he was proposing to attend had already been officially dissolved by papal decree, it was necessary for the Cardinal and his companions to make their journey as quickly and as inconspicuously as they could. It was always possible that Eugenius IV, through his agents, might interfere with their passage or even forbid Capranica to leave the country. Their idea was to make for Genoa by ship from Piombino, and tentative arrangements to charter a vessel had already been begun. The Lord of Piombino, Jacopo Appiano, professed to be a friend of Capranica, but secretly he forbade any ship to take the Cardinal on board. This deception became plain as soon as Capranica's party arrived at the port. Leaving Aeneas and his other secretary Piero di Noceto in charge of the household, Capranica went with a single companion down to the beach. Here they found a pinnace and rowed out in it to their ship, that could be seen lying some way off shore, and scrambled on board. As soon as Appiano realized that he had been outwitted he lost interest in restraining the rest of the party—'not thinking it worth while to chase the feathers when he had lost the flesh'[11]—so he allowed them to depart. By this time it was evening; Aeneas and the rest of the party could go no further than the island of Elba before night fell. They had to lie under the open sky in cold and discomfort, but when day dawned they were able to join Domenico Capranica in his ship.

Their troubles, however, were only now beginning: worse was to come. A great gale blew up and the ship was driven far out of her course. Recalling this storm some thirty years later, when he was writing his *Commentaries,* Aeneas declared that 'terrible storms battered them, carrying them within sight of Libya, to the great terror of the sailors lest they should be forced into a barbarian port. But wonderful to relate, almost incredible to hear, yet it is true: in a day and a night after they left Italy they were carried between Elba and Corsica to Africa, then back again to Italy as the winds changed, drifting rather than sailing between Corsica and Sardinia.' It seems that the story grew with the lapse of years: the account of the voyage that Aeneas wrote to the podestà of Piombino as soon as he arrived in Genoa[12] is very much more moderate. The hardships they had endured together brought Aeneas and his fellow-secretary Piero di Noceto into a friendship that turned out to be life-long.

Aeneas found Genoa a wonderfully rich city, 'as superior to Florence as Florence is to Arezzo', and Milan still more magnificent. The party stayed here a short while and Aeneas met for the first time the Duke of Milan, Filippo Maria Visconti. Just before they set out for Basel, in March 1432, Aeneas found a messenger to carry his letter to a friend in Siena, one Giorgio Andrenzio who had been a fellow-student and who evidently knew the Piccolomini family at Corsignano. The letter is mainly concerned with Aeneas's sorrow at parting from his home and friends; he asked Giorgio to comfort Silvio Piccolomini, ending with the words: 'I pray you to greet all our friends, and when you meet with my father console him as well as you are able.'[13] Aeneas's spasm of homesickness was soon forgotten in the excitement of setting out on the first of his many journeys across the Alps; all his other emotions gave way to wonder at the beauty and splendour of the St Gotthard pass.

When Capranica arrived at Basel he at once succeeded in gaining recognition of his Cardinal's rank, but it proved a hollow victory. Eugenius IV retained the fruits of his benefices and also put a stranglehold on his private fortune, forbidding Capranica's relatives to help him financially. The Cardinal was so poor that he could not pay his servants or maintain his household any longer; so Aeneas,

Piero, and the rest had to leave his service and make new arrangements for themselves while Capranica returned to Rome to make his peace with the Pope. For a short time Aeneas served Nicodemo della Scala, Bishop of Freising, and accompanied him to the Diet of Frankfurt. On returning to Basel, however, the Bishop lost interest in the Council and withdrew to his diocese, leaving Aeneas to find fresh employment. After some consideration of his future and prospects, Aeneas joined the household of Bartolomeo Visconti, Bishop of Novara, where his chief work was 'to compose and sign letters'.

Much of Bartolomeo's time was spent at Milan, so Aeneas was able to make his first essay in persuasive eloquence in this city, during a disputed election to the Rectorship of the famous and venerable Studio at Pavia. Pavia had always been very closely dependent upon the Duke of Milan; on this occasion both contestants for the office of Rector were members of his government. One was a Milanese noble of the house of Crotti, the other 'from Novara and of humble rank'. The aristocrat was strongly fancied and was already wearing the insignia of office, but Aeneas chose to support the candidate from Novara and had the great pleasure of winning the title for him by a speech of such eloquence that it left his opponents dumb and thwarted[14]. This was Aeneas's first successful pleading of a cause; it was a foretaste of his rhetorical triumphs in years to come.

Soon afterwards the Bishop of Novara became discredited and was accused of intriguing against the Pope on behalf of the Duke of Milan[15]. There seems to have been some substance in this charge[16] although it is probable that Aeneas was—as he claimed—ignorant of his master's designs[17]. It was necessary for him, however, to transfer his allegiance elsewhere as quickly as he could. Piero di Noceto had already entered the service of Cardinal Niccolò Albergati and he recommended the Cardinal to employ Aeneas as his secretary. This was a suitable and happy post for Aeneas: Albergati was a charming man, highly intelligent and generous to young scholars and artists, although he observed very strictly the rule of the Carthusian Order in his own conduct of life. He wore a hair-shirt beneath his gorgeous robes, he slept on a straw palliasse and would never eat any meat. Like Aeneas's first employer, Cardinal Capranica, he was a strict disciplinarian. His rule was maintained by a future Pope* who, as Tommaso Parentucelli, administered Albergati's household for twenty years. Tommaso and Aeneas respected one another's abilities, although they never became really congenial companions. It was, however, a great pleasure to Aeneas to be reunited with Piero di Noceto; the four years he spent in Albergati's service gave him a priceless opportunity of developing his special gifts of friendship and diplomacy. During this period of his life he stored up a great wealth of experience of men and affairs.

Aeneas joined Cardinal Albergati in Florence and went with him to Milan. Thence they set out for Basel by the Great St Bernard pass, making a detour in order to visit Amadeus VIII, Duke of Savoy, in his hermitage set in a woodland glade on the banks of the Lake of Geneva. Albergati and his companions took ship for Thonon. The Duke walked a mile through the woods to meet them. 'It was a thing worth seeing,' Aeneas wrote, 'and one which posterity will hardly find credible. The most powerful prince of his age, feared in France and Italy, one who had been wont to adorn himself in cloth of gold and go surrounded by a throng of court-officials, with axes carried before him and companies of soldiers and a crowd of potentates following behind, now preceded only by six hermits, followed by a few priests, dressed in a cheap and humble gown welcomed the apostolic legate . . . The hermits wore on their breasts a golden cross. That was the only sign of rank they kept.'[18]

A few years earlier, in 1431, after he had reigned for forty years, the Duke had announced his retirement from the world. With six selected companions, all widowers and all of noble birth, Amadeus had settled at Ripaille in beautiful rustic surroundings. Here he proposed to lead the life of a hermit, complete with the appropriate gown and staff. This action had excited much comment and Aeneas was extremely anxious to see for himself how the experiment had worked. Many believed that Amadeus was inspired by genuine piety; they accepted the simple explanation that the ducal hermit and his friends were bent upon a religious if not particularly ascetic rejection of worldly aims. Others saw the Duke's rustication as the first step towards fulfilling a high ambition. Already there were ru-

---

* Pope Nicholas V, 1447–1455. His birthplace was Sarzana, where his father practised as a surgeon.

mours 'begun, so many said, by fortune-telling women with pro-
phetic spirits, such as the mountains of Savoy abound in, that
Amadeus would be Pope'. In later years Aeneas referred to them as
'witches, who . . . foretell the future by means of trickery and devil-
ish arts'. Eight years later the prediction was fulfilled when Amadeus
was summoned from his fastness by the Fathers of the Council of
Basel in order to become the anti-Pope Felix V. At this first visit
Aeneas's shrewd observation told him something of what was afoot
and he surmised that Amadeus's renunciation of the world was
tinged with exhibitionism. Aeneas's dry comment was that Amadeus
and his fellows lived 'more voluptuously than penitentially'[19]; he
did not, however, go as far as did Piero di Noceto, who wrote on the
wall with a stick of charcoal a tag from Cicero[20] to the effect that no
unrighteousness is greater than hypocrisy.

Taking their leave of the seven hermits, each of whom retired
into his private suite, the Italians continued on their way to Basel.
In June the Cardinal set out for Arras, where he was to attend the
famous Congress. The party sailed down the Rhine as far as Cologne, then mounted horses and rode through Aix, Liège, Louvain,
Douai and Tournai. Finally they came to Arras 'where all of France
and England were gathered and awaiting the Cardinal'. This was
all new country to Aeneas, and some years later he wrote his impressions of the German towns in the *Germania*[21], perhaps the best
of his geographical descriptions. The 'splendour and beauty' of
Strasbourg, the canals there that reminded him of the saltier and
worse-smelling waterways of Venice, the 'nobility' of Cologne, all
stirred Aeneas to admiration and enthusiasm. By the time he
reached Arras he was prepared for a brilliant assembly in a worthy
setting, and this, indeed, he found. Political intrigue was smothered
in the magnificence of banquets and tournaments, although there
were many among the nine thousand strangers in the city streets
who wondered what would be the outcome of the Congress and how
it would affect the interests that they represented. To Aeneas, who
had no personal stake in the matter, it was all part of a spectacle to
be enjoyed and ultimately to be reproduced in his excellent and
fluent prose.

CHAPTER V

The Embassy to Scotland

And just as our people marvel at Ethiopians or Indians, so they stared in amazement at Aeneas, asking the priest whence he came, what he had come for, and whether he knew the Christian faith. – AENEAS SYLVIUS PICCOLOMINI, *Commentaries*

The chief purpose of Cardinal Albergati in attending the Congress of Arras was to end the Hundred Years' War between England and France. He went a long way towards fulfilling it by effecting the long-sought reconciliation between the French king and Philip the Good, Duke of Burgundy. This took place at Arras on 21st September 1435, and provided an occasion for Aeneas to dash off some verses on the blessings of peace in a letter addressed to the Duke. Aeneas did not stay on at Arras until negotiations had been completed, for he was instructed to go to Scotland as an emissary to arrange some secret business on behalf of the Cardinal Legate. Ostensibly, the object of his mission was to persuade King James I 'to restore a certain prelate to royal favour'[1], but there can be little doubt about its real significance. Aeneas was to persuade the Scottish king to make a number of raids across the Border so that English troops would have to be sent to the northern counties and therefore could not be used for an expedition into France. The idea was ingenious, and likely to succeed, but Aeneas's part in the plan had to be kept secret lest it should come to the ears of the English. In the *Commentaries* he is unwontedly discreet; his friend and biographer Campano was much more outspoken[2], setting out the terms of the mission very clearly.

Aeneas made his way to Calais and waited there to take ship for

England. The English authorities at Calais were always liable to
make difficulties for anyone they suspected was a potential spy or
enemy agent[3], so Aeneas found himself detained in his lodgings,
unable either to get a passage across the Channel or to return to
Arras. Fortunately for him Cardinal Henry Beaufort* was returning
to England at this time; he had known Aeneas at the Congress and
was able to arrange for his release. He also gained permission for
him to sail to Dover. Leaving the port immediately upon landing,
Aeneas set his course for London. Here he applied for letters of
safe-conduct to Scotland, not realizing how deeply suspect his mission must appear to the English government. The safe-conduct was
refused, so the only course open to him was to abandon his plan of
travelling directly through England to the Border. Instead he decided to recross the Channel in order to take ship directly to Scotland from the port of Sluys. 'To return', he wrote, 'was unpleasant
but unavoidable.'[4]

During his stay in London Aeneas made full use of his chance
to see the sights of the city. In the *Commentaries* he specially noted:
'the noble temple of St Paul's, the marvellous tombs of the Kings
[at Westminster], and the river Thames which flows less swiftly
than it rises; the bridge that is like a city.' In the sacristy of St Paul's
he was so deeply impressed by the beauty of an ancient manuscript
he saw there that he wrote a description of it, sixteen years later, to
his friend Johann Hinderbach[5]. This codex was a Latin translation
from Thucydides, by an unknown author, dating from the ninth
century. Aeneas admitted that he coveted possession of such a treasure. All through his life he admired books no less for their beauty
than for their contents, as he showed when he chose them for his
library and when—despite the cares and preoccupations of the
Papacy—he took a detailed interest in the writing and illumination
of the *corali* for his cathedral at Pienza. See Chapter XVIII.

Before he left England Aeneas found time to visit the village of
Strood in Kent, 'in which, as the story goes, men are born with
tails'[6]. He made no comment on his findings here but pressed on to
the 'golden shrine of St Thomas of Canterbury'. This, he considered,

* Bishop of Winchester. Beaufort was not only a prelate, he was also a prominent political figure, and he had extensive trading interests, being himself the
owner of several ships. He was at this time veering towards a policy of peace
with France although he had not yet found support for his views in England.

stole the glory from both St Paul's and Westminster, and he noted with admiration the jewels that covered the shrine—diamonds, pearls, and glowing crimson carbuncles.

The coast was now near at hand; before long he was able to find a ship to carry him to Bruges. After a calm passage, Aeneas and his party landed safely. At once he set out for the busy harbour at Sluys, in search of a ship that would take them to Scotland. In this they were successful, but Aeneas was now committed to the most dangerous and terrible of all his voyages. Within a day or two of leaving Sluys the ship encountered contrary winds that freshened to a gale; she was driven off course to a point near the Norwegian coast. For fourteen hours Aeneas was in constant fear of death. No sooner had they weathered this storm than they were struck by another which battered the ship for two whole nights and a day. 'So far into the northern ocean was that ship carried that the sailors could no longer read the stars and lost all hope of salvation.' At this point, racked as he was by anxiety and nervous exhaustion, Aeneas made a vow to Our Lady that if he reached land safely he would make a barefoot pilgrimage to her nearest shrine. As the mountainous seas abated, the ship could be turned back to her course, and after eleven days the coast of Scotland was sighted. Next morning, on the twelfth day out from Sluys, they made the port of Dunbar and dropped anchor there. Aeneas at once set out for Whitekirk where, he was told, he would find a church dedicated to the Blessed Virgin.

It was a ten-mile walk over a very rough track, the going made worse by ice and snow. Slowly and painfully Aeneas completed the journey, barefoot as he had promised, in the greatest anguish. After two hours' rest in the church he was still so weak and stiff 'from the wintry cold' that his servants had to carry him to shelter and it was a long time before he recovered the use of his limbs. Indeed, he suffered continually from rheumatic pains in his ankles and feet for the rest of his life, and often had to seek treatment at the spas of Petriolo and Viterbo in an effort to alleviate the pain. When a famous doctor, Giovanni Matteo de Ferrariis of Grado, he was Court Physician to Francesco Sforza and much admired for his skill in diagnosis, dedicated to Aeneas his translation from Avicenna he made a great point of his interest in the Pope's complaint: 'to be sure, most holy Father,' he wrote[7], 'when I heard about your unfortunate trouble in the sinews or joints of your feet, all my care and all my concern was for getting rid of it or, at least, for improving the condition. That is what I most ardently desire, for there was no reason why a weakness in your feet should redound to the glory of Almighty God, nor did it seem very useful.' Dr Giovanni Matteo towards the end of his treatise noted Aristotle's advocacy of mineral water and sulphur baths and advised the Pope to immerse his feet constantly in very hot water[8].

When at last his infirmity would allow him to do so, Aeneas pressed on to the court of James I of Scotland. The King received him with courtesy and friendship. The second of Pinturicchio's frescoes gives a delightful, if idealized, picture of their conference. King James is represented with dignity and a fine presence (although Aeneas afterwards described him as 'small and fat, hot-tempered and greedy for vengeance')[9]; he appears to be listening attentively to the eloquence of the fair-haired Aeneas. James I, with bitter memories of his eighteen years' captivity in England, was predisposed to agree to Albergati's plan for distracting England's attention from the French adventure by stirring up trouble in the north. The Scots made a series of forays across the Border, burning and looting and retreating again as quickly as they had come. Exaggerated rumours travelled south to the Lancastrian government; it was difficult for the English to know how seriously these raids should be resisted. Only the sudden death of James I—he was murdered less than a year after Aeneas's visit—prevented this Border warfare from becoming a serious embarrassment: as it was, it served Albergati's purpose very well. Aeneas was reticent about the outcome of his mission; in the *Commentaries* he merely remarked: 'When at last he was admitted to the King's presence he obtained everything that he had come for.' He was also given money for his expenses; for the return journey King James allowed him fifty nobles and two horses for his personal use.

From the account that Aeneas wrote of his travels in Scotland, the shrewdness of his observation of the landscape and the people stands out very strongly. It would seem that here lay his real interest. Few pages in the *Commentaries* are more vivid than those describing Scotland and her inhabitants. Aeneas rewrote and expanded his impressions in the *Europa*[10], written in the year that he became Pope, but the fuller version adds little information and lacks some of the spontaneity of the first draft. Aeneas thought poorly of the civilization of the Scottish court; he affirmed that the King himself enjoyed less comfort in his surroundings than did one of the meaner citizens of Nuremberg[11]. Aeneas found Scotland generally a cold land, deficient in crops and largely without trees. '. . . The commoners are poor and uneducated,' he wrote. 'They stuff themselves with meat and fish, and look on bread as a delicacy. The men are small of stature and brave, the women white and beautiful and very prone to love. To kiss a woman means less there than to touch her hand in Italy. They have no wine except what is imported. Their horses are all hackneys by breed and small. A few are kept for stud, the rest are gelded, and they are never groomed, whether with iron or wooden combs, nor yet do they have reins. . . . Hides, wool, salt, fish and pearls are exported from Scotland to Flanders. Nothing gives the Scots more pleasure than to hear the English abused.' Aeneas also noted the use of peat for fuel, distinguished firmly between highlanders and lowlanders, and observed for himself the winter solstice. He made an expedition in search of barnacle geese (*Branta leucopsis*) to find out if there was any truth in the legend that they were born from the fruit of a certain tree growing on a river bank: this fruit, it was alleged, fell into the water, came to life, and turned into birds. 'But when he went thither and made inquiries, eager for a miracle, he found it was a lie, or, if true, removed yet further to the Orkneys.'[12]

There was no time to visit the Orkneys, nor was it an attractive prospect in midwinter. Now that his official business was completed, Aeneas decided that he would leave Scotland and make his way back to Basel. The skipper of the ship that had brought him to Dunbar offered a return passage in the same cabin, but Aeneas had no mind to try a further voyage that might prove even more dangerous and would perhaps end in disaster. 'I'd rather try the mercy of men,' he said, 'than of the sea.' As it happened, the ship did run into foul weather and sank with her master and all save four of her crew, so that Aeneas was justified in believing that he had been saved 'by divine consent and favour'[13].

Before starting his homeward journey Aeneas disguised himself as a merchant, in order to avoid awkward questions that might be asked on the English side of the Border. For the same reason he travelled by an unusual route. It seems from his description that he came by the Solway and landed at Bowness, for he says he had to make his way over the river in a boat. Had he crossed the Tweed in the ordinary way he could have passed by one of the fords that were in frequent use[14].

Aeneas gives a lively account of his first night in England. At about sunset he came to a large 'villa'*, or settlement. Here he was offered hospitality in the house of a peasant; this he accepted gladly, for he was very tired after the long journey. While he and his companions sat at supper with his host and the parish priest, many villagers came to stare at the strangers. They brought presents of hens and geese for the visitors to eat, but offered them neither bread nor wine. Among his provisions Aeneas had some red wine and fine white loaves; these he gave to the villagers, causing them amazement and delight since they were unused to such luxuries and some had never before seen white bread, much less tasted it. Everyone ate the evening meal with great contentment. After the feast had continued well into the night Aeneas was beginning to long for sleep. The men and children, however, rose abruptly and departed, saying that they would go to a peel-tower some way distant to take refuge in case the Scots should come over the Solway at low tide, in search of plunder, as they sometimes did. The women, most of whom were 'girls or handsome matrons', were left sitting round the fire; Aeneas was told to stay with them and assured that no one would suffer harm—'since they do not count rape as harm'. For hours they sat in the firelight, talking interminably of many things. The interpreter wrestled with the women's uncouth speech, labouring to promote understanding, while the women chattered and cleaned their hemp as though just beginning their day's work. Aeneas was nearly prostrate with fatigue and had much ado to keep his eyes open. At last he was escorted by two young girls to a chamber strewn with straw; he was too tired to notice whether it was clean but there was certainly a strong smell of goat.

The two maidens offered to sleep with Aeneas, but his mind was just then, as he frankly said, 'less on women than on the thieves whom he expected to see at any moment', so he drove them away, disappointed and grumbling. The forward manners Aeneas had

---

* Aeneas used the word 'villa' in the sense of 'a group of houses or buildings set among fields'. *Cf.* Ducange *sub verbo*. I am indebted to Miss Flora Grierson for this note.

discerned in Scottish girls had educated him to feel little surprise at
these advances: he had already left behind him in Scotland a *pignus
amoris* that he mentioned in a letter to his father written eight years
later[15]. On this occasion, however, he remained solitary among
the cows and goats 'who, furtively snatching at the straw of his
bed, quite prevented him from sleeping'. During the night there was
a disturbance, with barking dogs and hissing geese adding to the
clamour, but the interpreter brought Aeneas reassuring news that
it was a false alarm. At last he was able to get a few hours' rest before rising and setting out for Newcastle.

The austere character of the country impressed Aeneas very
strongly; he found it 'wild, uncivilized, and never visited by the
winter sun'[16]. It has been suggested[17] that Aeneas cared so little
for these northern parts because he found the people alien to his
nature and their customs repugnant: moreover the climate and the
landscape formed a harsh contrast to southern Tuscany. To some
extent this may be true, but there is a more rational explanation to
be found in a letter that Aeneas wrote to his cousin some eighteen
years later[18]. Here he tells Goro that during his tour of Scotland
he was tormented by toothache and did in fact lose most of his
teeth, 'not without excruciating agony'. Incessant neuralgia, as well
as the fog that wreathed the hills, may well have coloured Aeneas's
impressions of Scotland and Northern England and caused him to
take a prejudiced view of the inhabitants.

After passing Durham, where he paused to visit the tomb of the
Venerable Bede, Aeneas came to York. This was far more to his
taste, and he describes the Minster with much feeling, writing of
'a chapel full of light, whose walls are of glass held up by extremely
slender pillars'. An amusing and fortunate encounter was with a
justice in Eyre who was travelling to London: he accompanied
Aeneas all the way to the capital without penetrating his disguise.
The judge was deeply interested in foreign politics, and told Aeneas
exactly what he thought of the Congress of Arras. Englishmen were
particularly furious at the doings of Aeneas's master, Cardinal Albergati of Santa Croce, for they knew he had robbed England of
her ally the Duke of Burgundy by reconciling him with the King of
France[19]. The judge 'uttered many curses' on the Cardinal of Santa
Croce, and told Aeneas he was a wolf in sheep's clothing.

When he arrived in London Aeneas found that a royal permit

was needed for leaving the country; he did not trouble to apply for this as 'it did not seem advisable'. It seemed to him a simpler process to bribe the officials at Dover to let him pass, and he found no difficulty in so doing. Aeneas sailed to Calais and then made for Basel, where he expected to find Cardinal Albergati. In this he was unsuccessful, so he went to look for the Cardinal at Milan at the same time as Albergati was returning from Florence over the Alps by another pass. Since he could not find Albergati in Milan Aeneas turned his face northwards again; ascending the stony gorge of Gonda, he went up over the Simplon pass, through Brieg, and down to the valley of Sion. Thence the way was easy to Basel; soon he had joined his employer and was reporting to him the results of his mission. Henceforward Aeneas would be closely concerned not only with the Council of Basel but also with the affairs of Germany. Not until he became Bishop of Trieste and afterwards of Siena would he be able to breathe the air of his much-loved Italy for more than a few weeks or months at a time when he might be sent there on the Emperor's business. After he became Pope, however, Aeneas ranged about his native land as far and as often as he could, often to the annoyance of his household and entourage. Never would he allow his physical infirmities to keep him at home when he wanted to be abroad, and no man ever made better use of his opportunities to observe and to enjoy the changing scene.

CHAPTER VI

A Pen for Sale

Now I shall tell briefly what happened at Basel and how Aeneas there won renown. – AENEAS SYLVIUS PICCOLOMINI, *Commentaries*

I

Even before he left Basel to attend the Congress of Arras, Aeneas had begun the first draft of his *History of the Council;* he also wrote long descriptions of the town and its inhabitants in some of the most vivid of his letters. His first impression was of cold north winds, of bitter nights, and of melting snow in early spring, when the bridges were carried away by the swollen waters of the Rhine, so that Basel became two separate cities, one on either bank of the river. As for the people, he found them mild and law-abiding, docile in the face of authority, hard-working and with a high standard of material comfort. Their rich furniture and substantial meals seemed to satisfy their ambition, for Aeneas found that their culture was low—they cared nothing for poetry and had never heard of Cicero. The chief citizens entertained one another to dinner in well-heated halls, where the silver plate was as good as anything to be seen in Florence and song-birds in decorative cages charmed both eye and ear. The churches were thronged, not only at festivals, and Aeneas was fascinated by the high wooden box-pews where rich men's wives shut themselves in, accompanied by all the maidservants of their household—'like bees in a hive'.

Aeneas considered that Basel was an excellent place in which to hold a General Council, for it was a natural centre, being midway between Denmark and Sicily, Spain and Hungary[1]. He was full of enthusiasm for the Council, and optimistic about its prospects,

without fully understanding either its nature or its scope. Nor did
he perceive that the more striking its early success the more cata-
strophic might be its ultimate failure. Like an impulsive research-
worker rushing to announce his findings to the world, without fully
considering their import, Aeneas dashed off the opening sequences
of his *History of the Council*. As it happened, he was obliged to
interrupt this work when he entered the service of the Bishop of
Novara, so that his first impressions of Basel that were meant to
be an introduction to his *History* stand by themselves as a journalist's sketch and—as such—have a spontaneity and freshness pro-
phetic of the qualities found later in his *Commentaries*.

The whole Conciliar movement had grown out of the past history
of Church and State, with roots that were deep and widely spread.
Its declared aim was to reform the Church from within, for it sprang
no less from dissatisfaction at long-standing abuses than from the
shame engendered in the minds of both churchmen and laymen
by the desertion of Rome, in favour of Avignon, as the Papal residence. At first it seemed that the Council of Basel had even less
chance of success than had its predecessors. The intellectuals of
the University of Paris, who had put forward with such enthusiasm
the idea of a General Council in the early years of the century, were
now either dead or senile: the next generation was disillusioned
and could see more clearly how easily such a conference might be
wrecked by nationalism and self-interest. The first impetus was
lost; although the need for reform was as urgent as ever, it was no
longer an exciting new idea. An abortive meeting had been held at
Siena in 1423; the only valid result of this was the issue of a general
summons to a further Council designed to be held at Basel seven
years later. This period of preparation did little to build up hopes of
success: indeed, such hopes ebbed away as the time for the Council
of Basel drew near, and the general expectation was that it would
be as futile as its predecessors.

Opening as it did in such an unpromising way it might seem that
the Council of Basel was foredoomed to failure. Had it not been
for the wisdom and insight of its first President, the Council might
well have ended as soon as it began, but Cardinal Giuliano Cesarini
as soon as he took office showed himself to be a leader with rare
genius. The Cardinal arrived in Basel early in September 1431, at a
time of grave crisis. A few weeks earlier the Bohemian heretics, the

followers of John Hus, had won a notable victory at Tauss over the 'crusaders' sent to exact their obedience. Cesarini realized, far more clearly than did most of his contemporaries, that Bohemia could never be brought back into the Church by force and that only by goodwill and understanding could any acceptable compromise be reached. Within two years he had brought the more moderate Hussites close to a settlement with the Church. This was based on tolerance and forbearance, conceding Bohemia special privileges, yet yielding nothing to the extremists of either side and allowing no tampering with the essential doctrines of the Church. These concessions, the 'Compacts', gave a real chance of unity: had they been honoured and duly implemented they could have brought about a lasting peace. Even the temporary truce and breathing space that was the fruit of Cesarini's far-sighted plan did much to show what could be achieved by the Council and rallied to it support that had hitherto been wavering and timid. This was a personal triumph for Cesarini, and for a time it seemed that he would be able to bring about the other reforms for which he strove—above all, a reconciliation between the Fathers of the Council and Pope Eugenius IV. At its inception the Council was composed of three bishops, seven abbots, and a number of professional canon lawyers, but as Cesarini's fame as President of the assembly spread through Europe more and more delegates converged upon Basel. When Aeneas Sylvius accompanied Capranica there he found 'a huge number of bishops and abbots from every part of Christendom'[2] already in residence and eager for discussion.

In 1423, as a first-year student at Siena, Aeneas had witnessed the action of the Council that sketched the agenda and meeting-place for the next assembly. He had been interested in the movement without ever imagining that he himself was to play a part; now that he found himself at Basel, in an atmosphere of revived hope and expectancy, he gave rein to his natural enthusiasm and became its champion. Above all, Aeneas was able to indulge in hero-worship of the President, who represented all the qualities that he most admired. Cesarini was a man of singular charm, his personal gifts of beauty, dignity and eloquence being matched by his deep learning, his loyalty, and above all his complete sincerity. Added to these he had the graces of tact, humour and courage of a high order. All these characteristics were blended in a man whose whole being was concentrated on peace, yet he met his end on a battlefield—leading a crusading army against the Turks at the battle of Varna on 10th November 1444.

In no time at all Aeneas was writing letters to his friends describing the day-to-day happenings at Basel, and what amounted to unofficial dispatches to the Signoria in Siena. He was already immersed in his *History*, although he laid it aside whenever Capranica or Albergati or some other client or employer was willing to pay for his services. His pen was for sale and he would accept any brief that was offered him: he could argue upon any given premises and he exulted in his own gifts of eloquence and adaptability. To suggest that Aeneas marshalled his arguments to suit the cause of the moment and thereby showed that his principles were elastic or impermanent is to misunderstand the whole situation. Just as he had thrown himself heart and soul into the election of the Rector of Pavia—not because the issue concerned him in any way, but because he saw a chance of practising his eloquence—so he would support any cause that gave him an opportunity for exercising his very notable talents. Like any other professional advocate he preferred to speak or write in support of matters congenial to his own sympathies, but he had to earn his living and that was his first care. His employers found him quick and exceedingly hard-working: there can be no doubt that Aeneas gave them conscientious service.

II

When Aeneas left Basel for Arras, signs had already begun to appear of the tension that was the main cause of the Council's failure: when he returned there in the spring of 1436 it had become plain to everyone. The gentle and moderate Cesarini was no less anxious for reform than were the extremists, but he saw—as they did not— that it could best be brought about by reasonable discussion. The leader of those who wanted to curb violently the papal power was the Cardinal of Arles, Louis d'Allemand, who had behind him the University of Paris and almost all the French clergy. Though personally a man of integrity and ripe learning, Louis d'Allemand was moved by a furious hatred of Pope Eugenius IV. Through his influence the Council, in June 1435, put out a decree by which *annates* were abolished and thus the Pope was by a stroke of the pen de-

prived of his main source of income. Since it has been calculated
that the total papal revenue for 1436 amounted to less than 60,000
gold florins[3], it is not surprising that Eugenius IV was hard put to
it to meet his day-to-day expenses, or that he was willing to sell
offices as and when he could find a bidder.

Public opinion began to veer round to the Pope's support, turning
inexorably against the extremists, though as yet they had lost none
of their vigour. If Cesarini was disappointed by the temper of his
colleagues, he was still more discouraged by another matter which,
seeming at the time of minor importance, in the end proved fatal.
This was the selection of a site for the long-desired Council called
to consider the union of the eastern and western churches, a project
very dear to Cesarini and for which he had laboured throughout
his life. For the past two years negotiations had been going on to
induce representatives of the Greek church to come to Basel for discussions. This they were unwilling to do, but in April 1436 they
agreed to take part in a Council if it were held in some Italian city
—or in Savoy—provided that all their expenses were paid. At once
Aeneas saw an opportunity for furthering the interests of his native
city. He wrote to the Signoria at Siena suggesting that they should
advance the necessary 70,000 ducats. Milan, Florence, and Venice
had promised money provided that the Council was held elsewhere—each city being bitterly jealous of the other two—and so
reap the great benefits that would accrue from the presence in their
city of a large number of strangers, with rent to pay and money to
spend, in addition to the fame and prestige that such a conference
would bring. His eloquence, however, fell on deaf ears. The Republic, foreshadowing their unwillingness to accept the authority of
Aeneas when he became Bishop of Siena, now refused his advice.
Less than half the required sum was all that the Signoria would
offer, so the chance was lost.

Instead of brooding on his failure, Aeneas used it skilfully to
further his career. Since his own city would have no share in the
proposed Council he turned his advocacy to promote the claims of
Pavia, where he had already enjoyed one rhetorical success. On
this occasion he sat up all night composing the oration he would
give next day. When the time came for him to speak, Aeneas addressed the Fathers of the Council for two hours, and commanded,
he tells us, 'the deepest attention and admiration'[4]. Copies of this

oration were afterwards distributed; he had at last made his mark in the assembly. Aeneas already held the not very significant post of cantor; thereafter he became scribe and abbreviator and was appointed to a number of committees.

Although the oration had brought him unqualified praise, Aeneas was not able to persuade the Council to choose Pavia as a meeting place for east and west.[5] The Duke of Milan, Filippo Maria Visconti, however, was so pleased by his efforts that he presented him to a provostship in the church of S. Lorenzo in Milan. The chapter of S. Lorenzo had already made their own choice, nor were they pleased by the Duke's selection of Aeneas, a stranger and a layman. It needed the full weight of the Duke's influence to secure the appointment for his protégé, who came speeding to Milan from Basel to take up his office. The matter was then settled to the satisfaction of everyone except the rejected candidate.

Aeneas was preparing to return to Basel, where matters were coming to a crisis, when he suddenly fell ill with a severe fever and dysentery that 'made him delirious and carried him . . . to the very door of death'[6]. He was saved only by the ministrations of the Duke's own doctor*, who came to see him every day and gave him very potent medicine. Aeneas lay ill, he tells us, for seventy-five days; all this time he resisted the efforts of well-meaning friends who urged him to put himself in the hands of an enchanter said to have cured two thousand of Niccolò Piccinino's soldiers as they lay fever-stricken in their camp. At last he decided to defy the malady and, rising briskly from his sick-bed, he mounted his horse and set out across the Alps. Fresh air and exercise did more for him than could either doctors or enchanters; by the time he arrived at Basel Aeneas had completely recovered. Indeed, he was able immediately upon arrival to preach a notable sermon on the feast of St Ambrose of Milan, 4th April 1437, 'being heard by everyone with incredible attention'[7].

Meanwhile, the dissensions at Basel became daily more bitter and intense. It was not that Cesarini had lost any of his skill in exposition: people would no longer listen to him. The French party wanted the next Council to be held at Avignon even though the

---

* 'A delightful person, Filippo of Bologna, who later served Pope Nicholas.' *Commentaries*, Book 1.

necessary subsidy would not be forthcoming; they voted solidly for
this location while others declared their vote illegal and themselves
advocated either Florence or Udine. The position was chaotic,
voices and tempers rose to a high pitch. As Aeneas wrote to his old
friend Piero di Noceto[8], the Fathers of the Council who had come
to Basel in the cause of peace had to be restrained by the local
magistrates from bloodshed. When the rival decrees were published in different parts of the Cathedral at the same time, conflict-
ing *Te Deums* resounded discordantly, and the bishops seemed to
be donning their vestments as armour and their mitres as helmets.
As the summer months slipped by, all hope of reconciliation between the Council and the Pope seemed to have died. Cesarini
realized that he could do no more: regretfully he relinquished the
office of President in favour of his rival, Louis d'Allemand. Sad and
disillusioned, Cesarini rode away to the south[9], leaving the futile
battle to be continued by the pamphleteers and the hot-headed
supporters of the Cardinal of Arles. Matters reached complete
deadlock when the Council summoned Eugenius IV to appear at
Basel to answer the charges brought against him. The Pope retali-
ated by publishing a Bull that dissolved the Council and destroyed
its entity. Many of the more moderate delegates left in disgust; the
complete disintegration of the Council was clearly only a matter of
time.

Had Aeneas accepted Cesarini's offer of money for the journey
and a horse to ride, and left Basel in the Cardinal's company, it
might have been better for his reputation. On the other hand, he
might have perished with Cesarini on the field of Varna six years
later, instead of living on to see his own crusading hopes dissipated
in the sea breezes of Ancona. As it was, he found himself so deeply
committed by his writings and his speeches to anti-papal propa-
ganda that there was small hope of any advancement in his career
were he then to try his fortune south of the Alps. Although Aeneas
was fast losing faith in the Council's ability to carry out its aims he
still clung to the ideals of unity and reform. Also, moribund as it
was, the Council still provided him with a living. He now held the
office of abbreviator major, which required him to draft letters for
the Fathers and to represent them on embassies. He had also
become a member of the Committee of Twelve—'an office', he

wrote[10], 'of great importance'. To resign from these posts seemed suicidal from a material point of view, nevertheless Aeneas had already begun to cast about for some means of breaking the bonds that confined and chafed him[11].

III

The summer of 1439 produced a poor harvest, so that famine soon raged in Bavaria. In their weakened state people had little resistance to the pestilence that followed. Before long, all the Upper Rhine was infected. In the city of Basel deaths from plague rose to a peak of three hundred a day. Many friends of Aeneas succumbed; he watched faithfully by two of them until they died. Not surprisingly he himself caught the infection soon afterwards. When Aeneas felt the fever rising he urged his companions to leave his bedside; one of them did so, but the more constant Andrea Panigali remained to nurse Aeneas and to carry out the doctor's remarkable but effective treatment. The choice had lain between two doctors, one a Frenchman from Paris who was 'learned but unlucky', the other a German 'uneducated and fortunate'. Perhaps recalling how his life had been saved in childhood by the natural wisdom of his godfather in Corsignano, Aeneas chose 'good luck rather than learning' and submitted to the prescribed poultices of 'chopped-up pieces of juicy green radishes' alternating with 'bits of damp chalk'. As his delirium rose it became clear that Aeneas was very ill indeed; a report of his death was carried to Milan where the chapter of S. Lorenzo elected a new provost in his stead. After six days, however, the fever left him and Aeneas became convalescent. In gratitude he offered the German doctor six gold pieces as his fee, but 'the latter, with good faith and charity marvellous in themselves and in a doctor perhaps unheard of'[12], refused payment. When Aeneas pressed the money on him, the German agreed to accept the six gold coins but in return he bound himself upon oath to treat 'six poor invalids for nothing'.

During his illness Aeneas had lost his provostship, for the canons of S. Lorenzo would not be persuaded to reject their own nominee a second time. The Council, however, showed him signal favour in bestowing on him a canonry and prebend in the cathedral of Trent. Aeneas was still a layman, and there were many other and more

appropriate candidates for the office, so that the appointment is a
measure of the Council's opinion of his value and abilities. In Trent,
also, the chapter had already made an election, so it was necessary
for Aeneas to 'placate' the canons and win them to his side. This he
seems to have done with little difficulty. The Basilean Fathers also
invited him to become one of the thirty-two electors who would
choose a successor to the recently 'deposed' Pope Eugenius. They
even offered him permission to assume Holy Orders up to the rank
of deacon all in one day, in order to qualify for this office, but Aeneas
would have none of it. He resolutely refused to enter Holy Orders
for such a reason: it must be credited to one who was admittedly
anxious to get on in the world that he would not go against his conscience in this matter.

The electors' choice fell, as most men thought it would, upon the
hermit of Ripaille. Since Aeneas, in attendance upon Cardinal Albergati, had visited Duke Amadeus in his retreat on the shores of
Lake Geneva the rumour that here would be found the next Pope
had spread and multiplied. The Duke accepted his election with
conventional humility although few who knew him doubted that it
was the culmination of much careful preparation and planning.
Taking the name of Felix V, the new anti-Pope at once tried to
build up his position. One of his first actions was to invite Aeneas
Sylvius to become his secretary; despite his earlier doubts about
the integrity of Pope Felix, Aeneas accepted the position in the be-
lief that it would bring him fame and fortune. Neither hope was
realized. To be secretary to an anti-Pope who spent his time in
Basel or roving about the banks of Lake Geneva was a very different
matter from filling a high position in the Roman Curia, as Aeneas
found only too soon. Eugenius IV clung steadfastly to his position
while the wavering adherents of the Council of Basel, shocked by
the impious action of the electors in naming an anti-Pope, withdrew their support or even transferred their allegiance. Aeneas
found that Felix V had been a far more impressive figure when he
dwelt in his hermitage. The shaving of his beard, when he was received into the conclave, symbolized for his secretary's critical eye
the deterioration in his bearing. 'For the barber's knife had removed what had been his true and most suitable ornament, his
long and copious beard which concealed all the faults in his face

and seemed to give him a kind of majesty. When he appeared without it his small face, crooked eyes (for he had a squint), and hanging cheeks gave him the appearance of an unsightly monkey.'[13]

Aeneas has very little to say in the *Commentaries* about this period of his life, nor did he write any particularly lively letters at this
time. Either his duties kept him so closely occupied that he had no
opportunity to put his impressions upon paper, or these were not
strong enough to make him desire to do so. In the course of his employment, however, Aeneas was sent on various embassies, making
contact with influential people and finding many new friends.
When the Emperor Frederick III received his crown at Aix, Aeneas
was present at the ceremony and afterwards consorted with a number of the Emperor's counsellors. He was particularly attracted by
Bishop Silvester of Chiemsee—'that serious and learned man'—and
the influential Archbishop of Trier 'who united nobility with virtue'[14]. Both these friends urged him to throw in his lot with the
newly crowned Frederick. As a new prospect began to open before
him, Aeneas prepared to leave the dullness of unfruitful service in
the household of an anti-Pope for the unknown opportunities of an
Emperor's court.

It was easier to make the decision to change his employment
than to carry out his design. Felix V, although he had shown small
appreciation of Aeneas's services, was very unwilling to let him go.
'He could not by his efforts get permission to depart' till his friends
interceded for him and he was grudgingly dismissed. Nevertheless,
Aeneas saw the advantages of keeping a foothold in the camp he
was leaving and was careful to retain a nominal position in Basel.
This proved very useful to him later when he was negotiating on
behalf of the Emperor; it also made him able to perform a service
for the Imperial Chancellor concerning the appointment of a new
Bishop at Freising.

Before he shook the dust of Basel from his feet, Aeneas's literary
energies found vent in the *Dialogues on the authority and deeds of
a General Council* that he wrote in 1440, and the same year saw his
better-known history of the Council—*De gestis Basiliensis Concilii*[15]. Aeneas was now on the threshold of discovering how deeply
he had misjudged the issue: it is likely that the setting out of his
arguments in favour of the Conciliar idea—in the first of the *Dia-*

logues between the papal champion Nicholas of Cusa* and an anti-papal secretary—clarified the position in his mind. The later *Dialogues* were concerned with more general topics such as the nature or eloquence or the delights of living in the country; in these Aeneas showed where his true interests lay and they foreshadowed many passages found later in the *Commentaries*. One chapter of his life was closing, another beginning. Aeneas left Basel with the Emperor's train in November 1442, his hopes as high as they had been when he rode out of Siena with Cardinal Capranica, but he left behind him a trail of speeches and writing that would have been more easily forgotten had they been less pungent. That the Council of Basel had no future was by now freely admitted: unfortunately for Aeneas, whose too-loyal support had lasted too long, it had a highly coloured past.

* Originally Nicholas of Cusa had been one of the strongest supporters of the Conciliar movement but, like Cesarini, he transferred his allegiance when the extremists went too far. The other speaker in the *Dialogue* was Stefano da Caccia.

CHAPTER VII

The Emperor and the Poet Laureate

. . . We, with our own hands, decorate our Aeneas with the evergreen leaves of the laurel, so that his name and honour may flourish for ever, and that his brilliant example may encourage others of like talent. — *Regesta Chronologico-Diplomatica Frederici III*[1]

I

On 27th July 1442, Aeneas Sylvius received an acknowledgment of his literary qualities that filled his soul with joy. This was the day on which he was crowned Poet Laureate by the Emperor, to the applause of all the courtiers and officials. Pinturicchio has represented the scene in one of his frescoes, the fair-haired Aeneas kneeling before Frederick III who holds the laurel wreath poised above his head. Such public recognition of his talent, that made the poet one with the great names of classical antiquity, brought him close to his hero, Petrarch. Aeneas had always seen in Petrarch not only a great poet but a guiding star; to be ranked with him in such a way was a symbol of triumph. It is true that the poet's crown was not everything that Aeneas believed it to be, but in the summer of 1442 it seemed to him the beginning of a new and glorious phase in his career as a humanist. To the Archbishop of Milan[2] he wrote in the first flush of success: 'You must not be surprised to see me sign myself "poet", for this is Caesar's will.'

Ten years later Frederick III crowned a Neapolitan poet[3], who had made an oration in his honour, as casually as he knighted two professors of medicine as he passed through Ferrara: such ceremony meant little more to him than an inexpensive reward for services rendered. He certainly did not see Aeneas Sylvius as a beacon shedding light through his uncultured court; he was not conscious of any darkness there, nor of any deficiency in literary studies, because his own interests were quite different. Frederick III was a curious character, self-absorbed, undemonstrative, with a streak of avarice in his nature that made him difficult to like and brought him unwilling service. His tastes were bucolic; he was fond of hunting and of gardening and he took trouble to see that his estates brought in a maximum yield. Jewels and precious stones he loved, but more for their monetary value than because they brought him aesthetic pleasure. According to the chronicler Niccola della Tuccia, Frederick III was not ill-looking, though his nose was 'un poco grosso'. At forty years old he had a fair skin, dark glittering eyes, and a red beard[4]. The French Ambassador[5] painted a very unattractive portrait of the Emperor, finding him unworthy of the great position he was called to fill and emphasizing his meaner qualities, his avarice, his deceit, and his credulity. The Frenchman may well have been prejudiced; he probably underestimated Frederick's intelligence, being misled by his gloomy and ponderous manner. No one, however, could possibly have found him witty or amusing: Aeneas Sylvius showed some optimism in believing he could stimulate Frederick into taking a personal interest in classical antiquity or elegance of style.

With his customary zeal Aeneas wrote and dedicated to the Emperor a tract, in his favourite dialogue form, very soon after entering the Imperial Chancery. In it he showed, among other things, that he was beginning to be able to take an objective view of the Conciliar movement. It was called the *Pentalogus*[6] and purported to be conversations or colloquies between the author and four other persons upon topics of the day. It is mainly concerned with politics, but touches also upon the relative merits of force of arms and humanistic education. Aeneas hints at the value such study might bring to the Emperor himself, both as politician and diplomat. Of the five characters in the *Pentalogus* two are bishops—one of them Aeneas's new friend the Bishop of Chiemsee, the other his old employer Nicodemo della Scala, Bishop of Freising—the remaining three are the Emperor, his Chancellor, and of course Aeneas himself.

Frederick's Chancellor at this time was that vigorous and confident man Kaspar Schlick, whose quick mind was coupled with great administrative ability. In the Imperial Chancery he was the immediate superior of Aeneas and was quick to recognize and use his assistant's special gifts. Moreover, he himself was half Italian and had accompanied the Emperor Sigismund to Siena in 1432, where he had lodged with Aeneas's uncle and aunt, Niccolò and Bartolomea Lolli, in the very house where Aeneas had spent his student years. Indeed, Schlick made friends with the family to such an extent that he was invited to become godfather to Goro's sister's child, naming him Kaspar after himself. 'And these things made Kaspar even fonder of Aeneas.'[7] From the first the two men appreciated and respected one another's qualities; it was no accident that Aeneas chose Schlick for the hero of his *novella*[8] and it is clear that the Chancellor was amused and gratified to be identified with Euryalus. He had a coarse strain in his nature and was very little interested in humane letters; as a patron Schlick lacked the qualities that Aeneas had admired so much in Cesarini but nevertheless it was he who made tolerable for the sensitive Italian the brutishness of Frederick's court.

It was not long before it was brought home to Aeneas that he had exchanged the frustration of his life at Basel for something even less palatable. Instead of being a leader of social and intellectual life as he had hoped to be, with scope for oratory and the writing of concise reports and minutes, Aeneas found that he was just another clerk in the already over-staffed Chancery. His poet's crown might have been a wreath of nettles for all the interest it aroused. His presence excited not admiration but resentment among his colleagues, for the more officials there were the fewer were their rewards. Most of them had no fixed salary; they were paid by piecework for the documents they drafted and could only count upon their board and lodging. Some of the clerks had grown hoary in Imperial service; others were so young and callow that Aeneas at thirty-seven, experienced and sophisticated as he was, felt as though he belonged to a different race. A Bavarian named Wilhelm Taz was in charge of the clerks at this time; between him and Aeneas Sylvius an initial distaste for each other soon ripened into strong personal enmity. 'And he abused Aeneas in a remarkable manner' so that 'in all things [Aeneas] came last, and neither at table nor in the dormitory had a place worthy of his rank, and was hated, despised, and mocked at like a heretic or a Jew.'[9]

With his fastidious tastes Aeneas suffered real hardship from the coarse food and dirty tablecloths; he hated the stale eggs, rancid butter, black bread, and the incessant smell of cooking fish that was 'strong enough to stay a serpent'. Nor did he appreciate the beer and cider that were consumed in such huge quantities. As Canthara the procurer says in Aeneas's play *Chrysis*[10]: 'I leave such drinks for Germans and Bohemians'. The squalor of his meals and the slovenly manners of his German companions made Aeneas homesick for the simple fare of his childhood days in Corsignano, when hot chestnuts and home-grown apples were washed down by draughts of milk or water from swift flowing streams. At night he suffered from sharing not only his room but even his bed with colleagues who at best snored throughout the night or more often lay in a drunken stupor, mumbling obscenities as they slept. Miserable as he was in these sordid surroundings, Aeneas could still make them into a good story; his letter to Johann von Eich on the *Miseries of Courtiers* has much in it that is autobiographical. This work became almost as popular as *The Tale of the Two Lovers;* while developing the fashionable theme of 'nobiltà' Aeneas exposed the hollowness of courtly life in so amusing and realistic a way that it appealed to men of all conditions and classes.

The *Miseries of Courtiers* is no self-pitying cry from a gifted man who finds himself too good for his job. Just as he had set himself to conquer uncongenial subjects in his student days, so Aeneas now strove to make a success of his new position. 'He laid back his ears,' he tells us, 'like an unwilling donkey when too heavy a burden is laid upon its back.'[11]

During Schlick's absence at Nuremberg on the Emperor's affairs Aeneas had made it his business to gain a mastery of all aspects of work in the Imperial Chancery. On his return the shrewd Chancellor was quick to appreciate Aeneas's diligence and skill. Finding him 'ingenious, industrious, and a patient worker' Schlick thereafter set an even higher value on his services. Indeed, on his next absence he put him in charge of the Chancery. The displaced Wilhelm Taz left Imperial service in great chagrin. A few months later Aeneas painted a ribald portrait of him in his play *Chrysis*, where he was so easily identifiable as Archimenides that a contemporary wrote 'W.T.' beside his name in a copy of the comedy that is now in Prague[12]. Thereafter, Aeneas's position was secure: although his work was still far from congenial, conditions improved considerably. To follow his own metaphor, Aeneas pricked his ears and began to step out merrily.

To some extent Aeneas found satisfaction in writing various dialogues and treatises, mostly in letter form. *Pentalogus* was followed the next year by no fewer than four works—the *Nature and Care of Horses* and three others that were perhaps the most popular he ever wrote°. *The Tale of the Two Lovers* is discussed in Chapter III for, although it was written in 1444, it belongs to the Siena of Aeneas's student days and owes nothing—beyond the model for its hero—to his sojourn in Germany. It is to be noted, too, that Schlick through his Italian mother, as well as by nature and education, was more Latin than German in his attitude to life. Besides the *Miseries of Courtiers* Aeneas in the same year produced his comedy named *Chrysis*. In a letter written in April 1444 to a friend at Wiener-Neustadt[13] he referred to this project; by 1st October it was finished and in circulation[14]. The plan of his play had, however, been in his mind for some time, for he sketched out some of the personalities that he intended to introduce, as early as mid-January 1444, in a letter to his old friend Piero di Noceto[15]. A number of the author's acquaintances can be identified in the characters of *Chrysis,* among them the Johann von Eich to whom the *Miseries of Courtiers* was inscribed; he is thought to have been the model for Charinus. Aeneas's rather serious-minded friend Michael von Pfullendorf ('who loved the gentler muses and pursued the study of the humanities')[16] was critical of the play, but most people found it amusing if not edifying. As one of the characters (Sedulius) says in the first act: 'This is no place for Cato but for Pandarus.' There is very little action in the play, and the situations are repetitive, but the characters are shrewdly drawn. Although the humour must have been much more apparent to Aeneas's contemporaries, who would recognize the topical allusions and enjoy the portraiture, it is still possible to find pleasure in this light-hearted trifle. The cook, Artrax, for instance, has his counterpart in all ages. He is an amusing rascal who tastes his dishes so extensively that he has to try to persuade his

° At any rate during his lifetime, for the *Commentaries* suffered so much mutilation and bowdlerizing that they have only recently become available as a whole. See Select Bibliography 1.

employers that the cranes he is serving them are 'monopedous—the sort of bird that hops about on one leg'[17].

Chrysis was composed in imitation of Plautus and has much in common with contemporary Latin comedies written by dons or students. It belongs in spirit, as in time, to the phase of Aeneas's life when he produced his famous *novella*. Some of the best of the *Epistolae* were also written during these years; it seems that his unhappiness and lack of companionship moved Aeneas to seek relief in the written rather than the spoken word. Instead of dissipating his ideas and phrases in oratory or conversation he set them down on paper, to the great benefit of posterity.

II

From time to time Aeneas Sylvius had been sent abroad by Pope Felix on missions and embassies of minor importance. In the cold and unfamiliar cities he was even more lonely than at Basel or later in Vienna or Wiener-Neustadt: this made him ready to respond warmly to any gestures of friendship that were made to him.

On one occasion, at Quinquagesima, in February 1442, just before he entered Imperial service, Aeneas had to go to Strasbourg as the anti-Pope's ambassador. He had been there seven or eight years earlier, with Cardinal Capranica, but he knew none of the townspeople and had to stay disconsolately indoors with nothing to do. To his great delight he found also staying in the inn a Breton[18] woman named Elizabeth whose husband 'Melineus' seems to have been a merchant or commercial traveller. She was as charming as she was witty, 'neither plain nor elderly', above all she spoke Tuscan extremely well. This was, as Aeneas said, a talent very rare in those parts. To hear himself addressed in his own tongue, in so humorous and delightful a fashion, brought the exile much joy and kindled in him passion and desire. Elizabeth had evidently travelled far and wide with her husband; she and her five-year-old little girl were staying in Strasbourg in the innkeeper's care while the husband was absent on business. Aeneas compared her conversation with that of Cleopatra, seeing himself as a combination of Antony and Julius Caesar. He 'grew hot and burned for the woman' and tried with all his might to win her regard by elegant compliments. For three days she held him at arm's length, till the night before her departure, when Aeneas besought her to leave her bedroom door unbolted. Elizabeth offered him no hope at all but Aeneas did not despair. Finally he succeeded in inducing her to become his mistress. This was on the night of 13th–14th February; the child conceived on St Valentine's Day was born in Florence the following November.[19]

When news came to him of the boy's birth, together with assurance that it really was his child, Aeneas sent a long letter to his father in Corsignano[20] describing his reactions. Shame at his sin was tempered by joy in his achievement, and the first thought in his mind was how best to provide for his little son. 'I beg you, my father,' he wrote, 'to accept your grandson and bring him up till he is old enough to come to me and be educated by me.' Silvio Piccolomini did not receive the news with unmixed pleasure. He seems to have reproached his son in a letter no longer extant, for Aeneas began Epistle No. 78 by saying: 'You write that you do not know yet whether to be glad, or sorry, Father, that the Lord has given me a child.' He continued: 'But I see cause for gladness and none for sorrow. For what is sweeter to mankind than to beget in one's own likeness and, as it were, continue one's stock and leave someone after one's death? What on earth is more blessed than to see your children's children? For my part I am delighted that my seed has borne fruit and that some part of me will survive when I die; and I thank God who has made this woman's child a boy, so that another little Aeneas will play about my father and mother, and give to his grandparents the comfort which his father should have supplied. For if my birth was a pleasure to you, who begat me, why should not my son be a joy to me? And will not my baby's face rejoice your heart, when you see me in him? Will it not make you happy when the little one hangs about your neck and charms you with his baby ways? But perhaps you will say it is my offence you mourn, because I have begotten a child in sin. I do not know what idea you have of me. Certainly you, who are flesh, did not beget a son of stone or iron. You know what a cock you were, and I am no eunuch nor to be put in the category of the cold-blooded. Nor yet am I hypocrite who wants to seem better than he is. I frankly confess my error, for I am no holier than David the King nor wiser than Solomon.'

Aeneas saw his mistress only once after the birth of their son, when she visited him in Basel. His plans for the child's upbringing could not be carried out, for Elizabeth seems to have kept the boy with her until he died, some time within the next fourteen months. Thus neither of Aeneas's bastards survived, the boy born to him in Scotland in 1436 died shortly after birth, and his strong desire for a son to succeed him went unsatisfied. All his life he had a great love of children; his affection for his two sisters' boys showed itself in the pains he took over their education, and he was particularly fond of his sister Caterina's* daughter Antonia. She in her turn married and had a child; Antonia and her mother brought the baby boy to see Aeneas after he had become Pope[21], telling him they had called the infant Silvio after his great-grandfather as Aeneas had suggested. The Pope was delighted by his great-nephew whom he found 'a bright and very lovely infant . . . he had not yet reached his twentieth month, and was imitating everything he saw and showing many signs of intelligence. And he gave the Pope a great deal of pleasure.'

Aeneas was no longer a young man at the time of his affair in Strasbourg; when he wrote the second letter to his father[22] he was approaching forty. He was not too old, however, to compose a love-letter for the young Duke Sigismund of the Tyrol, who wished to write a persuasive epistle to his lady love but whose pen lacked the facile elegance so characteristic of Aeneas's writings. In later life this letter proved almost as embarrassing to the Pope as his novel or his play: it was rather unfairly quoted against him during the Congress of Mantua by a German named Gregory Heimburg. Gregory was a very able lawyer; intellectually he was a worthy rival of Aeneas, in personality the strongest possible contrast. In an incisive sketch of Heimburg's character[23] Aeneas admitted his attractive appearance and vigorous, forthright eloquence, but deplored his obtuseness and the coarseness of his manners. 'In speech and gestures he lacked restraint, deferring to no one in his judgement . . . he chose freedom in everything, had no *civiltà*, and felt no shame for his ignorance.' This is a classical example of the prejudice and distrust that existed between Italians and Germans and shows how difficult and uncongenial it was for Aeneas to work in harness with such men.

* Aeneas built a palazzo in Siena for Caterina: it is now the Banca d'Italia.

The six years' sojourn at Basel, followed as it was by eight more years of exile in Germany, while it extended Aeneas's horizon and taught him much of men and affairs—knowledge that was to prove valuable indeed when he should become Pope—it continually heightened his longing for his native Italy. Unlikely as it seemed at the time, a train of events had already begun that would lead Aeneas southwards across the Alps on an embassy that was to be the turning-point in his career. He had successfully used his powers of persuasion to secure for Schlick's brother a benefice made vacant in 1443 by the death of Aeneas's old patron Nicodemo della Scala. This was the rich bishopric of Freising; Schlick was naturally grateful and as a reward he saw to it that Aeneas was chosen as Commissioner to attend the Diet held at Nuremberg in August 1444. Here a further effort was made to end the Schism, for European opinion was by now turning sharply against the Council of Basel. Support for Eugenius IV, too, was growing as more and more people became aware of the futility of the efforts of Felix V to assert his authority. In Aeneas's mind, however, the doubts that assailed him about the legality and efficacy of the Council of Basel had not yet hardened into opposition. He puts the matter very fairly in Book I of the *Commentaries*. '. . . the great Basilean ardour had not yet left him, nor had he found reasons why he should support Eugenius's cause. Knowing only one side of the question he belittled the other. But later he gradually changed his mind, when he perceived that the Basileans were avoiding an issue.' Aeneas has sometimes been accused of opportunism in transferring allegiance from the Council he had supported so warmly to the Pope he had reviled. As has been pointed out earlier, however, his first concern was to make a living as a skilful advocate. It must not be forgotten that his fundamental ideal was unity within the Church, nor that his efforts to promote this unity through the Council were just as sincere, and stemmed from exactly the same cause, as his attempts in later life to repress heresy in Bohemia and elsewhere. It was the same man, true to the same ideal, who dashed off pamphlets supporting Conciliar reform, who also spent himself leading Christendom in a crusade against the Turks.

The idea that he might one day enter Holy Orders may have been in the mind of Aeneas for some years, for he was careful never to contract a marriage, unlike his friend Piero di Noceto who had married a Florentine lady 'endowed with every talent other than riches', as he wrote to Aeneas in November 1443[24]. In his answer to this letter Aeneas replied: 'So far I have avoided taking Holy Orders because I fear chastity; although it is a virtue worthy of praise . . . it is becoming to philosophers rather than to poets.' The allusions to Venus and Bacchus gradually become less frequent in Aeneas's letters; a more serious and philosophical trend is discernible. A few months after he had put the finishing touches to *Chrysis* he wrote to a friend in Prague[25], asking him to buy a Bible containing both Testaments in the volume, for he had heard that they could be obtained there quite cheaply. 'As I grow older,' he wrote, 'secular knowledge neither delights me nor becomes me. I desire to steep myself in the Gospels . . . I do not know how I can please God better than in the study of letters: as the Bible contains the first principles of sacred learning I wish to have a copy in my possession.' Nearly eighteen months passed before Aeneas actually took Orders, but he was obviously feeling his way towards this end.

It may well be that the licentious character of his comedy marked a critical point in Aeneas's sexual life and that extreme disillusion accounted for his cynical attitude to love. At the same time, *Chrysis* must be viewed in the perspective of Aeneas's environment and the sophisticated tastes of his contemporaries: too much should not be made of its immoral theme since this was a commonplace in humanistic writings of this period. It does seem, however, that setting the matter down in writing cleared his mind and made Aeneas ready to think out his convictions with fundamental honesty. The change in his attitude to his religion, the putting of first things first, had probably begun much earlier—long before he himself was conscious of it. Even in his early letters there is often a hint of serious purpose that is at times incongruous to the light-hearted tone he uses. This is more noticeable in letters written to correspondents like Hinderbach or Carvajal: Schlick seems always to have called out the worst in Aeneas, despite his sterling qualities of loyalty and uprightness that the younger man admired and tried to emulate. Sudden as the change in Aeneas's life seems, when it is examined more closely signs are found that point clearly to his great destiny, signs that have been misunderstood in much the same manner as Vittoria Piccolo-

mini misinterpreted the pre-natal dream—the vision of the future
that she mistook for a miserable nightmare.

In March 1446 Aeneas was ordained deacon in Vienna; it is certain that his ordination as priest took place within the year but the
exact date is not known[26]. Henceforward not a breath of scandal is
connected with his name; Aeneas had enjoyed his amours, admitted
his error, and now he resolutely closed this chapter of his life. He
even ceased to describe himself as 'poet'. Gluttony and drunkenness
had always been abhorrent to him, sloth was foreign to his nature.
In these respects, then, he had no occasion to change his way of
life: after he became Pope he still preferred simplicity to elaboration and beauty to magnificence.

Even before he was ordained, Aeneas held at least two livings.
Such an irregularity was not at all unusual—it would be easy to find
far more glaring instances of a layman holding ecclesiastical prefer-
ments. Nor was it thought reprehensible, except by the sternest
reformers. Aeneas's first parish was awarded him by the Emperor;
it brought him an annual stipend of sixty gold ducats. The church
of Sarantanerthal stood high in the Alps between Italy and Germany. For three quarters of the year the steep valley leading to the
village was frozen and impassable; Aeneas has recorded a vivid
impression of his parishioners and their pursuits[27]. 'The natives stay
at home all through the winter', he says, 'making chests and other
works of carpentry very skilfully, which in summer are sold at
Bozen and Trent. They spend a lot of time playing at chess and
dice, and at the former they are exceedingly clever. No fear of war
preoccupies their minds, no desire of honour tortures them, nor are
they worn out by the hunger for riches. Their wealth is their flocks,
which in winter they feed on hay, and on these they live . . . Those
who dwell at a distance from the church lay the bodies of their
dead under the open sky during the winter, so that they freeze and
are preserved till the summer. Then the parish priest goes round
the parish and forms a long funeral procession, and saying the last
words he buries many corpses at a time in the cemetery. The rest
follow the service with dry eyes. Happiest of mortals, if they but
knew their own good and would refrain from lust. But living in
common night and day as they do, they commit rape and adultery
everywhere, and no maid goes a virgin to her wedding.' Himself a
countryman, Aeneas could appreciate the peacefulness of life in a

remote village, but he was quite ready to leave this parish for another that was offered to him in Bavaria, close to the River Inn. This was St Mary of Aspach, in the gift of the Bishop of Passau. The first steps had been taken in his new career; from this time forward his promotion was steady, though not so rapid as to suggest that it was undeserved.

IV

The Diet of Nuremberg had demonstrated once again the intransigence of the Basilean Fathers. It was plain for all to see that the best hope of ending the Schism lay in a direct personal approach to Pope Eugenius. Few were surprised when Aeneas was chosen by the Emperor to head a deputation to Rome; its aim was said to be to secure papal consent for a fresh Council, but everyone knew that the real object was to establish friendly relations between Emperor and Pope. At first sight it seemed that Aeneas, considering his recent championship of the Basel Council, would be putting his head into the lion's mouth. Indeed, his friends and relations in Siena besought him to turn back, when he passed through that city on the road to Rome. 'For, they said, Eugenius remembered nothing so well as injuries, and was cruel, and greedy of revenge.'[28] Aeneas, however, lacked neither courage nor self-confidence: he pressed on, with something of a swagger, and reached Rome in the early spring of 1445. Here he was met by an old friend, Gerardo Landriano, the Cardinal of Como, who introduced him to the Pope's presence.

After he had kissed the Pope's foot, and duly greeted him, and delivered the Emperor's letters, Aeneas addressed Eugenius IV on his own behalf. His words were few, he said, but worthy to be recorded: even if we doubt whether the speech was made exactly as Aeneas recalled it to mind when he was writing his *Commentaries,* it is clear that he made a brave and honest statement of his guilt and asked forgiveness without any hint of servility. 'They have not lied who informed against me,' he told the Pope. 'Many are the things that, while I was at Basel, I spoke and wrote and did against you. I deny nothing. And yet it was my intention less to hurt you than to defend God's church. For when I persecuted you I thought I was obeying God. I erred: who would deny it? And yet I erred not with

few or obscure men. I followed Giuliano of Sant'Angelo*, the Archbishop Niccolò of Palermo, and Lodovico Pontano, notary of your
see; these were thought to be the eyes of the law and the masters
of truth. Need I mention the schools of Paris and other universities
throughout the world, many of whom opposed you? Who had not
erred with such great names as these? But when I perceived the
errors of the Basileans, I confess that I did not at once turn to you,
as many did. Fearing lest I should slip from error into error, as often
men trying to avoid Charybdis fall into Scylla, I betook myself to
those who were considered neutral, in order that I should not pass
from one extreme to another without time for deliberation. And so
I stayed three years with the Emperor. There I listened to more and
yet more disputes between the Basileans and your legates, until no
doubt was left me but that the truth resides with you. And so it
came about that, when Caesar desired me to make this journey to
your Clemency, I willingly obeyed. For thus I thought I might be
restored to your favour. Now I stand before you, and because I
sinned in my ignorance I implore you to forgive me.'[29]

With some magnanimity Eugenius IV rose to the occasion. He for-
gave Aeneas freely, telling him: 'We, forgetful hereafter of past offences, shall love you dearly while you walk aright.' It was necessary
to stay in Rome for a few weeks while the Pope deliberated on his
reply to Frederick III; Aeneas found time to visit old friends and to
make many new ones. A fortuitous encounter showed how deep had
been the rift between the parties at Basel. Aeneas one day chanced
to meet Tommaso of Sarzana, who had served with him ten years
earlier in Albergati's household. He went forward to greet him, but
Tommaso 'shuddered at him' and would have none of his advances,
feeling that his friend was still a Basilean at heart. It was not till
some days later, when Aeneas was taken ill with a sharp attack of
colic, that Tommaso relented. He was now Bishop of Bologna and
a busy man; he could not come and see the invalid himself but he
sent his Spanish servant to wait upon him and offered to pay the
doctor's fees. After a few weeks their old friendship was resumed
without any reservations[30]. While Aeneas lay ill for twelve days, in
such pain that he often longed for death, he was visited daily by
Juan Carvajal[31], later one of his closest friends, and the Pope sent

---

* Cardinal Giuliano Cesarini: he had died the year before.

his own doctor to look after him. As soon as he was well enough, Aeneas sought another audience with Eugenius IV, when he was given letters to take back to the Emperor. On the return journey Aeneas visited his father for the last time, for Silvio was now becoming old and feeble; he died in 1450, while Aeneas was still in Germany.

Aeneas's mission to Rome proved its success almost immediately, for the Pope sent the newly created Cardinal Carvajal and the Bishop of Bologna as special envoys to the Emperor's Court: no choice could have suited Aeneas better. Friendly relations between Emperor and Pope were established, and soon these became highly cordial. The German Princes who acted as Electors to the Empire, however, were less inclined to give up their neutrality than was the Emperor himself. Aeneas once wrote to Campisio: 'As you know, the Germans are not easily brought to a conclusion; moreover, having reached it, they are harder still to move from it.'[32] It was not until the summer of 1446 that the Electors at last agreed to send their representatives to Rome, together with those from the Imperial Court. Among the German envoys was Aeneas's old rival, Gregory Heimburg; it amused Aeneas greatly to see him completely at a loss in Roman society, cursing and swearing and sweltering in the heat of the city streets. The chief purpose of this expedition was to invite the Pope to send his answer to the Electors' proposals directly to the Diet that would be held at Frankfurt immediately upon the envoys' return. Eugenius IV agreed without enthusiasm, dismissing the German delegation rather summarily, but he invited Aeneas to a special audience and had with him a fruitful discussion as to means of securing agreement.

His mission completed, Aeneas started back to Germany alone. Tommaso of Sarzana, who was to have accompanied him, was delayed in Rome but caught up with him at Siena and they travelled together nearly as far as Parma. They went on foot across the Apennines, sleeping in peasants' huts and living very frugally. The fatigue proved too much for Tommaso; Aeneas had to leave him, suffering from fever, in the region of Monte Sillano while he pressed on alone to Germany 'lest his delay should hinder the things that must be done'. Aeneas chose the route by way of Mantua and Verona up the valley of the Trent and over the mountains of Brixen. He took a day off to go stag-hunting with Duke Sigismund of the

Tyrol, the young man for whom he had written the famous love-letter, and had excellent sport in the valley of the Inn. After reaching Ulm in safety, Aeneas had to halt there to wait for companions before he could get through any of the passes leading to Frankfurt, for they were all held by robbers. To his great delight, his friends Schlick the Chancellor and the Bishop of Chiemsee arrived one evening, so that he was able to travel in their company to Frankfurt.

At this Diet Aeneas enjoyed one of his most notable triumphs, for he tackled the Electors singly and one by one persuaded them to accept compromise and to offer the Pope Germany's obedience. This was achieved mainly by persuasive eloquence, but flattery and cajolement had something to do with his success. In at least one instance[33] 'it was necessary to resort to gold, to which ears are seldom deaf', for 'Gold is the sovereign of Courts, ruling all things, and it conquered the Archbishop'.

For the third time in less than two years Aeneas took the road to Rome as the Emperor's representative. His stature had increased until he was now recognized by everyone as the most important member of the embassy. It was no longer necessary for him to struggle across the mountains on foot or to sleep in shepherds' huts at night. He rode at the head of sixty horsemen and stately lodging was provided. The party arrived at Rome early in the new year, 1447. On 12th January Aeneas visited the Pope in order to explain to him the significance of the Diet's proposals. After trembling in the balance, swaying this way and that, a settlement at last was reached. Eugenius fell mortally ill, so that matters were delayed until 7th February, but on that day the Pope summoned the delegates to his chamber and approved 'the whole formula', decreeing a Bull to that effect[34]. Aeneas's long-drawn-out efforts and his patience were now vindicated. As he claimed in his *History of Frederick III*[35] God had 'reunited the Church when it was weak and divided, and had brought the bark of St Peter into a safe harbour'. And he had allowed Aeneas to be its pilot.

While Pope Eugenius IV lay on his deathbed, bells and trumpets sounded in the streets and squares of Rome; there was a public holiday in celebration of the settlement, with bonfires blazing all over the city. Mass was said in the Lateran 'and Frederick and Eugenius were praised in a not inelegant sermon'. For sixteen days the Pope wrestled with his illness, strong fighter that he was, till at last he died on 23rd February. His struggles were over, his troubled reign had ended in triumph. His successor would have new problems to face, new enemies, new supporters. One thing was clear, however: the man who beyond all others had brought about the settlement would have great importance in future papal policy. Aeneas Sylvius was at the threshold of the Vatican, although another decade was to pass before he himself reached St Peter's throne.

CHAPTER VIII

Bishop and Cardinal

Aeneas Senensis, Bishop of the same city, deserves to be numbered among the illustrious men of his time . . . above all for his eloquence. – BARTOLOMEO FAZIO: *De Viris Illustribus*[1]

I

One of the last acts of Eugenius IV before he died was to raise Aeneas to the rank of apostolic subdeacon: Aeneas Sylvius was clearly marked for speedy promotion. When a rumour began to circulate that the Bishop of Trieste was dead, general opinion took it for granted that Aeneas would be appointed in his place. Although this rumour turned out to be untrue, in actual fact the Bishop did die within a few weeks and Aeneas did indeed prove to be his successor.

As soon as the ceremonies attending the funeral of Eugenius IV had been concluded the Cardinals went into conclave to elect a new Pope. They were immured as usual, Aeneas and a German named Prokop being installed as two of the guardians or doorkeepers. The Cardinals' only contact with the outside world was the daily admission of their food-boxes that were brought to each individually by members of his household. Popular opinion suggested that the next Pope would be Prospero Colonna, who was rich and powerful and whose family had been connected with Rome for many generations, even though this would mean the renewal of bitter party strife. The Cardinals' choice fell, however, upon the Bishop of Bologna—Aeneas's old friend and colleague Tommaso Parentucelli. He had been a Cardinal only since the previous December, so his election caused considerable surprise. In taking the name of Nicholas V it was generally thought that the new Pope was showing reverence for the saintly Cardinal Niccolò Albergati[2], in whose household he had served for so long, and who might well have himself become Pope (on the death of Martin V) had he not been absent on a legation in France at the critical time[3].

After the papal coronation[4], when by special invitation he had carried the cross before Nicholas V, Aeneas returned to Germany with his posts as papal secretary and subdeacon duly confirmed. Only three weeks later he was delighted to receive a letter from the Vatican ('without any fee')[5] appointing him Bishop of Trieste. The Emperor had already announced his intention of trying to secure this bishopric for Aeneas, as soon as the news of Bishop Niccolò's death had been confirmed. Pope and Emperor were acting in concert for the first time for many years; Aeneas felt that he, who had done so much to bring them together, was now reaping his reward. Even the Triestini, notoriously hostile to outsiders, accepted the appointment without grumbling.

The citizens of Trieste gave Aeneas a warm welcome when he celebrated there his first episcopal Mass, after receiving consecration at Vienna in the presence of Cardinal Carvajal, the apostolic legate. They set up a bust carved in stone in honour of their new Bishop, and it stands in the Piazza San Giusto to this day. Aeneas found unexpected pleasure in breaking away from courtly preoccupations and in having time for meditation and study. At Trieste he led a peaceful life far from the storms and intrigues of the Imperial Court, where Chancellor Schlick, who died in July 1449, to the great grief of Aeneas, had fallen out of favour and a faction mostly composed of Styrian nobles, interested in cultivating their fields rather than their minds and obnoxious to Aeneas, had become all-powerful. It was here, in his cathedral city, that news came to Aeneas of the final extinction of the Council of Basel and the resignation of anti-Pope Felix[*]. With great tact Pope Nicholas V had accepted election by the Council, who thereby saved their faces and then made a fairly honourable retirement. The formidable Louis d'Allemand left

---

[*] Who was, however, made titular Cardinal of Santa Sabina. This was in April 1449. He died two years later at Geneva, 7th January 1451.

Basel for his own diocese of Arles; the remainder of the Fathers withdrew from the city scarcely noticed and unlamented. Aeneas himself composed a balanced account of the life and death of the Council, *De rebus Basiliae gestis stante vel dissoluto concilio*[6], in which he developed the themes of his earlier writings on this subject and set the whole matter in perspective.

Some time between 1444 and 1450, most probably during his residence at Trieste, Aeneas wrote a series of short biographies of his most notable contemporaries, the *De Viris Illustribus*. To this period also belongs one of the most serious and substantial of his works—a treatise on the Roman Empire[7]. In a lighter vein is the essay on the upbringing of children[8] specially written for the boy-king Ladislas Postumus of Hungary and Bohemia. This child—as son of the deceased Albert of Hapsburg—was the heir of Austria; since he was the Emperor's cousin it was natural that he should be brought up as Frederick's ward in the Imperial Court. At four years old his high spirits and beauty had so captivated Aeneas that he wrote a charming letter to the Hungarian Archbishop, Dionys Szech, in which he described the young Ladislas riding around the palace on his wooden horse[9].

The book was finished in 1450; it does not differ greatly from other contemporary treatises on this topic—the education of princes was a theme closely allied to that of *nobiltà* and was a favourite subject for discussion in humanistic circles. The quality that gives the work special value is that Aeneas Sylvius had adapted general principles to meet the particular case of the young Ladislas. Occasionally he seems to forget the boy's tender age, but as a rule his admonitions are practical and realistic. 'It will be your destiny,' he writes, 'to defend Christendom against the Turk. It will thus be an essential part of your education that you be early taught the use of the bow, of the sling, and of the spear; that you drive, ride, leap, and swim. These are honourable accomplishments in everyone, and therefore not unworthy of the educator's care.'[10] When the young Ladislas died in 1457, Aeneas mourned him deeply. He had lost a friend and patron, from whom he hoped great things not only for himself but for all Christendom. Bohemia, however, suffered even more, for she lost the chance of having the enlightened ruler she so badly needed.

II

In the year of the Jubilee, 1450, there were the customary festivities in Rome when many pilgrims came there from distant lands. It was a period of change and mounting tension: by the time of the next Jubilee the whole world would have swept into a new age and men of the sixteenth century would look back a hundred years to see their ancestors as the last representatives of medieval society. To those alive in 1450, however, it seemed an era of great promise and greater performance. For Aeneas Sylvius it was an important year that saw a favourable development in his life both as ecclesiastic and diplomat.

To this time, too, belongs a curious and interesting work that has not had the attention it deserves. When he composed it, Aeneas was in a sombre mood; he had been greatly cast down by the death of Schlick the year before and was moved to write to Cardinal Carvajal a complaint that he now had more friends among the dead than among the living[11]. Using his favourite dialogue form he wrote a fantasy, *De Somnio*, that he sent to Juan Carvajal with the same letter[12]. Aeneas imagines himself walking in a dense wood* that has some of the attributes of Purgatory, for in it he sees a great number of his friends and patrons—among them the lately departed Schlick. The shade of the Chancellor speaks with Aeneas, referring to the year of Jubilee and regretting that most of the pilgrims will be more keenly interested in seeing the sights than in expiation of their sins. Aeneas is pleased to be greeted by San Bernardino who says to him: 'I used to know you as a young man in Siena, when you listened so intently to my preaching.' Aeneas looks in vain for Cesarini and is told that he has gone directly to Heaven from the battlefield of Varna. In his dedicatory letter Aeneas tells Carvajal that there is much wisdom in dreams, as the ancients have always held: this is what he himself has dreamed in a vision—can Carvajal interpret it for him more fully? This preoccupation with dreams, together with a tendency to give them deep significance, is characteristic of hu-

* Cf. the opening stanza of Dante's *Divine Comedy* (trans. Dorothy L. Sayers):

> '. . . I woke to find myself in a dark wood,
> Where the right road was wholly lost and gone.'

manistic thought in the middle decades of the fifteenth century. An Englishman in his early thirties, seeking favour at the papal court, made a translation of Synesius's *De Insomniis* that he probably intended to dedicate to Pius II had the Pope not died just before it was completed[13]. The author inscribed it instead to his successor, Paul II, writing in his preface that he had decided 'to bring knowledge of so useful, so inspired a book, which for so many ages had lain hidden in the deepest night of Greek, into the light of Latin'. Synesius's theory of dreams was based on Plato and had been amended by Aristotle; it later caught the attention of the great Platonist Marsilio Ficino who made his own version and dedicated it to one of the Medici[14].

Life in Trieste was tranquil rather than interesting; there were times when Aeneas thought wistfully of the comings and goings of visitors from many nations in the Emperor's Court. This can be deduced from his letters, which at this time were as flat and as ordinary as anything he ever wrote. Before the end of 1450 he was summoned by Frederick III and entrusted with a mission that Aeneas found highly attractive and that offered a good opportunity to exercise his talent for oratory. The Emperor wished to marry Leonora, niece of Alfonso, King of Aragon and Sicily. He chose Aeneas Sylvius to make the necessary arrangements, and invited him also to announce to the Pope his intention of coming to Rome to receive the Imperial crown. Aeneas found that one of his companions on this embassy was to be his old friend Michael von Pfullendorf, so he prepared for the journey to Naples with confidence and pleasure. It was indeed a delightful trip, in the nature of an unexpected holiday. The Portuguese envoys had already arrived at King Alfonso's court where they were heartily enjoying themselves; they were in no hurry to begin serious discussion. In the end, forty days were spent in amicable negotiations and conversation of a general character. It was Aeneas's first visit to Naples; in this stay he laid the foundations of friendships that would ripen when he returned there five years later. He made a notable oration in the presence of the King and a distinguished audience on the theme of 'the rank and virtues of the contracting parties': Aeneas noted with satisfaction that 'many copies were afterwards made of this speech'[15].

On his return to Rome, where he arrived towards the end of the Jubilee celebrations, Aeneas was able to announce full details of the betrothal and the plans for the coronation. It had been a perilous journey, for as he was travelling by the River Evola Aeneas's craft struck an overhanging branch in the darkness: for two whole hours the boat lodged on a submerged tree-trunk in imminent danger of overturning. With his instinct for dramatization, Aeneas made a good story out of his narrow escape, and characteristically he added: 'Since we are speaking of Aeneas's misfortunes it is only right that we should tell also of his good luck.' This was announced to him at Ferrara, as he passed through on his way back to Trieste; he was breaking his journey in order to pay a visit to his first cousin Jacopo Tolomei, a distinguished jurist and judge in that city and afterwards made by the Emperor a count of the sacred palace of the Lateran. Jacopo told him that news had come from Siena that Bishop Nevi had died there and that Aeneas had been appointed to the see. Pope Nicholas V had again proved himself a good friend to Aeneas, and appreciative of his talents, for he recommended the Sacred College to transfer him from Trieste to Siena even though the Sienese themselves were pressing strongly for the promotion of a local Abbot, Conte, Abbot of the monastery of San Galgano, who also was a Sienese citizen. When, however, they heard of the new appointment, and Aeneas arrived in person at the gates of the city, the volatile Sienese gave him a warm welcome. He was 'received by the clergy and people in procession under a golden canopy'[16], when he returned from Rome with the appointment secure and formalities completed.

This was in January 1451; when Aeneas returned to Siena the following October his reception was very different. In the first glow of enthusiasm the Sienese had been ready to offer their new Bishop anything he wanted; they had freely given a safe-conduct for the Emperor when he should come to Siena to meet his betrothed. For Leonora wished the marriage to precede the coronation so that she could be crowned as Empress. As the months passed, however, the citizens of Siena—in common with those of other territories—began to feel alarm at the prospect of the Emperor's visit. They feared for their independence and were particularly apprehensive lest Aeneas should persuade the Emperor to compel the Sienese to reinstate the noble families they had expelled. Their whole constitution might be in jeopardy. 'The year before,' he wrote in the *Commentaries*, 'no one could pay enough respect to Aeneas, none could praise him too much. Now, hated by all, none came to meet and do him honour when he entered the city, in his house there were few to welcome him, and in the streets he heard many abuse him. It was even rumoured that some had conspired to kill him. But Aeneas bore all with moderation, laughing to himself at his change of fortune.'

Although he put a good face on it, Aeneas felt deeply hurt by his rejection. He remonstrated with the Sienese, who somewhat modified their attitude without showing Aeneas any of the warmth for which he craved. To add to his troubles, Michael von Pfullendorf 'fell sick of a fever and breathed out his great and honourable spirit'; he was an austere person and had at times been critical of Aeneas's more flighty compositions, but Aeneas had grown to depend upon the integrity of his judgement and would miss him sadly. Now, all that he could do for his friend was to give his body 'a magnificent burial in the church of the Blessed Virgin'[17]. Feeling despondent and out of tune with the city fathers, Aeneas left Siena for Talamone where Leonora of Portugal was expected to land. Here he had to wait for sixty days, 'to the great boredom of himself and his colleagues', beguiling the time with expeditions to see the Etruscan remains at Ausedonia and other archaeological sites. Meanwhile, the Pope had become infected with the general panic that was spreading over Italy at the prospect of the Emperor's arrival[18]; he wrote to Aeneas that supplies of food were short in Rome and that it would be better if the Emperor's visit could be postponed. It needed all Aeneas's tact and persuasiveness to reassure him.

All this time the unfortunate Leonora was tossing on the sea, for contrary winds prevented her ship from making harbour; in the end it was decided to try for Livorno instead of Talamone. Frederick III also had been delayed; he did not reach Florence until the day that Leonora stepped ashore at Livorno. Aeneas hurried to Pisa to meet her, while the Emperor pressed on to Siena. It was now February 1452: on the 24th of that month the Emperor met and embraced his bride, 'in a spacious open plain' outside the Porta Camollia on the northern boundary of Siena[19]. It was a day of great pageantry that lingered long in the minds of all beholders. Pinturicchio made it the subject of one of his most successful frescoes: in the background can be seen the marble column that the Sienese erected some months later to commemorate the occasion[20]. Young Ladislas was there, distinguished from the crowd of German princelings and courtiers by his long golden hair and his grace and beauty. The bride was only sixteen years old; she won the hearts of the Sienese by her beauty and vivacity—even the phlegmatic Emperor was moved to leap from his horse and crush her in his arms. The festivities that followed this dramatic meeting lasted a full week. The daughters of the Sienese ladies who had dallied with Sigismund's troops now dazzled Frederick's bodyguard. The wife of one of the magistrates made an oration of such elegance and power that the Emperor offered her any reward that she might name: the chronicler Orlando Malavolti records that she chose exemption from the sumptuary laws so that she could flaunt her clothes and jewels exactly as she wished.

The good impression made by the Emperor, and the relaxation of tension when the peaceable character of his visit was appreciated, increased the stature of Aeneas. The Sienese recognized him as the Emperor's friend and were glad that their countryman should have such honour. Frederick showed Aeneas particular favour; as they rode together towards Rome over Monte Cimino and began to descend the slope to Viterbo he astonished him by uttering a prophecy. The Emperor told Aeneas that he foresaw his appointment as Cardinal and later as Pope; whatever the Bishop of Siena's private feelings may have been, all that he wrote in his *Commentaries* was that he 'listened as though to one who joked'.

After the party reached Rome there was much for Aeneas to do in making the final arrangements both for the marriage and for the coronation. 'He did much private business between the Pope and the Emperor,' Aeneas wrote, but his part in the actual ceremonies was that of an onlooker. He was shrewd enough to see that all this pageantry meant extraordinarily little. The iron crown of Lombardy, that should have been assumed at Monza or Milan, had to be received at Rome simply because the Emperor dared not challenge Francesco Sforza's authority in the Duchy of Milan. His lack of power was hidden under gorgeous medieval trappings, and ceremony cloaked unreality for the uncritical, but it was clear enough to those most deeply concerned that Frederick's coronation was no more than a charade. Even the insignia specially brought from Nuremberg, including the sword supposed to have belonged to Charlemagne, proved suspect. Characteristically it was Aeneas himself who examined the sword in a realistic way. 'I found,' he remarked[21], 'that it did not belong to the first Charles but the fourth, for I saw the lion of Bohemia engraved upon it.'

III

After the coronation the Emperor left to spend Easter in Naples, while the wedding guests departed for their homes—all but young King Ladislas who stayed on at Rome in Aeneas's charge. This boy was constantly the pivot of plots to steal his wardship from the Emperor. Such a scheme was afoot in Rome at this time, but a warning was brought to Aeneas so that he was able to keep the boy-king in safety by watching over him night and day. Ladislas could not even be allowed to go out hunting with the Cardinals for fear of treachery. Both he and Aeneas were relieved when Frederick returned from Naples and they all turned their faces northward. Nevertheless, Aeneas re-entered Germany with a heavy heart, for he hated to leave Italy for the cold and bleakness of the Emperor's residences, whether at Graz, or Vienna, or thirty miles away in the country at Wiener-Neustadt. Aeneas had at one time or another written charming descriptions of all these places, but he was older now, and ill, and disappointed: he longed above all for warmth and friendship. Now that Schlick and Michael von Pfullendorf were gone the German court seemed dull and empty and very very cold.

The deepest of his disappointments was that he had not yet received the Cardinal's hat, for Aeneas felt that this might well have been an appropriate reward for his recent efforts. The Emperor, never a forceful man, had tried tentatively to put forward his claims, and they had been voiced too by King Ladislas when he stayed in Rome. Piero di Noceto—now a close adviser of the Pope—did everything that he could to plead Aeneas's cause: for some reason, however, Nicholas V seemed determined to advance Aeneas no further. This is curious, because the bishoprics first of Trieste and then of Siena, though certainly not undesired, had been bestowed unsought. Aeneas himself gives no clue to show that there was any definite antagonism between Pope and Bishop; there does seem, however, to have been a certain coolness at that time, emphasizing the fact that their friendship had always been based upon propinquity rather than congeniality. It may well have been that Nicholas V still considered Aeneas frivolous and preferred to promote to the

Cardinalate more ardent churchmen or more experienced administrators. This Pope seldom bestowed even minor offices on his friends; in a series of Popes noted for their nepotism, Nicholas V only favoured his half-brother Filippo*, who was, indeed, a man of worth and ability.

In the opinion of Aeneas Sylvius, the one great blemish on the pontificate of Nicholas V was the shadow cast over Christendom by the loss of Constantinople in 1453. 'For many and great deeds was he famous and fortunate,' wrote Aeneas[22], 'but in the fall of Constantinople unfortunate, for this . . . branded his name with infamy.' Aeneas bracketed the Emperor with Nicholas V, claiming that his reign also was 'blackened with no small disgrace because of this great scandal to the Christian religion'. Indeed, Frederick III was, he thought, more culpable than Pope Nicholas, who had reigned only for a short time and had had little opportunity to help the Greeks in their struggle, whereas Frederick had for many years been tepid and vacillating in his support for the crusaders. After the battle of Varna, where Cardinal Cesarini had given his life for the cause, the Emperor had apparently lost all interest in the Hungarian resistance. It is true that he was moved to tears when news of the fall of Constantinople was brought to the Imperial Court at Graz, but he could not appreciate its full significance. It was Aeneas who at once realized the danger that faced Europe, disrupted as it was by jealousies and strife. 'Of the two lights of Christendom,' he wrote to Nicholas V[23], 'one has been put out.' Not only was he appalled by the physical threat, he grieved also for the destruction of Greek civilization and declared that it was a second death to Homer and Plato. His whole energy and powers of persuasion were thrown into the effort to set on foot a new crusade to win back this stronghold.

A Bull issued by the Pope on the last day of September 1453 called on all the Christian princes to offer their support, and the following spring saw a Diet called at Ratisbon to discuss ways and means. To the disgust of Aeneas, the Emperor made a feeble excuse for his non-attendance. Only Philip, Duke of Burgundy, showed any

---

* Filippo Calandrini, Bishop of Bologna, as Tommaso had been before him. He died in 1476. C. M. Ady, *Pius II*, p. 141, wrongly states that Filippo was the Pope's nephew.

enthusiasm; he appeared in person at the Diet and by his example induced other rulers either to come to Ratisbon themselves or at least to strengthen their delegations. The Franciscan friar, Giovanni Capistrano, an old friend and protégé of Aeneas, by his vigorous preaching stimulated support for the project among lesser people. But the rich and powerful who should have been the natural leaders, hesitated to commit themselves. Pope Nicholas felt a deep distrust of the Diet, for a Congress of this kind could, he feared, develop into a General Council and the lately healed wounds inflicted by the Schism might break out again. He was, too, an ailing man without the dynamic quality of leadership. The handsome young Duke of Bavaria was typical of many; he came to Ratisbon in search of adventure, but was soon diverted by the prospect of hunting; with his friends and followers he disappeared into the forest and the Congress saw him no more[24]. The wholly admirable speech made by Aeneas fell on ears attuned to other accents; he quickly realized that the Diet was foredoomed to failure. As he wrote to Capistrano early in 1455[25], pride, sloth and avarice were the three 'malignant plagues' that had wrecked its chances.

A further Diet met at Frankfurt in the autumn of 1454 to discuss the abortive proposals made at Ratisbon. By this time the shock of Constantinople's fall had weakened and the enemy still seemed far away. Rumours began to spread among the delegates that any money raised would only be spent for the benefit of the Hungarians who, 'because they could not defend their realm, wanted now to involve the Germans in their calamities'[26]. Again Aeneas spoke, again he commanded rapt attention. His speech lasted for two hours 'and so closely did they listen to him that not one even cleared his throat; none turned his eyes from the speaker's face, none thought his speech was anything but short'. Many praised this oration or circulated copies of it, though few really appreciated its import. Others who made good speeches 'were heard with boredom and derision'; when the Bishop of Pavia tried to lighten the occasion by introducing a flight of fancy he was condemned as frivolous. The delegates were determined not to be pleased and not to agree: some promises were renewed, a new congress was planned, but everyone went home with a feeling of strong dissatisfaction.

At the next meeting, in Wiener-Neustadt, matters seemed more promising and the passionate exhortations by Fra Giovanni won

notable response. Aeneas felt that some measure of success might
now be achieved, but everything was jolted to a halt by the Pope's
death on 24th March 1455. This 'in a moment cut short the web it
had taken so long to weave'. The Diet seized on the opportunity to
shelve the Turkish question[27]; all interest was now focused upon
the election of a successor to Nicholas V. Aeneas had lost a good
friend whom he had always respected rather than loved; like many
others he expected that the next Pope would be another colleague,
with whom he had much more in common and who fully shared
his enthusiasm for the new crusade. This was Cardinal Bessarion
of Nicaea, a Greek monk of the order of St Basil who had been made
Cardinal-Archbishop by Eugenius IV. He was a very distinguished
scholar and a man of high integrity; he seemed an obvious choice
and at the first scrutiny stood high above all others. Cardinal Alain
of Avignon, however, threw his influence against Bessarion, pointing
out that the Greek showed his alien character by retaining his beard,
and said: 'Behold the poverty of the Latin Church who cannot find
a man worthy of the Apostolic throne unless she looks to Greece!'[28]
In the next scrutiny the bearded Bessarion was passed over in favour
of an ancient Spaniard from Valencia, named Alfonso Borgia. He
was a nobleman who had in earlier years been known as an excellent
lawyer; in 1455 he was past seventy and, according to Aeneas,
'nearly decrepit'. He was, at the time of his election, Cardinal of the
Santi Quattro Coronati. Borgia took the name of Calixtus III; immediately upon his accession he made a vow that he would direct all
his energies against 'the impious Turks' and the collection of an army
to fight them became his ruling passion.

Aeneas, together with an old friend and correspondent of his,
Johann Hinderbach, was directed to go to Rome as ambassador
carrying Germany's obedience to the new Pope. This was a congenial mission; Aeneas set off for Italy in the summer of 1455 in high
spirits. Calixtus III cared little for literature and less for the fine
arts, nor was he interested in German or any other politics. His one
preoccupation was the defeat of the Turks, not by the summoning
of Congresses, but by the old-fashioned means of force of arms.
Aeneas made a passionate oration in support of this aim; many
copies of it were circulated and in due course it was printed inde-
pendently of his other famous speeches. The Pope welcomed this
backing; he showed that he was well-disposed to Aeneas, whose

thoughts began to turn again towards the Cardinal's hat he so deeply
desired. When it became known that Calixtus did indeed intend to
create new Cardinals during the next Advent, general opinion was
that Aeneas's name would be found among them. But only three
new creations were made, two of them the Pope's own nephews and
the third a young Portuguese with royal blood in his veins. They
were Luís, Cardinal-presbyter of Santi Quattro Coronati, Rodrigo,
Cardinal-deacon of S. Niccolò, and the Portuguese Don Jayme of
San Eustachio. Rodrigo Borgia afterwards became Pope Alexander VI.

Aeneas hid his vexation and disappointment as best he could,
making a dignified withdrawal to the Court of Naples. Here he was
able to conduct negotiations on behalf of Siena. It is interesting to
compare a letter that Aeneas wrote on this occasion to the Priori of
Siena[29] with an earlier one sent from Milan on 17th November
1433.[30] In the first instance he was self-consciously trying to make
an impression upon the city fathers in the hope of furthering his own
career, then beginning to unfold. The dispatch is carefully worded
and written in an exquisite hand that appears to be completely different from the fluent character of his autograph twenty-two years
later. By 1455 Aeneas was sure of his position and able to dash off a
bulletin that told the Priori in a few words exactly how matters
stood and what they might expect. Writing at four o'clock in the
morning he tells them: 'Master Bindo has returned from Gaeta . . .
the rumour is that he has done well, which I hear with immense
pleasure if it means that he brings peace to our city. I hear that he
has sent certain very swift couriers to you who will give you all the
news in his letters. So I need not set myself to guessing, which is for-
bidden to man.' By this date Aeneas had written so much and so
quickly, and his gouty fingers were so stiffened, that his handwriting
had lost its pristine elegance. It was still, however, a good and legi-
ble hand, full of character and typical of the writer. When it is laid
beside two other autograph letters also written to the Priori—one
from Rome on 28th January 1457 and the other from the baths at
Viterbo just before he became Pope[31]—Aeneas's handwriting is
seen to have become definitive, just as his relationship with the
Signoria had crystallized into a consistent condition of armed friendship.

After much persuasion Aeneas succeeded in inducing King Alfonso of Aragon to make peace between his beloved city and the condottiere captain Jacopo Piccinino who had been ravaging Tuscany. Hitherto, Alfonso had been disinclined to hear the Sienese case, but when Aeneas arrived to treat with him 'he received him with smiling countenance and honourable words, for as soon as he beheld him the King said: "Now we may speak of peace, since a mediator that we love has come." '[32] Even so, it was difficult to engage the King's attention, for he was greatly taken up with the charms of a new mistress named Lucrezia, so that the ambassadors had to follow him from Naples to Pozzuoli and back to Torre del Greco, or wherever Lucrezia happened to be. While he waited for the conduct of his business Aeneas took the opportunity to visit Salerno and Amalfi, where were the tombs of the Apostles Andrew and Matthew. He made expeditions, too, to 'the skeletons of ancient cities' in the district, and went to find the source of the River Sarno. The court at Naples pleased him greatly; he met again a friend of his student days[33], consorted with poets and painters, and enjoyed the conversation of his highly civilized companions. Above all, he found Alfonso everything that he expected a humanist prince to be: magnanimous, intelligent, and many-sided in his interests. In the *De Viris Illustribus*[34] Aeneas described Alfonso as: 'small in stature but immeasurable in spirit, contemptuous of danger . . . a great benefactor, fond of consorting with men of noble minds, never idle'. He also believed that he had found in the king a recruit for his crusading army. When Aeneas returned to Rome after this, his second, visit to Naples he felt refreshed and fortified and full of hope for the future.

Aeneas's fortunes had, indeed, taken a turn for the better. Not long after his return it was whispered to him that he would soon be created Cardinal. As before, he waited for confirmation of the news before openly rejoicing. This time, all was well. On 18th December 1456 Aeneas Sylvius was admitted to the Sacred College as Cardinal Priest of Santa Sabina. At the same time Giovanni Castiglione, Bishop of Pavia, also entered the Cardinalate, a self-important colleague of whom Aeneas had no high opinion. As he had once written to the Bishop of Fermo, Aeneas had found difficulty in living on the income from his benefices[35]; now that he had to support greater dignity he was compelled to seek for vacant canonries and so forth to satisfy his needs. No one has accused him of being greedy or grasp-

ing; it was a plain cold fact that he was a poor man whereas most
Cardinals were as wealthy as they were powerful. There is still a
hint of the impoverished Sienese student in the Cardinal of Santa
Sabina, but just as he had not allowed poverty to cramp his style
when he was young, so he now contrived to build himself up a position where his lack of means counted for very little. This he did by
the exercise of courtesy, tact, and geniality. His opinions were sought
and respected, particularly on matters concerning Germany. Indeed, he became a kind of specialist in Imperial relations. Aeneas
had always made friends readily; his tolerance was as notable as his
power of persuasion—both these qualities were rare in the Sacred
College and were therefore greatly prized. Young Rodrigo Borgia
was as different as any man could be from the German Nicholas of
Cusa, or the saintly Carvajal, yet all three Cardinals were Aeneas's
constant associates and he mixed on easy terms with all of them.
Servants, clerks, and secretaries delighted in giving him devoted
service, for never was there a more considerate employer. In the
two years of his Cardinalate Aeneas won golden opinions from
everyone in the Roman Curia, not least from the old Pope who still
had enough wits to see that Aeneas and Aeneas alone would be
willing and able to continue the Turkish campaign upon which his
mind was fixed. The Cardinals knew him as an excellent companion
and colleague; it may well be that those whose thoughts were bent
upon electing him to succeed Calixtus believed that they could
manipulate his policy as they wished. How wrong they were they
were shortly to find out.

Meanwhile Aeneas served his apprenticeship, observing, learning, and forming his own judgements. It was a fruitful time for his
writings, which were no longer inspired by escapism and nostalgia,
as in 1444. Now he had mellowed and matured; the *Germania*[36] is
the happiest of all his works, the *History of Frederick III* the most
penetrating[37]. The *Europa*[38] was compiled at this time too; it is
hardly more than a collection of material for an ambitious work
that was never written, but it contains some brilliant thumbnail
sketches[39] of people and places. The tragic death of Ladislas Postumus, King of Bohemia, in the winter of 1457 turned Aeneas's
thoughts sharply to the country in which he had always felt a deep
interest. He began to write the *History of Bohemia*[40], a book that
he meant to dedicate to Alfonso of Aragon. The dedicatory epistle

was, indeed, already completed when that great king and patron of
letters died in June 1458. Aeneas at this time was taking baths at
Viterbo, where he was having treatment for his gout; it is here that
he wrote the early chapters of the *History*.

Here, too, came the news that Pope Calixtus III had died on 6th
August of the same year. At once Aeneas prepared to leave for
Rome. He was joined by Cardinal Filippo of Bologna who had been
staying at Bagnoregio to escape the summer heat. Together they
travelled from Viterbo to Rome, to be greeted by the news that
Cardinal Capranica, Bishop of Fermo, had died within a few days
of the Pope. Now, indeed, the matter of Calixtus's successor was
wide open and, as Aeneas put it: 'all the city hung upon the event'.

CHAPTER IX

The Papal Conclave, 1458

The said Pope Pius was crowned in Rome, with the highest honour . . .
whereat all Christendom was very pleased, because he was well known to
everyone. – *Chronicle of Niccola della Tuccia*, 1458[1]

The Sacred College went into conclave on 16th August, ten days
after the late Pope's funeral; there the Cardinals would remain in
isolation from the world until they could agree upon a successor to
Calixtus. At this time they numbered twenty-four, but only eighteen
were present. Two Frenchmen and one German stayed in their
own countries, Aeneas's old friend and mentor Nicholas of Cusa
remained in his diocese of Brixen, and Cardinals Carvajal and
Scarampo were in command of papal forces, the one in Hungary
and the other at sea.

The Cardinals fell naturally into three groups, the Spaniards,
Frenchmen, and Italians, with the two converts from the Greek
church—Bessarion and Isidore of Russia—taking up an independent
and detached position. The Italians were subdivided: as ever the
Orsini and Colonna families were at enmity, as were the candidates
from Genoa and Milan. The Venetian Cardinal Pietro Barbo*,
nephew of Eugenius IV, and Filippo Calandrini of Bologna—half-
brother to Nicholas V—each had his own following. The last of this
group, other than Aeneas himself, was Cardinal Tebaldo, a creation
of Calixtus III by way of a reward to his brother, the chief papal
physician. The two Borgias and Don Jayme, together with two
older Spaniards, had little hope of succession but might well swing
the balance one way or the other. In the French faction the most

---

* Afterwards Pope Paul II.

powerful of all was the Cardinal of Rouen, strongly supported by his colleague, Alain of Avignon. The rich and powerful Guillaume d'Estouteville of Rouen was a man of great ability and dynamic character. From the first Aeneas recognized Estouteville as his chief rival: the death of Domenico Capranica had left the election theoretically very open, but it is clear that the choice really lay between these two.[2] Political or national trends were less important on this occasion than were personal prejudices, except in the mind of Bessarion who could think only of plans to further the crusade.

Aeneas entered the conclave with a feeling of quiet optimism. He could not but remember the Emperor's prophecy at the time of his coronation; he refrained from boasting but felt obliged to write in his *Commentaries*: '. . . most men foretold that Cardinal Aeneas of Siena would be Pope'. Nor was this opinion unsupported by evidence, for the Milanese ambassador wrote to his master that since the death of Capranica had ruined their plans he was transferring Milanese support either to Cardinal Colonna or to Aeneas. 'The Cardinal of Siena seems to me the more probable choice,' he wrote on 14th August, 'since all parties are inclined to agree upon his election'; he added that this candidate would have the full support of the new King of Naples, Alfonso's illegitimate son Ferrante[3]. This monarch was assured of Aeneas's friendship, should he become Pope. There would, however, be strong papal support for his rival, René of Anjou, if any French sympathizer were successful. It was therefore to Ferrante's interest to support the claims of Aeneas as forcefully as he could. Francesco Sforza foresaw great danger to Milan from too-powerful French interests, so he too brought his influence to bear in favour of Aeneas. Although he would have preferred to see the Milanese Giovanni Castiglione, Cardinal of Pavia, as Pope, Sforza was shrewd enough to recognize that Castiglione was unlikely to be chosen, so he gave unqualified backing to the Cardinal of Siena.

Before the proceedings actually began, the Bishop of Torcello, Domenico de' Domenichi, a very able and upright man, preached a sermon to all the assembled Cardinals. They were then free to make arrangements for settling in to their allotted quarters. Each had his own cell, opening off a large hall in the Vatican palace where they were at liberty to walk about and hold semi-private conversations. As may well be imagined, there was much lobbying and jockeying for position at this stage. The cells were provided for eating, sleeping, and meditation; all meetings were held in a smaller hall, where there was a chapel adorned with frescoes recently painted by Fra Angelico. On the first day of the Conclave proper certain 'Capitulations'[4] were drawn up that would be binding upon the new Pope: each Cardinal had to swear that he would observe them all in the event of his election. The Capitulations in 1458 included a promise to further the crusade, to reform the Curia, and to provide a monthly allowance to those Cardinals like Aeneas whose stipends were inadequate. The whole College must be consulted in matters of the first importance, such as the declaration of war. Since there were no sanctions that could compel a headstrong Pope to conform to any of these rules, and the most that the Cardinals could do was to 'admonish him in love', the Capitulations were of very little practical use. They were, in fact, no more than general recommendations of the course of policy it would be advisable to pursue.

The following day the first scrutiny was held immediately after Mass. This was a preliminary round of voting; it had no binding effect upon the direction in which votes would ultimately be cast. The supporters of Estouteville were content to bide their time; 'whether from design or malice'[5] no one voted for him on this occasion. If there had been overwhelming support for any one candidate —if, in fact, he had received the statutory two-thirds of the votes (in this instance, a round dozen)—the first scrutiny would also have been the last. Here, however, two candidates had five votes apiece, none of the others achieving more than three. The leaders were Aeneas himself and Filippo Calandrini of Bologna: either of these could be promoted by the method known as *per accessum* had the other candidates been willing to agree, but to this many of the Cardinals were bitterly opposed. The *accessus* was normally the result of informal discussion, when it could be discovered whether any member of the college would be willing to transfer his vote to a stronger candidate, in order to reach agreement. It was now clear that this election was to be fiercely contested; Aeneas and Calandrini had done no more than establish their candidature, the hidden forces and pressures would now become apparent.

'So they went to dinner,' wrote Aeneas, 'and then many groups were formed. The men having most power in the College, whose authority and wealth gave them distinction, summoned the others and demanded the apostolate for themselves or for their friends. They implored, promised, threatened; some even without a blush, and forgetting all modesty, spoke in praise of themselves and claimed the pontificate. So did Guillaume of Rouen, Pietro of San Marco, and Giovanni of Pavia i.e., Estouteville, Barbo, and Castiglione. . . . Each sang his own praises. Great was their rivalry and extreme their diligence.' Most vocal of all was the Cardinal of Rouen, who recognized Aeneas as his chief rival and made a bitter personal attack upon him. 'What is Aeneas to you,' he asked, 'that you think him fit for the pontificate? Will you give us a Pope lame in both feet and poor? How will he who is penniless assist our penniless Church? How will he who is sick cure her sickness? He has just come from Germany, we do not know him. Perhaps he will even carry the Curia thither. Where is his learning? Shall we put a poet in St Peter's place, and rule the Church by the Laws of the Gentiles?' He then put forward—with some crudity—his own claims. 'I am the senior Cardinal,' he declared, 'you know that I am not imprudent, and I am learned in pontifical law. Royal blood flows in my veins, and I am rich in friends and money with which I can bring help to the impoverished Church. I have also not a few ecclesiastical benefices which, when I resign them, I will divide among you and others.' Whether they were moved by his eloquence or charmed by his promises, frightened by his threats, or simply of the opinion that he was bound to be successful, several of the Cardinals made up their minds to vote for Rouen. He and Cardinal Alain of Avignon won over the waverers by conferring with them singly or in groups. With mounting indignation Aeneas reported: 'A number of Cardinals met in the latrines and there, as being a private hiding-place, agreed together how they should elect Guillaume to be Pope, and bound themselves with signatures and oaths. Relying on them he straightway began promising priesthoods, magistracies, and offices, and divided his provinces among them. A worthy setting for the choice of such a Pope!'

By nightfall Rouen was assured of eleven of the twelve votes he needed. There was no time to be lost: when Cardinal Calandrini of Bologna woke Aeneas from his sleep to come and offer the twelfth vote that would make Rouen Pope, the election seemed over. But Aeneas was a man of spirit, nor would he win the cheap and temporary gratitude of his rival by acceding to him. To Calandrini who, as Aeneas recognized, was speaking purely as a friend, he exclaimed: 'You, if you are a Christian, will not accept as Christ's vicar one whom you know to be a limb of the devil.' These bold words put new heart into Calandrini, for he was a timid person, much gentler than his choleric brother, Nicholas V. The Cardinal of Siena had shown him that there was, indeed, an alternative choice. As dawn broke, Aeneas sought out Rodrigo Borgia, asking him whether he had sold himself to Rouen. 'What would you have me do?' replied Borgia cheerfully. 'The affair is settled. A lot of them met in the latrine and decided to elect him. It is not to my advantage to remain among the few who lack the favour of the new Pope. I run with the majority and have looked after myself.' After this frank avowal Rodrigo went on to say that he was counting upon the Chancellorship that had been promised to him, but Aeneas pointed out that this office was far more likely to be given to Alain of Avignon who was closer to Estouteville and more certain of reward. 'Will the Frenchman be more friendly to the Frenchman or the Catalan?' he asked, and told Borgia that he might hold Rouen's promissory note, but that Avignon would have the Chancery.

On no occasion did Aeneas show his talent for diplomacy more strongly than in his tactical battle for the Papacy. One by one he approached those Cardinals who had been his supporters but who had been won over by the bribes or browbeating of Rouen. He knew the Cardinal of Pavia to be a stupid and conceited man, and knew, too, exactly what to say to him. Aeneas quoted the example of Castiglione's uncle who, as Cardinal of Piacenza, never rested until he had secured the election of Martin V and brought back the Papacy to Rome in triumph. 'He', said Aeneas, 'brought the Apostolic Curia from Germany back to Italy, and you, his nephew, will carry it out of Italy into France . . . what a splendid bridegroom you have chosen for the bride of Christ, when you entrust her to a wolf!' Giovanni Castiglione was moved to tears by Aeneas's stern comments, but replied that he could not retract his promise without behaving as a traitor. 'To which Aeneas replied: "It has come to this . . . that whatever you do will incur the charge of treachery. Now you have got to choose whether you would rather betray Italy, your country, and your church, or Rouen." Convinced by these words, Pavia thought it less disgraceful to abandon Rouen.' The Cardinal Pietro of San Marco showed more independence of judgement than did Castiglione, and less cynical self-seeking than Rodrigo Borgia. Since he saw clearly that he himself had no prospect of election, Pietro Barbo came out strongly in favour of Aeneas. First he told all the rest of the College of the secret agreement made in the latrines, then he summoned seven of them to a meeting in the cell of Cardinal Fiesco of Genoa, and exhorted his hearers to vote in favour of Siena.

The time for the second scrutiny was drawing near; the Cardinals assembled in the Chapel of St Nicholas with a strong feeling that the crisis was upon them. The golden cup in which the slips of paper would be put was set upon the altar. It was guarded by three Cardinals appointed to see fair play. One of them was Rouen himself, the other two were Isidore the Cardinal-Bishop of Russia, and Prospero Colonna. One by one the Cardinals rose from their seats and advanced in order of seniority to toss their papers into the cup. Aeneas noticed that Rouen was pale and trembling with emotion. When all had voted, the three Cardinals in charge emptied the cup onto a table set in the middle of the Chapel and read out the names written on the slips. Aeneas and the others prudently made notes of the names as they were announced. This was just as well, for when Estouteville of Rouen counted the votes he gave the number of those who had chosen Aeneas as eight. 'Look more carefully at the papers,' said the Cardinal of Siena, for he knew that nine votes had been cast for him. 'Rouen said nothing, as though he had made a mistake.'

Nine votes had indeed been cast for Aeneas, only six for Estouteville. The College now agreed that they should try to reach a decision *per accessum*. All sat motionless in their places, pale and silent. Only the movement of their eyes showed that they were alive. More and more tense did the silence become, everyone waiting for the more senior members of the College to make the first accession. But it was young Rodrigo Borgia who suddenly sprang to his feet and offered his vote to Aeneas. 'And his words were like a sword through Rouen's heart.' Again there came a long silence, but now the Cardinals were eyeing one another and communicating by nodding. Two of those who did not wish to vote for Aeneas broke the tension by leaving the room hurriedly, 'pleading the calls of nature', but since no one followed them they soon returned. At last the aged Tebaldo tottered to his feet. 'I too yield to Siena,' he declared. 'At that a greater panic filled them all, they lost their voices, like men in a house that is shaken by a mysterious earthquake. For Aeneas lacked only one vote, since twelve made a Pope.' To give the deciding vote was generally thought to be good policy, for the final accession might win a reward from the victorious candidate, while there was a certain glory in being the creator of the new Pope. Prospero Colonna had a fine sense of personal importance: he decided to make the announcement of the twelfth and final vote. In the words of Aeneas: 'He rose and would have given his voice solemnly, as is usual, but he was seized about the middle by Nicaea [Bessarion] and Rouen, who rebuked him harshly because he wanted to yield to Aeneas. And when he persisted in his intention they tried to drag him forcibly from the room, that even so they might snatch the pontificate from Aeneas. One on the right, one on the left, they tried to lead him away, but Prospero, caring nothing for their insults and foolish words . . . , turned to the other Cardinals and cried—"I too yield to Siena, and I make him Pope." At this the spirits of his adversaries failed them and all their schemes were broken.'

In a moment the whole situation was changed, the tension eased, the conflict forgotten. 'With no dissentient voice' the Cardinals acclaimed Aeneas Sylvius as Pope, and prostrated themselves at his feet. Then Bessarion, only a few minutes after the unseemly brawl with Colonna, made a speech that was honest and magnanimous, in keeping with his rugged character. Speaking for himself, as well as for all Rouen's supporters, Cardinal Bessarion assured Aeneas that they had a high opinion of his character and abilities, declaring that their opposition had been solely on the ground of his physical disabilities. 'Had you been healthy of body,' he told Aeneas, 'there was no one whom we had judged preferable to you. But since God is pleased with you we must perforce be pleased also. The Lord who has chosen you will himself supplement the defects of your feet, and you will not punish our ignorance.' To this Aeneas made a graceful reply. 'You estimate us, Nicaea,' he said, '. . . much higher than we do ourselves. For you attribute to us only the defect of our feet: we are well aware that our imperfection stretches far and wide.'

Without any more ado Aeneas donned the white robe, or tunic. When he was asked by what name he would be called he had his

answer ready. 'Pius,' he said. It is not for posterity to say whether
he was thinking less of the early Christian martyr Pope Pius I than
of Virgil's hero Pius Aeneas. Taking up a pen the new Pope signed
the Capitulations he had helped to plan. It was a solemn moment,
the strife of the election was stilled, all were now at least outwardly
united in support of a figure they could all respect.

According to Campano[6], Aeneas wept at his election, deeply
stirred by a variety of emotions. In Rome there was joy that an
Italian would be Pope, in Milan and Naples deep satisfaction. The
Sienese, who had cold-shouldered Aeneas in the past, welcomed
the election of Pius II with feasting and fireworks and unbridled
enthusiasm.[7] People danced in the streets, there were pageants and
orations in his honour, and on the day of his coronation a solemn
thanksgiving in the Duomo. 'Throughout Italy there was great festivity,' wrote the Prior of Viterbo in his *Chronicle*[8], 'and all Christendom was happy at the news.' Only in Florence were there glum
faces; this was not from any personal rancour, it was due simply
to the long-standing rivalry with Siena. A young Englishman in
Ferrara wrote home to his patron: 'I am very well aware that before
you read this letter you will have heard the news of the new Pope's
election. But I am inclined to think that you cannot yet have realized with what heartfelt joy this election has been greeted by the
whole of Italy.'[9] The writer described the four days' celebration
ordered by the Marquis Borso d'Este, the singing, the horseraces,
and the gorgeous bonfires when 'wild youths' tore down wooden
porches and snatched boats from their moorings in the near-by river
to feed flames 'that nearly touched the sky'. A cosmopolitan party
of pilgrims returning from Jerusalem heard the news in early October from the sailors on board a Venetian galley: they too found it
'very delightful tidings'[10].

As for the Roman populace, they had awaited the result of the
Conclave with mounting excitement, until it was announced to them
from a high window of the palace. Some of them mistook 'il Senese',
the Sienese Cardinal, for 'il Genovese' and rushed off to the house
of the rich Archbishop of Genoa to loot his possessions. This was
the custom of the mob at every papal election; Pius II observed
ruefully that they did not find much of value in his apartments,
although they were so rapacious that they carried off 'even the

marbles'*. Pius thought it a disgraceful practice and regretted the loss of his books, which were appropriated from his cell by the servants attending the Conclave. He was, however, greatly moved by the reception given him by the common people. 'Everywhere was laughter, joy, voices crying: Siena, Siena, oh fortunate Siena.' When night fell, 'bonfires blazed at every crossroad . . . neighbour feasted neighbour, there was not a place where horns and trumpets did not sound, not a quarter of the city that was not alive with public joy. The older men said they had never seen in Rome such popular rejoicings.'

The following evening the chief citizens came to the Vatican on horseback, carrying burning tapers in their hands, to salute the Pope with solemn reverence. Elated as he was, Pius was deeply aware not only of the dignity but of the responsibility of his position. There were storm clouds in the sky when he rode out of Siena with Cardinal Capranica, twenty-seven years earlier; now that he had succeeded to the position that would have been Capranica's there were darker and more dangerous portents to be faced. Pius had qualities of abounding courage and self-control, patience, humour and judgement: in the future he would need them all. It was a time of surpassing difficulty when there was no room at all for complacency. The man who said in all sincerity that his infirmities were not confined to his feet was not ill-equipped for battling with such forces. At least he had the will and determination to do his utmost to protect the Papacy and to reinforce its wilting powers.

* I.e. statuary.

PART TWO

THE POPE
1458–1464

CHAPTER X

The Congress of Mantua

. . . the Pope replied: . . . 'Our religion is in peril, attacked by the Turks
against whom this congress has been summoned. If we go forth the temporal power of the Church is in danger. But this has been often lost and
as often recovered. If once we lose our spiritual power it is [uncertain]
whether we can ever recover it. Let these fleeting things perish, provided
we retain those more substantial ones.' And without another word he
started on his journey. – AENEAS SYLVIUS PICCOLOMINI, *Commentaries*

I

It was not long before the Cardinals began to realize that they had
elected less of a King Log than a King Stork. Those who thought
that the enthusiasm shown by Aeneas for his project of a crusade
had no deeper value than an election promise were quickly disillusioned. Immediately after his election Aeneas proved beyond
all doubt that the eloquence of his orations had been sincere and
that destruction of the power of the Turks really was his dearest
ambition. The new Pope appreciated that there was no time to be
lost; no one had a greater sense of urgency. Pius threw himself into
the business of preparation with an efficiency that astonished those
of the Cardinals who had looked on him as a literary adventurer
with no ambitions except personal ones.

Remembering the amateurish and fumbling efforts to reach
agreement upon important matters, both at Ratisbon and at Wiener-
Neustadt, Pius determined that the congress he was about to call
should be differently conducted. Practical matters must have far
more prominence, a lower value should be set upon vague promises.
In short, good intentions unsupported by a firm offer of men and

munitions would not be enough. If the princes he intended to summon were genuinely unable to attend the new conference, they must be bound by any undertakings given by their envoys. Pius avoided the mistake of imagining that he could himself, simply by virtue of his position, provide the necessary leadership. Advice and co-operation from the rulers of France, Spain, Germany and England were essential for his plan, as well as support both practical and moral from the Italian despots and republics. As he wrote in the *Commentaries*: 'Pope Pius . . . put not his confidence in himself alone, that is, in the strength of the apostolic see; for to subdue the Turks seemed a task not for this Kingdom or that, but for the whole of Christendom. So he considered it necessary to obtain their advice whose help he was going to ask, and decided that a congress of princes and free peoples should be summoned, at which they should discuss together their common salvation.'

At a very early stage in his pontificate Pope Pius composed a series of letters, written in moderate and tactful terms, in which he set out the position and invited all rulers to show their goodwill by attending his conference in person. He was far too intelligent a diplomat, and too experienced, to try to rush his collaborators into a position that they might be unable or unwilling to maintain. It is a measure of the distance he had travelled that Pius was content to use persuasion rather than to resort to the emotional appeal that in his younger days would have been his instinctive choice of weapon. His honest realism made him tolerant of the doubts and difficulties that must beset those who were to be asked to put the needs of Christendom above the interests of their own countries or provinces. No one saw more clearly than he that apathy and self-interest might bedevil his Congress, but he was the last man to be daunted by such considerations.

A well-intentioned amateur diplomatist who tried at this time to further the cause of the crusade was the Milanese poet, Giovanni Stefano Cotta. Putting aside the eclogues he was writing for Francesco Sforza[1], Cotta embarked upon seven exhortations, in the form of letters addressed to various princes, in which he begged them to take up arms against the Turks.[2] These recently discovered epistles are something more than a literary exercise; they represent the reactions of an ordinary man of letters confronted by a situation that he did not entirely comprehend but whole-heartedly deplored.

Cotta's first epistle was, as might be expected, directed to the Pope himself: the last, 'to all Christians'. The remaining five he inscribed to the rulers who seemed to him most influential: the Emperor Frederick, Charles King of France, the Dauphin, King Ferrante, and Francesco Sforza. These were, in fact, five of the people from whom Pius II had the keenest expectations; in the end they were those who disappointed him most deeply.

It was personal interest combined with a short-sighted view of the prospect before them that had prevented the leaders of Christendom from implementing the conclusions of earlier Congresses. There was another reason, too, why they did not take the Turkish menace seriously. This was plain ignorance of the facts. Little more than sixty years had passed since the disastrous battle of Nicopolis[3], when a hundred thousand crusaders had been outmanoeuvred, outfought, and finally routed by the better-disciplined Turks. The news was long in reaching western Europe, for those who survived the battle—except the few nobles considered worth a ransom—were nearly all decapitated or sent to slavery in eastern lands. A few stragglers made their way home, starving and exhausted by the rigours of winter in the mountains of Hungary, only to be greeted with ridicule and disbelief. When at last the full extent of the calamity became known, attention was fixed upon finding means to pay the huge ransoms that the Turks demanded rather than upon the implications of the defeat. The humiliation of the Christian forces was forgotten long before the ransom money had been collected[4]. Those who could have testified to the accuracy of the Turkish bowmen, and to their iron discipline combined with ferocious courage, were either dead or enslaved. The stay-at-homes clung to the absurd idea that the Ottoman Turks were a disorderly rabble, persuading themselves that primitive weapons and tactics were adequate for Christian knights to employ against such heathens.

The grandsons of the defeated crusaders soon forgot the half-learned lessons of Nicopolis; they still felt sure that a few catapults could match the formidable artillery of the Turks. This blind overconfidence was, as it usually is, based on a complete lack of comprehension. Even so, the Christian leaders might have taken advantage of a second warning when Cardinal Cesarini's army was defeated at Varna. This was not nearly so important a battle as

Nicopolis—it was scarcely more than a trial of strength during the
chronic skirmishing between Turks and Hungarians—but it showed
once again how notably the crusaders underestimated their enemies
both in strength and quality. Only in Hungary, the last European
outpost against the Turkish invaders, was there any realistic appreciation of their military skill on land, although the Genoese and
Venetians had a wholesome respect for Turkish naval strength.

On at least two occasions before their successful siege in 1453
Turkish sultans had come near to capturing Constantinople. In 1402
Bajazet I might well have overpowered the Greek defenders had
he not been obliged to turn aside in order to contend with a dangerous Tatar invasion of Asia Minor[5] under the famous Timur—
that 'Tamerlaine the Great' whose name has passed into legend.
At the Battle of Angora in that year the Sultan's men were decisively
defeated and Bajazet himself taken prisoner. This setback, together
with the courageous defence of Hungary under the Transylvanian
hero John Hunyadi, father of Matthias Corvinus, a generation later,
postponed Turkish victory for fifty years. At the time Mahomet II
made the final assault upon Constantinople the Greeks were already
disheartened. They had received neither the men nor the money
they had expected from western Europe. Only about four hundred
men-at-arms from Genoa helped to defend the city as the walls
were pounded and shattered by heavy Ottoman artillery, specially
cast for the purpose at Adrianople[6]. The doomed Greeks, under
their Emperor, Constantine XI Dragases (1448-1453), fought
bravely enough and it was not until the siege had lasted seven and
a half weeks that the invaders were able to storm into the city. It
was the last chapter in a tale of shame.

The question was whether it might also be the opening chapter
of a new story of Turkish aggression and advance into Europe.
This was the fear that had obsessed Pope Calixtus III and was, indeed, present in the mind of anyone able to take an objective view
of the future and willing to face alarming facts. Pius II saw more
clearly than did most of his contemporaries that the crusading movement was now far less of a holy war for the recovery of the custody
of the Holy Places from Muslim hands than a military campaign in
defence of Christendom[7]. As long as the Holy Land remained subject to Mahomet II his power outside its borders must be reduced
before any reconquest could be undertaken.

Such a realistic and common-sense standpoint was not new; it had been long the opinion of experienced travellers although few of them had been able to make their voices heard. A Cretan named Emanuele Piloto wrote (before 1441) a long and most admirable treatise addressed to Eugenius IV advising him how best a crusade should be conducted[8]. For more than thirty years Piloto had lived in Mohamedan territories, having started his career as Genoese consul in Alexandria. He really understood Muslim civilization, his deep knowledge making him adopt a much more liberal attitude towards the 'Saracen' races than was common at this time, but small heed was paid to his warning. Of those who were not directly inspired by commercial motives, as were the merchants of Genoa, Venice, Pisa and Ancona, many still thought in terms of a war of revenge for the cruelties and insults endured by earlier crusaders. It may be remarked that the cruelties were by no means all upon one side: it had been the massacre by the crusaders of prisoners taken in a skirmish before the battle of Nicopolis that had hardened the heart of the Sultan Bajazet and led him to order wholesale slaughter of the Christians.

Although he himself had not had opportunity to travel in the Levant or in the Holy Land, Pius II was always ready to listen to first-hand accounts of oriental territories. Often he put the information to good use, as in his *Asia*, the work that inspired explorers and geographers for several generations to come*. In a letter to the Franciscan preacher Capistrano the Pope put the blame for the fall of Constantinople squarely where it belonged[9]. 'If we were humble, energetic, and magnanimous,' he declared, 'we could collect an army which could crush not only the Turks but also all other unbelievers.' In his zeal to learn the relevant facts Pius paid close attention to the harrowing tales recited by refugees and was perhaps too ready to accept them at their face value. More than once he was deceived by impostors on their first appearance, for he was so deeply distressed by the plight of Christendom that his customary astuteness forsook him for the time being. Some account of these 'impostorous envoys' will be found in later pages; of the refugees who worked upon the Pope's easily aroused emotions the most genuine

---

* Including, perhaps, Christopher Columbus. See A. W. Berg: *Aeneas Sylvius in seiner Bedeutung als Geograph*, Halle, 1901.

as well as the most notable was Queen Charlotte of Cyprus, whose appeal for help came at an opportune time in stimulating zeal for the crusade when it seemed to have died away.

The queen's visit to Rome, however, lay several years ahead; in 1458, immediately after his election, Pius II had to generate initiative and enthusiasm without any extraneous help. To those of his advisers who, remembering the failure of the Congress of Ratisbon only five years earlier, begged him to postpone his scheme for organizing the defence of the Christian world, Pius had only one reply. He must and would put first things first. Even before establishing his temporal power, before there had been time to conquer or placate the discordant elements in Rome, Pius decided to take the first steps towards a new crusade. He felt certain that it was his mission to convince the Christian rulers that their duty lay in coming not next year but immediately to the aid of the Church. His whole energy and his formidable eloquence was to be turned to their persuasion. Already plans had been made, tentatively by Nicholas V and more strongly by Calixtus III, to hold a further Congress. Calixtus, old and feeble as he was, could readily be roused to enthusiasm when the idea of a crusade confronted his groping mind. It was, indeed, the one topic on which he thought clearly and strongly. He, at any rate, never made the mistake of believing Aeneas's speeches and writings on this subject to be conventional exercises or merely occasions for displaying the Sienese Cardinal's eloquence. He took Aeneas seriously and rightly regarded him as the strongest advocate in the whole of the Curia, for, although Bessarion was equally fervent and had much better first-hand knowledge of the situation, he was a poor orator and totally lacked the compulsive eloquence in which Aeneas excelled.

No one who reads the little tract *de captione urbis Constantinopolitane* can fail to be impressed by Pius II's sincerity. It is vigorous and forthright, and his description of the storming of the city is as vivid as anything he ever wrote. This pamphlet quickly went through several editions and seems to have reached a wide public[10]. In it the author's indignation against Mahomet II at times outruns the elegance of his style; once he is led to refer to the sultan as 'crudelis et sanguinarius carnifex'. This immoderate language is in strong contrast to the restrained and balanced arguments that he afterwards advanced in his *Letter to Mahomet*[11].

To find a meeting-place for all those embassies Pius II hoped would attend his Congress was far from easy. The city first suggested was Udine in the province of Trieste. This seemed appropriate, since near-by Venice was the power most deeply concerned. The Venetians, however, cared more for their commercial dealings with the Turks than for joining whole-heartedly in the crusade: as Pope Pius remarked (*Commentaries*, Book II): 'They did not love the Christian religion so much as they feared the Turks.' They rejected the proposal with vehemence, nor would they allow the Congress to be held elsewhere in their territory for fear of compromising their position. Some of the Cardinals believed that the Congress should meet in Rome, others suggested a site in Germany or France. There were long discussions and much impassioned argument before agreement could be reached. The first invitations that were sent out offered Udine or Mantua as alternative locations, for the Venetians did not reject Udine until after Pius II had actually set out on his progress northwards[12]. In the end Mantua was chosen because it was convenient and accessible, with good communications both by road and river, and because its ruler was an enlightened person ready to play host to a great variety of delegates. Pius II was personally pleased with the choice of Mantua, for it seemed to him 'a very ample city, set in fertile soil . . . and it provides this advantage, that supplies from all over Lombardy may be brought there by ship.' As early as 22nd October 1458 he had written a letter to Lodovico Gonzaga, Marquis of Mantua, telling him that Mantua was his foremost selection for the Congress, and assuring him that he looked forward to his reception there[13].

The Cardinals grumbled at the prospect of so long a journey but as they could offer no alternative plan they had to allow themselves to be talked into agreement. The Romans also were highly dissatisfied, for they realized that they were bound to lose material benefit, as well as prestige, through the absence of the Curia. Dr Daniel Waley has pointed out the great economic importance to Roman tradesmen, bankers, and inn-keepers of the residence of the papal household[14]. Not only did they supply the prelates themselves with goods and services, but also the multitude of strangers seeking a hearing for their various causes. The bankers in particular depended upon the loans made to the Pope himself, or to the Cardinals, or to needy visitors who found they had overspent the allowances they had brought with them: cost of living, fees, and dues being far heavier than might have been expected.

Many Roman citizens professed to believe that the Pope would never return home, 'heavy [as he was] with years and sickness'. Some even affirmed that the whole thing was part of a plot by the Pope to enrich Siena, his native land, and that he intended to transfer the apostolic see there or elsewhere—perhaps beyond the Alps. Memory of the residence at Avignon was still green in men's minds; it is not surprising therefore that 'those who were more sensible came trooping to the Pope, opposed his departure, asked him to stay in his own city, and promised much if he would remain.'[15] Pius had to delay his journey until arrangements could be made to reassure them. First of all the Pope bound the local landowners upon oath to keep the peace during his absence, then he appointed a skeleton staff to carry out the duties of the Curia under the authority of Cardinal Nicholas of San Pietro in Vincoli as his spiritual vicar. The college of Judges were ordered to remain at their posts. Pius tried to ally himself with the most powerful of the civic parties by appointing Antonio Colonna, Prince of Salerno, Prefect of Rome. He was the brother of Cardinal Prospero, who had given Pius II the decisive vote in the Conclave of 1458. He promised that any papal election—should he happen to die during his travels—would indubitably be held in Rome[16]. These were common-sense dispositions, but they had to be makeshift in character, as were the temporary settlements of political matters in Naples and Sicily. Outstanding problems had to be shelved, not solved, as the day of departure drew near.

II

At last, on 20th January 1459, Pope Pius left the Vatican. He went at nightfall to the church of Santa Maria Maggiore on the Esquiline, where he spent the following day preparing for his journey and blessing 'a vast and weeping crowd'. He himself was moved to tears, the whole cavalcade setting forth in dismal spirits. 'His friends opposed him,' we read, 'and by many stratagems sought to delay the Pope. They reminded him that the winter was severe, the ranges of the Apennines were frozen, his journey was full of a thousand dangers. And when these objections proved vain there were not wanting some to cry: Well, Pope, if no thought of your body holds you back, think at least of the church of Rome, entrusted to your care, think of the plots laid against her. Who will protect the patrimony of St Peter when you are absent? As soon as you have crossed the Po hungry wolves will fall upon your realm. For what land is more full of tyrants, not to say brigands, than yours?'[17] Undaunted by these arguments, though heavy at heart, the Pope took leave of his people. Then, accompanied by the six Cardinals (Guillaume d'Estouteville of Rouen, the Breton Alain of Avignon, Filippo Calandrini of Bologna, Pietro Barbo of San Marco, Prospero Colonna and Rodrigo Borgia) he had chosen to attend him, he turned his face northwards and set out for Mantua.

The first night of the journey, 22nd January, was spent at Campagnano, a village sixteen miles distant from Rome. Here the whole party was splendidly entertained by the Archbishop of Trani; Giovanni Saracini, who was the papal *spenditore* or treasurer, on this occasion wrote in his account book that nothing had to be paid out, since all expenses had been covered[18]. Next morning the whole party had shaken off their gloom. Although his way now lay through country dominated by the condottiere Jacopo Piccinino the Pope went on 'full of hope, nor ever thought that God's help could possibly fail him'[19]. His faith was promptly vindicated when news came that Piccinino had yielded the town of Assisi that he had annexed previously from the Papal States.

Recalling his dissatisfaction with Siena, for the commune had not yet allowed the banished nobility to return, the Pope decided to avoid that city and to travel by way of Perugia and Arezzo towards Florence. Crossing the Tiber presented little difficulty, for near the town of Magliano a wooden bridge had recently been built. The Pope and his companions passed over it, pausing only to admire the festoons of ivy and green branches with which it was adorned. By 24th January the party had reached Narni. Here, all the country people thronged about the Pope, wishing him long life and happiness and strewing his way with aromatic herbs. Many houses were decorated with garlands and ribands, while the streets were carpeted with precious cloths, so delighted were the people to welcome their Pope. In Terni, too, the citizens fought each other with swords for the privilege of laying hands upon his horse. Soon the citadel of Spoleto came into view, a fortress that dominated the

pleasant valley leading to it. Here the Pope was well received and
the two days he spent in the town were among the happiest of his
tour. The Cardinals, too, enjoyed this halt, for Pope Pius gave a
special feast for his companions and so far departed from his austere
custom as to 'eat merrily' with them. Before he left Spoleto Pius
received three messengers carrying replies to the letters of invitation that he had written from the Vatican. The first was a procrasti-
nating answer from the Emperor excusing himself from coming to
Mantua in person, the second a more emphatic refusal from the
Venetian Senate. Only the last messenger brought tidings that were
pleasing to the Pope. The city fathers of Siena had suffered a change
of heart. Alarmed at the idea of friendly relations between the rival
city of Florence and the Papacy, and jealous perhaps of Arezzo
where Pius would doubtless be received with honour, the Sienese
made haste to invite the Pope to visit his own city forthwith. They
could not prevent the progress through Florence, but they could set
the pattern for the Pope's reception.

Pius allowed the Sienese messengers to believe they had persuaded him to change his plan, although he knew very well what
was passing in their minds. He did not, however, turn aside immediately but held his course for Foligno, Assisi, and Perugia. In
Perugia the Pope spent three delightful weeks: 'For though the
winter was very severe the city was adorned exactly as though it
were spring. All the place was green, and . . . in all the streets were
hung the insignia of the Pope and the golden crescent moons, i.e.
the arms of the Piccolomini. Military games were held, everything
seemed bathed in happiness.' Pius had arrived on the Vigil of the
Feast of the Purification, so he was able to bless and distribute the
candles. A few days later he dedicated the great church of S. Domenico, and his biographer Campano tells us that he ordered the
glazing of the great window behind the high altar[20]. While Pius
explored the town and wrote down in his *Commentaries* many interesting things that he had learned about Perugia's history, the
city 'famous both in arms and letters', and recounted the distinction
of her scholars, the bloody deeds of Braccio da Montone, the battles of the condottieri Piccinino, father and son*—he still found time

---

* Niccolò and Jacopo. Another son of Niccolò, named Francesco, 'though
brave and distinguished in warfare, succumbed to drunkenness and soon after
died'. *Commentaries*, Book II.

to receive various envoys. Delegates of Duke Louis of Savoy arrived to offer the Pope obedience, and he was visited also by the soldier-Duke of Urbino, Federigo of Montefeltro. The last was a congenial and welcome guest; he and the Pope had much in common and many topics to discuss. They became, indeed, close personal friends. To mark his pleasure in the Duke's company Pius made him a number of presents including a quantity of sweetmeats: 10 lb. of marzipan and half as much again of the little comfits—*coriandoli*—that belong to times of carnival[21].

At last the Pope decided that he must be on his way. Descending the steep hill from Perugia's fortifications, Pius and his companions followed the course of a rivulet that led them to Lake Trasimene. As the party approached its shores, their meditation on Hannibal's victory was interrupted by the sight of menacing clouds and lashing rain. It seemed impossible that Pius could cross to the island where he meant to spend the night with the Franciscan brothers who had a small friary there. But, as Pius reached the water's edge, the storm that had raged for several days suddenly abated. The wind dropped and the waves disappeared from the lake: 'as the Pope went on board the sea grew calm like a tamed animal. On every side the waves were stilled, a marvellous calm fell, so that a great catch of fish was taken while they sailed to the island.' Next morning Lake Trasimene, 'so stormy and intractable all the winter', lay smooth as glass, but as soon as Pius and the Cardinals had landed on the further shore, a raging wind sprang up 'so that those who were following the Pope only just escaped drowning'. Pius was encouraged by the local fishermen and villagers to believe that a smooth crossing had been miraculously contrived for him. Following the line of the Chiana, Pius reached Sienese territory at Chiusi. This he rated 'a wretched little town', and he was disappointed to find that no trace remained there of the ancient labyrinth that Pliny had said was not least among the wonders of the world. 'And that no traces of it have survived,' the Pope said dryly, 'might seem another wonder.'

From Chiusi Pius and some of his followers set out for Sarteano; the rest of the party followed the road to San Quirico d'Orcia, where they put up at the Eagle Inn[22] for two nights while the Pope went on to Corsignano to visit his friends and relations. On Thursday, 22nd February, the two parties came together as the cavalcade headed northward for Siena. As they approached Buonconvento news arrived that the Bishop of Padua was dead. Pope Pius impetuously granted the vacant bishopric to Pietro Barbo, the Cardinal of San Marco, who was riding by his side, and the next morning held a consistory with the five other Cardinals to settle the matter. The see of Vicenza, vacated by Barbo, was transferred to the Pope's notary, Gregorio Corario, and Corario's monastery in Verona became available for Pius's own nephew. The Pope imagined that this complicated transfer would please everyone, particularly the Venetians 'to whose nobility the Cardinal belonged. But to them nothing seemed more grievous, for they were stirred by rabid hatred and civil discords of which the Pope knew nothing.'[23]

As he spent the night of 23rd February six miles short of Siena, Pius was unaware of the seeds of discord he had sown that day, nor did he appreciate until many months later the intransigence of the Venetians. It seemed to him as he entered his own city—'beautifully adorned and making holiday'—that he brought with him peace and goodwill. Those who resented his presence in the city at first kept silence amid the general rejoicing. By his own account[24] Pius then made some very ill-timed references to the restoration of the nobility, and his graceful speech in praise of the Sienese failed to placate the city fathers. The Prior accepted the gift of the golden rose that the Pope presented to him in person, listening to the speech with its effective quotation from Sallust* with close attention, but at the end he made a curt reply. All those who disagreed with the proposed readmission of the nobility at once 'blasphemed the Pope and criticized his speech'. Pius, however, continued to press the nobles' claims until a compromise was reached which granted them partial recognition. Although Pius was shrewd enough to realize that his success was very meagre, and probably temporary, he granted the city perpetual tenure of the fortress of Radicofani, a grim stronghold set upon a spur of Monte Amiata, as a pledge of his approval. At the same time he made Siena a metropolitan see, subjecting to it the dioceses of Grosseto, Massa, Soana, and Chiusi, under the new Archbishop Francesco Piccolomini, whom he had appointed to the bishopric when he himself became Pope.

While the Pope stayed in Siena a number of delegates arrived

---

* 'Small things grow great on concord, great things are destroyed by discord.' *Jugurtha* x, 6.

from many parts of Europe to do him homage. They came from the Imperial fiefs, from Castile, Hungary, Portugal, Burgundy and Bohemia. Pius received them all most graciously, and distributed to them gifts of money, candles, and sweets[25], according to the usual custom. On Saturday, 21st April, he gave the last of these audiences; two days later he and his followers set forth for Florence. His ears were ringing with the warnings uttered by the Sienese—that the road was dangerous, that the Florentines were cunning and inimical, and that he must beware of poison. Many had told him he was wasting his time in going to Mantua, 'whither very few would come', and had tried to discourage him from his project. Pius recognized these warnings from interested parties for what they were worth; he reported with a wry smile that there were some 'who made mock of Pope Pius, saying that he was wandering hither and thither as though blessing the crops'[26].

Ignoring the protests of those Cardinals who had become disaffected—in particular the ungrateful Barbo of San Marco—Pius pressed on to the outskirts of Florence. There came to meet him the Vicars of Faenza, Forlì and Carpi, and with them young Galeazzo Sforza, the eldest son of Duke Francesco of Milan. This fifteen-year-old boy had delightful manners and appearance: 'In his face and gestures was a gravity worthy of a prince. He spoke without preparation as another could hardly have done after much thought. He did nothing childish, nothing frivolous. It was astonishing to hear the opinions of age in the mouth of a boy, and the good sense of white hairs offered by one who had not yet a beard.' According to a contemporary chronicler, the Milanese princeling was accompanied by a hundred and fifty servants, all clad in pure silk[27], a discreet display of the riches and importance of the Sforza intended to impress not only Pius but also his hosts, the Florentines.

The Pope was carried in a golden litter, for he 'could not ride on horseback on account of his gout', preceded by priests carrying the Blessed Sacrament, and accompanied by the Vicars and many distinguished citizens. Sigismondo Malatesta of Rimini had now joined the throng; he was pressed into service as a bearer of the litter and was heard to say 'with some indignation: "Look how we have fallen! We who are lords of cities must now carry a litter." But he carried it, however unwillingly.' From all the neighbouring towns and countryside people had gathered to see the new Pope, who found time to note, as he passed by, the women's 'marvellous attire, with both foreign and native fashions', also 'their powdered faces'. At last his triumphal progress was halted at Santa Maria Novella, where lodging had been assigned to the Pope and his attendants.

The ten days that Pius spent in Florence were a time of relaxation in congenial surroundings. He knew the city well, from his student days, and had many friends among scholars and poets. In his *Commentaries* he wrote a shrewd appraisal of Cosimo dei Medici and a sympathetic portrait of Archbishop Antonino who died at about this time. Cosimo pleaded illness as an excuse for not coming to visit the Pope in order to pay his respects; Pius had some doubt about the genuine character of this sickness but reminded himself that the great Florentine was seventy years old and suffering severely from gout. Pius greatly enjoyed the beauty of the buildings and the splendour of the city, as well as the witty conversation of its inhabitants. He regretted their extreme preoccupation with commerce: 'they seem more bent on profit than is right,' he wrote, 'and for that reason when the chief citizens collected from the people fourteen thousand gold ducats with which to honour the Pope, they kept the best part of it for themselves, used some to give hospitality to Galeazzo and his retinue, and spent very little on the Pope. They . . . went to great expense [however] in providing games, when they brought lions into the market-place to fight with horses and other animals, and arranged equestrian contests for which prizes of great value were offered.'[28] The Pope's visit cost the Florentines nothing like the sum they had been obliged to pay out when the Emperor Frederick III brought his three thousand horses there on his way to Rome for the coronation, when their total expenditure came to no less than 20,000 florins[29].

There was no question, however, about the lavishness of the hospitality offered to the Pope and his entourage when they left Florence (on 5th May) and went to spend the night at the Medici villa of Caffaggiuolo. This was a very lovely castle built by Michelozzo on a spur of the Apennines in Val Mugello, about eighteen miles north of the city.[30] Vasari describes the gardens, full of fountains and aviaries, surrounded by the dark foliage of the ilex woods that were grouped around the moated villa. Here all expenses were paid and the party enjoyed sumptuous entertainment[31]. Refreshed

by their night's rest, the travellers set out in good heart to make
their way over the high pass and then were faced by a second steep
ascent, which they negotiated 'not without toil and discomfort' to
reach Pianoro at nightfall. According to the Bolognese chronicler
Ghirardacci, delegates from that city met the papal train at the
boundary between the lands of Florence and Bologna. They escorted the Pope to the city, where an uneasy peace reigned and
soldiers sent for the purpose by the Duke of Milan kept the various
factions from open combat. Technically Bologna was part of the
Papal States, and Nicholas V had used his experience as their
Bishop to persuade the citizens to accept papal suzerainty on 22nd
August 1447, but in practice control of the government lay with the
Bentivoglio family and their friends.

Pius wisely decided to make his visit a short one, of six days
only[32]. After blessing the people in the church of San Petronio he
withdrew to his lodging, where he gave audience to those who
wished to speak with him. The jurist lecturer Bornio da Sala made
a long speech 'not as he had been ordered to speak but as pleased
himself. For after praising the Pope as much as he considered fit he
spoke at length . . . about the fertility of the soil at Bologna, the
clemency of its climate, its pursuit of letters, its churches, walls,
public and private buildings.' He also surprised his hearers by
inveighing against civic strife, begging the Pope to end it if he
could. The Bolognese had been sullen and unresponsive before
Bornio made his criticism of their attitude and conduct: now they
were moved to fury and it was only the Pope's presence of mind in
inviting Bornio to accompany him to Mantua that saved the outspoken jurist from immediate exile[33]. Pius also attempted to placate
the citizens by presenting to the commune a hundred and eight
barrels of wine[34]. Four days later he left the city for the more congenial court of Ferrara.

It was with some sense of relief that Pius turned his back upon
intransigent Bologna, leaving the shadows of her gaunt walls and
fortresses for the placid river banks of the Reno and the Po. As he
approached Ferrara the Papal Vicar Borso d'Este rode to meet him
with a great company of courtiers and local gentry. At the southern
gate Borso knelt at the Pope's feet and presented him with the keys
of the city on a velvet cushion. Remembering how he had per-

suaded the Emperor to give him the title of Duke of Modena*, Borso felt confident that he could induce Pius II to promote him to be Duke of Ferrara and to give him wide powers at the papacy's expense. All his efforts were bent to further this ambition; he spared no expense and did everything he could to make the Pope's visit delightful and memorable. The Pope, however, knew better than most men when a hint should not be taken. He was quite shrewd enough to assess Borso's character and ambitions for what they were worth. 'Borso was a handsome man,' he wrote, 'above the average stature, with beautiful hair and a pleasant appearance. He was talkative and listened to himself when speaking, as though he pleased himself better than he did others. His mouth was full of flattery mixed with lies. He wanted to seem magnificent and generous rather than to be it . . . His people erected a statue in his honour in the market-place during his life, which represented him seated and administering justice, for there was nothing Borso liked as well as praise. . . . But when he asked unworthy things he found that with Pope Pius benevolence came after honour.'[35]

The Pope left his barge and was carried in a litter along streets canopied with cloths and strewn with flowers: 'everywhere were songs and masks and people shouting: Long live Pope Pius.' The eight days that Pius spent in Ferrara were filled with conversation, both public and private. There were the set pieces, the orations that reached a very high standard of eloquence, and what pleased Pius much more, long talks in private with his old friends[36]. It was very agreeable to him to renew contact with the great masters of the Studio, Guarino da Verona and the aged Giovanni Aurispa, now entering upon his ninetieth year. Pius noted in his *Commentaries* that Aurispa died soon afterwards as did two other 'most eloquent men'—Poggio the Florentine and Gianozzo Manetti who had been so pleasant a companion to Pius during his sojourn at Naples. The most notable oration of all was given in the Cathedral on 19th May by a learned and versatile Milanese doctor named Girolamo Castiglione who at that time was physician to Duke Borso. He was a man after Pius's own heart, interested in every kind of topic and willing to share his knowledge with non-specialists. It is typical of his atti-

* He was created Duke of Modena and Reggio, but he had to pay for this privilege an annual tribute of 4,000 golden florins.

tude that when—as a very old man—he made a pilgrimage to Jerusalem, he wrote an account of it in the vernacular[37] 'so that it
may be useful to all sorts and conditions of people' instead of ad-
dressing it exclusively to his own circle of friends.

The time passed pleasantly; shows and pageants and feasting at
the ducal court made agreeable distraction for the Cardinals while
the Pope continued to bargain with Borso d'Este and tried to extract from him support for the crusade. 'The Duke promised that
he would certainly come to the Congress of Mantua,' wrote Pius in
the *Commentaries*, 'as though he were more eager than any living
person to preserve Christendom,' but as soon as the papal train had
left the city Borso threw his promise to the winds and became absorbed in his favourite pursuits of hunting and wild-fowling in the
marshes of the Po estuary. From Ferrara Pius and his company
sailed up the Po towards Revere, while the Marquis of Mantua set
out to meet his visitors and their Ferrarese escort. Everyone from
the estates and the villages around came to the river banks to catch
a glimpse of the barges as they passed and to receive the Pope's
benediction. 'Trumpets on this side and on that filled with a marvellous clamour all the valleys round. Banners waved in the breezes
like a forest.' As the fleet passed the mouth of the Mincio, Pius decided to explore the lagoon on whose bank Virgil's villa was supposed to stand, for he could not resist the opportunity of making
this archaeological expedition. The Pope mused gravely before the
green mound where 'they say that there was once the home of the
divine Maro', then returned two miles to the manor house belonging
to the Gonzaga family, where he spent the night before entering
Mantua, the goal of his long progress. The journey, that had cost
nearly 6,ooo ducats and had occupied upwards of five months, was
almost at an end[38].

As he crossed the lagoon, that reflected in its waters the tall towers of the city, silhouetted against a sunset sky[39], Pius formed a
very favourable impression of Mantua—a town that he had never
seen before. 'It is ample,' he said, 'and can house a vast population.
In it are many splendid houses and palaces fit for kings.' His entry
to the city was triumphal, for many had come from neighbouring
towns to join the people of Mantua, headed by the Marquis and his
household, in paying honour to the Pope. Among the visitors was
Bianca Maria, the wife of Francesco Sforza, who had come for the

occasion from Milan. She was accompanied by her four charming
sons and her daughter Ippolita, who was as lovely as she was intelligent. Bianca joined the Marchesa, Barbara of Brandenburg, on a
platform that had been erected near the great church of San Pietro,
and here they awaited the arrival of the procession. At its head
there came the servants of the Curia, followed by twelve white
horses with golden reins and saddles. Pius described the scene in
the second book of his *Commentaries*:

'Then came the three standards. On the first gleamed the sign of
the Cross, on the second the Keys of the Church, and on the third
the five moons, which is the ensign of the Piccolomini family. And
these were carried by nobles wearing armour and mounted on
caparisoned horses. Next came a canopy striped in red and yellow,
and then the priests of the city in their holy vestments and carrying
the Sacrament. After these came the delegates of kings and princes,
and behind them a golden cross accompanied by the Apostolic
subdeacons, the auditors, secretaries and advocates of the Sacred
Palace. With these went a little golden chest borne on a white horse
and surrounded by many candles, in which was placed the Eucha-
rist, that is the blessed host of the Saviour, and over it was a silken
canopy. Next to this came Galeazzo of Milan (who had accompanied the Pope from Florence) and the Marquis Lodovico, and behind them the venerable order of the Cardinals. Then came the
Pope himself, seated on a lofty throne, gleaming in his priestly cloak
and mitre heavy with precious stones, and carried on the shoulders
of noble lords, blessing the people as he went.'

All the way from the city gate to San Pietro the houses on either
side of the street were decorated with tapestries and flowers.
Women and children crowded the upper windows and the roofs,
peering through the clouds of incense to catch a glimpse of the
Holy Father as he passed.

After hymns and prayers in San Pietro Pius gave plenary remis-
sion of their sins to all who were present; he then retired to his lodging in a palace near by. The following day Barbara Gonzaga, the
Marchesa, conducted her guest, the Duchess of Milan, to pay a
formal call upon the Pope. This occasion was graced by a Latin
oration delivered with eloquence and spirit by thirteen-year-old Ippolita Sforza. This girl was already a distinguished classical scholar
—ten months earlier she had written out her own copy of Cicero's

De Senectute[40], and when she was married a few years later to Alfonso of Calabria her father gave her a dozen books by Latin authors as a wedding present. Pius was charmed by the elegance of Ippolita's oration; his warm reception at Mantua and the congenial atmosphere of Lodovico Gonzaga's court* seemed to him to set the tone of his sojourn there. The Marquis was the most civilized of men. He owed his attitude of mind as well as his learning to the early training of Vittorino da Feltre, perhaps the most enlightened of all Renaissance schoolmasters. Vittorino had selected poor boys like Basinio of Parma, to give them free education on level terms with the young Gonzaga, so that from an early age these princes were able to appreciate the relative merits of character, intelligence, and *nobiltà* when opposed to self-indulgence and the hoarding of material possessions[41]. Nevertheless Vittorino encouraged in his pupils high standards of taste and the discrimination that led Mantua under the Gonzaga to become a centre of culture and the arts that was rivalled only by Florence. With his usual quickness of apprehension Pius at once responded to his surroundings. His hopes began to rise and it seemed to him that the Congress he had convoked might indeed result in real harmony among the leaders of Christendom. Now, he had only to wait upon their arrival.

III

Although his progress to Mantua had occupied more than five months, Pius II was several days early for the opening of the Congress. The day appointed was 1st June; it was marked by High Mass in the cathedral of San Pietro, celebrated, said Pius, 'with solemn magnificence'. It was typical of Pius that although he himself set little value upon outward show, disliked pomp, and had the simplest of personal tastes, when it came to the exaltation of the Papacy nothing must be omitted that could contribute to its dignity and splendour. The Bishop of Coron gave a sermon outlining the purpose of the Congress, then 'Pius from his throne signalled with

---

* The Marchesa was plain and homely, in her heavy German style a great contrast to her lively guest. She was nevertheless an excellent wife and mother, and much loved by her subjects. For a naturalistic family group of the Gonzaga see the painting by Andrea Mantegna in the Camera de' Sposi at Mantua.

his hand for silence, just as all were preparing to arise', and uttered an address to which, he said, 'the Cardinals and Bishops listened . . . with marvellous attention'[42]. All joined in praising the Pope and agreed that proceedings had opened most favourably; with this impression in her mind the Duchess Bianca returned to Milan with her children, intent upon persuading her husband to attend the conference and to play there his rightful part.

Several days passed without news of the arrival of any fresh delegates or even that they were on their way. Hopes declined; courtiers and Cardinals alike began to turn against the Pope in their disappointment and wrote grumbling and mischievous letters to their friends. 'They said that Pius had been a fool to come to Mantua . . . the place was marshy and unwholesome, everything was boiling hot; the wine was bad, and the rest of the victuals no better; many were sick, a great number had fever, and there was nothing to listen to but frogs.' From Rome* Cardinal Scarampo had written to the Venetians advising them to boycott the Congress, while Cardinal Jacopo Tebaldo at Mantua 'spoke poisonous words among his friends'. Pius described Tebaldo scathingly as 'a man of small stature and smaller wit', nevertheless these criticisms annoyed and disturbed him and it needed much resolution to face his disappointment philosophically. Even the staunch support given him by Bessarion and Carvajal, whose loyalty had its roots in a genuine enthusiasm for the Pope's projects, weighed little against the apathy of the Christian rulers who continued to linger at home while they waited to see what their colleagues intended to do. Most deplorable of all was the inaction of Frederick III. Gregorovius had said that 'history could never have beheld a greater caricature of the first and second Fredericks'[43] than this poor-spirited Emperor who prevaricated and procrastinated every time he received a summons to the Congress.

The delegates who had arrived at Mantua were few and unimportant, with the exception of those sent by Thomas the Despot of Morea, who persuaded the Pope—aided by the Duchess of Milan who paid for one third of the expedition—to send a token force of

---

* Where he had returned in February from his operations at sea: see Pastor, *op. cit.*, p. 63 n. *. He afterwards joined the Pope at Mantua where he continued to denigrate the aims of the Congress.

mercenaries to resist the Turkish advance. Pius probably hoped that this would set the pattern for his crusade, but the force was far too small and ill-disciplined. Indeed, the soldiers quarrelled 'whether from rivalry or greed of booty' and abandoned the venture without achieving anything. It was, as the Pope remarked, an ill omen for what had to be done.

While he waited with what patience he could muster, Pius occupied his time with letter-writing and expeditions to explore the countryside around Mantua. The letters were urgent summons to the princes of Europe, repeating former arguments or expressing them more strongly. Fifty-two have been preserved in a graceful manuscript now in Paris[44]. On the first page is a miniature of the Pope sitting at his desk, wearing the triple tiara and writing with his own hand this series of epistles. Each initial letter encloses a portrait of the person to whom the exhortation is addressed. It would be too much to claim that the miniature on fo. 1 is a lifelike portrait of the Pope, but it suggests very well the importance he attached to these letters and his hope that his correspondents would take them seriously and act upon the urgent advice that they contained.

When the Emperor's envoys did arrive, they were men of so little consequence that Pius straightway sent them home; on 6th July he wrote again to Frederick instructing him to appoint more suitable representatives. He even sent the Emperor a blessed sword and hat, in the hope of bringing home to him his duty and position[45]. Another delegation that seemed to the Pope unworthy was the embassy from England. In August 1459 the Milanese ambassador wrote to Duke Francesco saying that the English embassy was expected to arrive any day[46], for the English nobleman John Tiptoft, Earl of Worcester, had been named as the King's representative together with Lord Dudley, two prelates, and several others of considerable standing[47], as early as 25th July. Safe conducts had been issued, wages paid, and there seemed every likelihood that the English delegation would be important and forceful. But, for some reason that has never been explained, the Earl of Worcester—although he was in Italy at the time and probably no further from Mantua than the Studio of Ferrara[48]—never put in an appearance. Nor did the other members arrive: in the end England was represented at Mantua by two obscure priests whose names were not thought worth recording. When these presented their credentials, which had the usual endorsement *teste Rege,* Pius concluded that King Henry VI had been deserted by all his officials and so had been obliged to act as his own witness[49]. The Pope did not often show such unfamiliarity with customary procedure: his derogatory remarks about the English King may have been inspired as much by captiousness as by ignorance.

A number of delegates now came to Mantua from the shores and islands of the eastern Mediterranean, all with demands for protection although Ragusa alone offered co-operation in the struggle against the Turks. Already disputes about precedence were developing into wrangles based on national prestige, so that the Pope had to spend much of his time adjudicating these petty quarrels. The revised embassy from the Empire consisted of three eminent men all well known to Pius, and one of them—Johann von Hinderbach, now Provost of Trent—a close personal friend. They did not, however, 'carry quite the authority which the dignity and rank of such a congress seemed to demand'[50]. Again Pius sent a message to the Emperor, rebuking his negligence and parsimony, and pointing out that the way to Mantua from his dominion was no longer or more difficult than the road from Rome. The Duke of Burgundy also defaulted, less from lack of enthusiasm than from political entanglements at home. In his place Duke Philip sent his nephew John, Duke of Cleves, and with him 'many knights and other celebrated interpreters of divine and civil law' under the the leadership of the Bishop of Arras who was Papal Refendario and a man of considerable learning. This strong embassy did much to help the Congress, even though Burgundy was not present in person, for it was quite clear that he took the situation seriously and was determined to help provide men and munitions for the crusade as well as to promote unity within the Church. Most important of all, Philip took a realistic view and had instructed the Bishop of Arras to point out that not only must a huge army be gathered to fight the Turks but that the first cause for the Congress to tackle was the healing of dissension. For, 'It was not easy for anyone to draw his sword on an outsider when he was already at war at home with his own people'[51].

Some plain speaking by Pius II and much discussion and argument resulted in a firm promise of help from Burgundy, but as soon as this was settled the delegates proposed to leave for home. The Pope wished them to stay to meet the Dukes of Milan and Modena, whose arrival was expected any day, but after waiting fruitlessly for more than a week, the Duke of Cleves and most of his followers departed. 'It is no easy matter,' the Pope remarked ruefully, 'to bring great princes together.' In the end, the Duke of Modena never put in an appearance at all*, despite the promises given in Ferrara. Francesco Sforza, however, arrived a few days after the Burgundians had left. As he sailed from Cremona along the Po and up the Mincio, accompanied by a fleet of forty-seven vessels[52], Francesco greeted all those who had come out to meet him. They crowded the lagoon with their small boats and pinnaces, making a splash of colour against the pale landscape of the marshes. The Duke's company, we read, 'was vast and very noble, and there was not one whose clothes were not glittering with gold or bright with silver. On his arrival much was spread abroad about the dignity and glory of the apostolic see, and everywhere one heard men say: Look, how lofty and most excellent is the authority and majesty of the Bishop of Rome, to kiss whose feet so great a prince has come!'[53]

With Francesco's arrival the Congress entered upon its second phase, illuminated by new hope and a feeling of optimism engendered by the powerful personality of the Duke. He was a born leader of men and it is not surprising that Pius had already chosen him as supreme commander of the crusading army. On 17th September, nearly three months after he had first set foot in Mantua, Pius held a public consistory at which he welcomed Sforza as friend and ally, and listened to a discourse on behalf of the Duke given by his old master Francesco Filelfo. Afterwards Pius replied with a graceful speech in which he described Filelfo as the Attic muse, likened Sforza to 'another Ajax in battle', and recalled that his own uncle, Giovanni Tolomei of Siena, had served as an officer under Francesco's father. There was a genuine cordiality between Pope and Duke, although both knew that the real reason for Sforza's presence at Mantua was his determination to secure solid support for the cause of Ferrante in Naples in opposition to René of Anjou. This support Pius had already decided to give—in defiance of pre-

* Borso d'Este claimed that the astrologers at his court had advised him against making the journey at this time.

vious papal policy—but he was quick to see that he had here a useful bargaining counter and prepared to exchange it for Francesco's backing of his crusade.

News that Sforza had reached Mantua spread quickly; delegates from all the important Italian cities began to make their way thither at speed. Venice chose two distinguished citizens as envoys and sent them with 'a picked company of noble youths' and five hundred horsemen: Francesco Sforza met them outside the walls and conducted them to their lodgings. The Pope welcomed the embassy with a certain coolness, pointing out that although they were nearest to the Congress yet they were the last Italians to come. He decided that he would wait no longer for the French delegation, lest Sforza should depart before important decisions could be taken. 26th September saw the first formal session of the Congress: Pope Pius was moved to make one of the most striking orations of his whole career so that this date became a memorable one in the minds of all who heard him. After Mass in the Cathedral he began to speak; although his address lasted almost three hours it was listened to so attentively by his audience 'that not a word escaped them'. It was a personal triumph for the Pope, the more so because he had been suffering from a severe cough and it was feared that he might break down. 'Yet, by God's help . . . he did not cough once, nor showed the slightest difficulty.'

The Pope's speech[54] won fame outside the walls of Mantua. A chronicler in Verona wrote that Pius had delivered a most marvellous oration[55] and it was quickly circulated: many copies of it still exist in libraries over a wide area. All the fire and eloquence of which he was capable found expression in this speech; Pius looked back to the crusading Council of Clermont, four centuries earlier, and passionately hoped that he could rekindle the vital spark. He was followed by Cardinal Bessarion, who added to a sincerity as strong as the Pope's an even deeper knowledge of the circumstances. But of inspiration he had none. Bessarion droned on for a further three hours, in deplorable Latin[56], developing 'many arguments' until his audience was stunned and exhausted, and much of their fervour had evaporated. Francesco Sforza wrote home to his wife[57] of 'the Pope's long and splendid oration'; to him it seemed to have lasted for only two hours. Sforza himself spoke (in the vernacular) 'with a soldier's eloquence' offering his services and his possessions to the Christian cause. He was followed by the Hungarian envoys who spoke bitterly of the Emperor's vacillations, a criticism that Pius thought to be ill-timed. He told the Hungarians that their remarks were irrelevant to the purpose of the Congress and wound up the day's meeting with the words: 'let us finish what we have begun, and cease all disputes in this place, nor listen to a word of evil.'

Next day there was a council of ways and means, Sforza taking the lead and affirming that attack on the Turks must be made by land and sea. The Venetians contended that thirty armed galleys and eight frigates would be enough, Sigismondo Malatesta—speaking with 'a soldierly and headlong eloquence'—confined his remarks to suggestions of how men and arms could best be raised. Pius then summarized the proposals. Fifty thousand troops would be needed and money to pay for them must be found at once. He proposed a three-year tax of one-tenth on the revenue of the clergy, a thirtieth on laymen, and five per cent on all possessions of the Jews[58]. Only the Venetian and Florentine envoys raised objections; in a private meeting the latter were persuaded to agree but the Venetians remained obdurate. In principle they approved the crusade, in practice they wished to do nothing that might interfere with their Levantine trade. As Pius put it: 'their words were different from their thoughts'.

On 3rd October Francesco Sforza left Mantua to return to his home. He felt, with some reason, that he had done all he could and that little would be gained by waiting for the dilatory envoys of the French King and the Emperor. The Pope himself felt the need for a holiday; in the middle of the month he withdrew for a few days to the convent of S. Maria delle Grazie, five miles outside the city. Rumours reached him, however, that the French delegation was at hand, so he returned to Mantua in some haste. Pius had every reason to expect intransigence on the part of the Frenchmen, not only because of his support of Ferrante of Naples in opposition to the French René, but from the old arguments concerning the Pragmatic Sanction of Bourges*. He resolved to strike the first blow, so as soon as the envoys arrived the Pope warned them that he would not discuss the Sicilian question, or even admit them to his presence,

---

* For a discussion of this matter see pp. 176–7.

until they offered their allegiance. The Bishop of Paris 'spoke at
length in praise of the Pope and about the eminence of the apostolic see and the glory of his own King and realm'. In his reply Pius
sternly criticized the attitude of France; while accepting the Bishop's compliments he reminded him that whosoever rejected papal
authority was anathema. Perhaps the Frenchmen were taken aback:
they had no answer ready and astonished everyone present by their
meek and submissive attitude. There could be no doubt that the
Pope had won the first round of his battle.

Meanwhile, a new and worthier delegation had arrived from the
Emperor, and envoys had come to Mantua from Castile and Portugal as well as from a number of German cities and princes. Among
these was Pius's old rival and enemy Gregory Heimburg, who represented Duke Albert of Austria and also spoke for Duke Sigismund
when he arrived a short while later. Before he could welcome the
new arrivals, Pius was laid low with 'a severe complaint of the stomach', probably stone, from which he suffered excruciatingly from
time to time and his cough returned in a more violent form. The
French believed that his illness was a diplomatic one, feigned to
avoid awkward commitments. Pius, when he heard this, struggled
from his bed exclaiming: 'Though I must die in the middle of the assembly, yet shall I reply to that proud-stomached delegation. Pain
will not subdue my spirit, nor sickness make me seem afraid of
them.' For three hours the Pope harangued the assembly; as he
spoke and warmed to his subject the pain left him and he was carried away by his own eloquence. He strongly defended his support
of Ferrante in Sicily, and followed up this hammer blow by a
stronger and harder one. He roundly condemned the Pragmatic
Sanction, by which 'the authority of the Holy See was impaired, the
power of religion weakened, the Church robbed of her freedom'[59].
Laymen had been set up as judges of the clergy: such a position
was intolerable not only to the Papacy but to all Christians. It must be
abandoned forthwith. This was a splendid speech; like the oration
of 26th September it was widely disseminated. The Frenchmen
pleaded for a private audience: here too they had very much the
worse of the argument. They turned then to excusing themselves
from offering help against the Turks on the ground of their preoccupation with the English war, but found the Pope implacable in
his determination.

Nor could the Germans find adequate excuses for their non-co-operation, although Gregory Heimburg did his best with taunts and sneers to confuse the issue. It must have been with some satisfaction that Pius celebrated his own birthday by putting Gregory under a ban so that he could not appeal—as he wished—to a Council. Young Sigismund of Austria, of whom Pius had once held high hopes, had become dissolute and selfish; only in the Margrave Albert did the Pope find anything of the magnanimous spirit that he sought. On the Feast of the Epiphany Pius awarded to Albert the sword of honour 'with which the worthiest of the secular princes present is wont to be adorned' and added to it on his own account the present of a cap of pearls. The delegates were now streaming away from the Congress with much greater alacrity than they had shown in coming. They were sped on their way by a feast provided from a present sent to the Pope by Francesco Sforza as soon as he reached home. This was a gift of three fat Milanese cattle, that had been 'fed on turnips, washed in warm water, and combed every day'. The beef made excellent eating, both princes and Cardinals declared that they had never tasted better. Pius, however, who did not care for meat and who had had to tip each of the bringers of the animals a hundred golden pieces, observed that 'it was no cheap present'[60].

Before the Congress closed, with a High Mass in San Pietro, Pius issued an important decree that had been in his mind for some time past and was the logical conclusion of his changed attitude to the Conciliar movement. Not content with calling the Pope a 'chattering magpie' and denouncing his decrees as 'cobwebs', Gregory Heimburg had threatened to appeal to a Council: his attitude as much as that of the French envoys, and of Duke Sigismund of the Tyrol (who was at odds with Cardinal Nicholas of Cusa concerning the bishopric of Brixen) had hardened Pius's resolution. On 17th January 1460, the Bull *Execrabilis* was published. This condemned in forthright terms (as 'an execrable thing') the practice of appealing from the Pope's authority to a general council, declaring that all who so appealed 'would be punished as fosterers of heresy and guilty of high treason'[61]. The wheel had come full circle: Aeneas who had risen to fame as the champion of the Conciliar movement was the same man as the Pope who now condemned it. Yet he was indeed the same man, inspired by the same passionate desire for the unity of the Church. 'And if any presume to attack it,' he concluded in time-honoured fashion, 'let him know that he will incur the wrath of omnipotent God and of the holy apostles Peter and Paul.'

Pius followed up *Execrabilis* with a realistic summary of the results of the Congress. He now knew where he stood and he had a very shrewd idea of the emptiness of the promises he had received. In material effects the Congress of Mantua was not much more substantial than those of Ratisbon and Wiener-Neustadt, but the Pope had emerged as a strong leader and there could be no doubt about his intentions. His position, too, had been strengthened by his attack on the Pragmatic Sanction of Bourges, soon to be abolished, and by his emphatic denial of the right to appeal from the Papacy to a Council. Personally he emerged from the Congress with increased stature; bitterly disappointed as he was by the flimsy response to his appeal for the crusade, at least he now knew where he stood. Now he must turn to the discord within his own dominions, but before Pius returned to Rome to take up this challenge he promised himself a leisurely progress visiting the cities of his beloved Tuscany, studying and trying to solve their problems and refreshing his own jaded spirits.

'When all had finished,' he wrote, 'the Pope bade the Cardinals, bishops, abbots and all the priests that were there to put on their sacred vestments, and he himself, descending from his throne, turned towards the steps of the high altar. There on bended knees, sighing and weeping, he chanted in suppliant voice for a long time verses chosen from the psalms which seemed suitable to the occasion, while the prelates and all the clergy made responses. When his prayer was finished he blessed the people, and in this manner brought to a close the Congress of Mantua.'[62]

CHAPTER XI

Springtime in Siena

Through this landscape went the Pope rejoicing. — AENEAS SYLVIUS PIC-
COLOMINI, *Commentaries*

I

At two o'clock in the afternoon of 24th January 1460, Pope Pius
and four of his Cardinals left the scene of the Congress and set out
by river for Revere[1]. The Pope himself remarked that in Mantua
the dust of summer was equalled only by the mud in winter; for
some time he had been longing for the firmer, drier ground of the
Apennines where the earliest signs of spring would soon be beginning to show. The season was, however, particularly cold: when
Cardinal Bessarion left for Germany, a fortnight after the Pope's
departure, he had to travel in a two-horse *chareta* since the weather
was too icy for him to ride on horseback with the rest of his party[2].
The River Po was more than usually swollen with winter rains; as
Pius and his companions passed down the River Mincio to its junc-
tion with the Po a few miles short of Revere, 'the courtiers were
astonished that the old Pope should start upon his journey in such
bitter weather, but he who had not shrunk from the cold on his
departure was not afraid of it now that he was returning.'[3]

As the procession sped down the river on the crest of the flood
they came within a short distance of the Abbey of S. Benedetto in
Polirone[4], where Pius had stayed within the community when taking a short holiday from the Congress. The Abbot, D. Teofilo of
Milan, had commemorated this visit by commissioning a white marble bust of his famous guest, which he set up in the Sala di Capitolo.
Here it stayed until 1796 when, during the Napoleonic Wars, it was

lost and for many years was thought to have been destroyed. But in 1924 the bust was rediscovered in the basilica and now Pope Pius— in his sternest mood—looks down from his niche in the nave of the church of S. Benedetto. Though his expression is formidable and austere, this is probably the best extant portrait of the Pope, for it corresponds very closely to contemporary descriptions of him at this time; as a likeness it is to be preferred to the better-known bust in the Borgia apartments at the Vatican that is thought to be by Paolo Romano.

The following day Borso d'Este, blandly forgetting that he had failed to redeem his promise, came to meet the Pope with a great concourse of ships, 'to such an extent that the entire surface of the river was shaken and tossed up by their oars. Banners of many colours blowing in the breeze made a wonderful effect, while flutes and trumpets and all kinds of musical instruments were set high on the helms and sounded in sweet concert. Various masques appeared of gods and goddesses, giants and virtues; boys and girls sang, while on the dykes that keep the river from overflowing men and women were seated as though for a spectacle, some crying long life to the Pope and some to Borso.'[5] None of this pageantry deceived the Pope as to the true character of Borso's welcome. He would not stay the next day in Ferrara, but required Borso to set his name—as last on the list—to the financial decree concerning tithes, etc. Pius noted in his *Commentaries* that although Borso was the last to sign, he was almost the first to break his word.

A difficult stage of the journey lay ahead. Sometimes at this time of the year the rivers were frozen so solid that it was possible to traverse them on foot[6], but it had been a bright winter until the rains came to flood the lagoons, so that the way was blocked by treacherous chunks of ice that sometimes had to be split with axes before a passage could be forced. When they reached the Reno they found the river completely frozen over. The Pope had to travel in a litter borne by his servants, since no vehicles had arrived from Bologna to transport the party. That night most of his companions slept in peasants' huts, though room was found for the Pope and his servitors in the country house belonging to Sante Bentivoglio. Remembering his surly reception in Bologna the previous summer, Pius would not consent to stay there but pressed on towards Florence, despite stomach pains and the discomfort of travelling through sleet and snow up the slippery slopes of the Apennines. At last they came to Florence, where the warmth of his greeting and the 'marvellous honour' paid to him did much to restore the Pope's spirits. Whether or no Cosimo dei Medici had been ill when Pius visited Florence in May 1459, on this occasion his behaviour was most courteous. The two statesmen had long and serious talks; they learned to appreciate one another's qualities and found that they had in common much more than the gout that crippled both of them. Nevertheless, Pius found the Florentines unwilling to be pinned down: he could not induce them to make any satisfactory reply to his suggestions. It was with some sense of relief that he left Florentine territory and three days later Pius entered his native Siena, just before the Feast of the Purification on 2nd February.

The grudging reception given him in earlier days was now forgotten and Pius entered his own city like a triumphant general, to be greeted by the townspeople with cries of joy, for in his own words: 'Everything was green, though February was as cold as ever, not a place was seen but was bright with flowers and strewn with aromatic herbs . . . while in the fields luxuriant crops were springing. The lie of the lands of Siena, especially in the neighbourhood of the city, is more lovely than can be described. The gently rising hills, covered with domestic trees and vines or else ploughed for sowing, look down on cheerful valleys . . . through which flow streams that never run dry. There are besides many woods of natural or artificial growth where birds sing very sweetly, and there is not a single elevation on which the citizens have not erected country houses. Here you will see fine monasteries where dwell holy men, there private dwelling-places built like castles.'

Before he had left Mantua, and at intervals during his twenty-two days' journey to Siena, news had been brought to the Pope of the open warfare that had broken out in Naples and of the machinations of Jacopo Piccinino the condottiere. For the moment he could do nothing in this matter, and even when Ferrante's troops were defeated by the Angevins five months later at the Battle of Sarno, 7th July 1460, he had to remain an onlooker. Pius wisely felt that his first preoccupation must be the restoration of his own health. It was essential for him to find alleviation from the excruciating pain he was suffering before he could hope to make statesmanlike decisions concerning political affairs. Before he left for the baths at

Macereto*, where he expected to find a cure, Pius tentatively raised the question of the readmission of the banned nobles to Siena: once again he was obliged to accept a compromise that promised much but achieved very little. Instead of alienating the Signoria by insisting on a discussion he felt would be unfruitful, the Pope then let the matter drop, though he resolved to return to the attack at a more propitious time.

Pius proposed to spend a month at the spa of Macereto in the hope of relieving his gout, neuralgia, and other maladies through immersion in the healing waters. 'This place', he wrote, 'is ten miles distant from [Siena], in a valley some two or three furlongs across and quite eight miles long. The fields are irrigated with a perpetual moisture by the River Merse, which flows down to the Ombrone and is rich in eels, very white and sweet though rather small. At its start the valley is highly cultivated and full of castles and villas, but where it ends near the baths it is wild, closed by a stone bridge of considerable workmanship and by shadowy and thickly wooded cliffs. The evergreen ilex clothes almost all the mountains that overhang the valley on the right, while on the left are acorn-bearing oaks and cork-trees. About the baths are modest houses that take the place of inns. Here the Pope spent a month, and though he bathed twice each day yet he never missed the Signature or other affairs of State. He would go out into the meadows and sit on the river bank, where there was more grass and greenness, and there he gave audience to delegations and suppliants. The wives of the peasants brought him flowers every day and strewed the path which the Pope took to the baths. And all the reward they asked was that they might kiss his feet.'[7]

When he found that the baths of Macereto failed to bring him relief Pius acted on the advice of the best doctors of the day and went for further treatment to Petriolo. This spa was perhaps the most famous of all Italy's health resorts in the middle years of the fifteenth century. Many sufferers from rheumatic diseases, and still more who had eaten and drunk unwisely and too well, found relief in the healing waters there. When Cosimo dei Medici's younger son, Giovanni, had occasion to take the baths at Petriolo his father

* Macereto, on the road to Grosseto, not Macerata which is in the Marches, near Ancona—also a spa, but not at this date.

wrote to him urging him to follow the prescribed treatment conscientiously: 'Be diligent', wrote Cosimo, 'in doing all that is necessary and come back as soon as thou canst . . . be careful to take thy baths properly so that they may be beneficial.'[8]

Pius found that the waters of Petriolo suited him better than those of Macereto; this he attributed to the fact that they contained more sulphur, even though the two spas were only five miles apart. He was happier here, perhaps because he felt better, taking more general interest in his surroundings. On 12th June two Florentine merchants came to Petriolo and displayed their wares before the Pope, trying to tempt him to buy an exquisite piece of tapestry worked in gold and silver thread. Pius agreed to take it and to pay the Florentines 1250 florins[9]. In such agreeable ways the time passed quickly, although the treatment seems to have been rigorous to the point of violence. For twenty days Pius endured 'hot water pouring through a pipe on to his head, for this the doctors said was healthy as there seemed to be too much moisture in his brain'. Whether or no this diagnosis was correct, Pius seems to have derived benefit from the treatment. On his return to Siena he stayed resting quietly with the Franciscan brothers; he built there a fountain in a shady part of their garden so that he might sup there during the hot weather. The fountain was destroyed one night by local hooligans whom the Pope described as 'pernicious youths': one of the very few strictures he was ever heard to utter concerning thoughtless and rowdy boys.

Spring gave way to summer, and still Pius lingered in Siena. Embassies came and went, Sienese citizens brought their problems to the Pope, offices of varying importance fell vacant and were filled, grave and even more grave news continued to come from Rome. The Feast of the Assumption was celebrated on 15th August with particular solemnity because it was the second centenary of Siena's great day, the battle of Montaperti when the Sienese had begged Our Lady's help against the Florentines and defeat had been turned into victory. The votive wax candles were offered, the Palio* was run in the Campo, the citizens made merry and a great bonfire on the summit of Monte Amiata lit up the night sky. This marked the

* The customary horse races for the prize of a length of cloth (or *palio*). See W. Heywood, *Palio and Ponte*, London, 1904, pp. 55–67.

climax of the Pope's visit; immediately afterwards he began to make
preparations for departure. It was not, however, until 10th September that Pius actually left his beloved city, restraining his tears while
all the courtiers wept at leaving 'so delightful a spot and so pleasant
a people'. The cavalcade left Siena by the southern gate and headed
towards the Pope's beloved mountain. When he arrived at Corsignano Pius felt very ill, with pains in his arms and chest. For nearly
a fortnight he lay ill in bed, then resolutely took up again his re-
sponsibilities and made his first positive move to avenge the defeat
of Ferrante's forces at Sarno, by sending 'a vast company of soldiers'
to aid him, under the command of Roberto da Sanseverino.

From Corsignano the Pope descended to the Val d'Orcia, then
climbed the steep slope of the hill crowned by Radicofani, the
strong fortress he had given to Siena for her defence. On he went
through Abbadia San Salvatore to Proceno 'once a noble town and
almost impregnable, encircled on all sides by lofty cliffs'. Here the
people had turned out in force to welcome the Pope; they had prepared dinner for him on the banks of a stream, under shelters of
green branches. That night the Pope spent at Acquapendente, the
next at Bolsena, and then he made his way to Orvieto. Pius wrote
a splendid description of this natural fortress and its cathedral, 'second to none in the whole of Italy'. He showed his flexibility of mind
in admiring the sculpture of his own day and declaring that the
artists were 'not inferior to Pheidias or Praxiteles. Those statues
seem to live. The faces and the limbs of men and beasts are carved
so well out of the white marble that art appears to have equalled
nature. Only the voice is wanting to make them alive.' Pius noted,
too, that it was at Orvieto that there were preserved the traces of
the miracle of Corpus Domini, the vision vouchsafed to a priest of
Bolsena who had doubted the Real Presence. The feast was insti-
tuted by Pope Urban VI. Nicholas V had restored some of the
bedrooms in the Bishop's palace: Pope Pius rested here for three
days, enjoying the beauty of the city and tasting its mellow wine
which was, he said, 'not contemptible'. More important, before leaving Orvieto he did what he could to reconcile the warring factions
in the city and prepared the way for peace between the parties[10].

While he stayed in Montefiascone a few miles short of Viterbo,
Pius lodged in a ruinous palace, 'but as he could not bear the violence of the winds, for that place is like a cave of Aeolus, he went

on next day through spreading fields to [Viterbo]'. Here a deputation from Rome met the Pope and begged him to make haste, for Rome would soon be utterly destroyed by faction and turbulence. Only the bodily presence of the Pope could save her. So flattering a message, brought as it was by young, noble, and highly decorative envoys, moved Pius to eloquence of a high order and he made to the people of Viterbo one of his more notable orations. The citizens were sorry to lose their distinguished guests, for since the Cardinals had been billeted on private citizens the visitation had been the excuse for much display and festivity in which all had joined. On Saturday, 4th October, the feast of San Francesco, the Pope gave benediction after Mass to the huge congregation[11]. Then, after dining at midday, he climbed into his litter and the procession wound through the city gate and along the road to Rome. The progress to and from Mantua was over at last.

II

While he lingered in Siena and enjoyed its delights, the Pope still brooded on the failure of his Congress to initiate a crusade, turning over in his mind new schemes for furthering his purpose. Instead of being daunted by the difficulties in his way he was stimulated by them to seek a new approach. Pius was not so blinded by prejudice that he failed to recognize in the Sultan Mahomet II not only a fine general but also a man of brilliant intelligence. The thought occurred to him that so able and reasonable an opponent might well be open to persuasion if a formula were offered to him that would appeal directly to his intellect. Pius knew very well his own gift of presenting an argument in the most attractive light: how would it be if he could persuade the Sultan to renounce his faith, and to accept baptism as a Christian? From an implacable foe he would immediately become an ally and all cause for rancour between Christians and Muslims would be ended. If the arguments for Christianity were sufficiently skilfully set out and the climax reached by flawless reasoning, surely Mahomet could not refuse to accept this logical conclusion?

His supreme faith in the humanistic approach, by means of eloquence and an appeal to historical precedent (had not Constantine and Clovis received baptism and thereby brought whole nations

to the faith?), blinded Pius to the absurdity of expecting Mahomet II
to yield to an overnight conversion. He was not totally ignorant of
Mahomedan aims and ideals, for he had studied the treatise written
by Cardinal Nicholas of Cusa on the Koran and drew from it some
of the theological reasoning that he used in his own *Epistle* to the
Sultan[12]. Nevertheless, the Pope was very wide of his mark in attributing to Mahomet the habit of mind of an Italian humanist;
although the *Epistle* as an exercise in the art of rhetoric and the
skilful arrangement of arguments and illustrations is among the best
he ever wrote, failure was inevitable. Indeed, it is not known
whether it ever reached Mahomet's eyes[13]. As Professor Isidoro del
Lungo once said: 'Ah, if only Mahomet had known Latin!'[14]

Several years had elapsed since Constantinople fell; the emotional
Aeneas Sylvius who had deplored the Sultan's actions and moral
character at the time was older now, and wiser, and sat upon the
papal throne. It is not surprising that the tone of his letter is more
liberal than that of the pamphlet dashed off in the heat of the moment. Nor was it only expediency that made Pius address the Sultan
in moderate and respectful terms, for although he still recognized
Mahomet II as the arch-enemy of the Christian Church he fully
expected him to accept and appreciate the Pope's own position.
'Leave the shades of darkness,' he wrote, 'and seek the light, for . . .
if instead you shall reject our counsel your glory will dissolve into
smoke and you—becoming ashes according to the destiny of mortal
men—will perish utterly and for ever.'[15]

Pius dwelt movingly upon the horrors of war: all bloodshed and
violence could be avoided if only Mahomet were to become a Christian. Power and glory could be his, too, for he would be recognized
as Emperor of Asia and of Greece—all through the medium of the
small basinful of water needed for his baptism. The virtues of a
philosopher were his already; by accepting Christianity there would
be added to them the theological virtues—faith, hope, and charity
—that together make a perfect man. The Pope supported his analysis of Christianity, and his argument to exalt the Bible above the
Koran, with apposite historical incidents and allusions. He quoted
from many classical writers, both poets and philosophers, and pic-
tured the Golden Age that must follow Mahomet's conversion. There
would be blossom in the wilderness, swords would be discarded or
turned into pruning-hooks, the leopard would lie down with the
lamb and the lion with the calf—all the familiar images adorn his

description, but there is also a freshness and exuberance about it that make the *Epistle* extremely easy to read. It must have seemed to the writer—as, indeed, to posterity—a very persuasive piece of work.

It has been assumed[16], on what appears slender evidence, that the *Epistle* was written in 1461 and was probably inspired by emotional chivalry when the Pope was confronted by the Queen of Cyprus and heard from her own lips the story of her sad plight. It would seem more reasonable to suppose that Pius left Mantua with his mind full of the disappointments of his Congress, with false promises that he knew would never be implemented still ringing in his ears. Surely this was the time when he would cast about for some new means of achieving his ends? As he recalled the frustration of his hopes he would be ready for an entirely new approach to the problem and it is natural to suppose that he impulsively set down what was fermenting in his mind. This conjecture is supported by the statement of 'Bernardos' who wrote a copy of the *Epistle* that is now in the Bodleian[17]; he says categorically on fo. 85 that it was composed in Siena during the year 1460[18]—that is, between the dates of 30th January, when Pius arrived in that city, and 10th September, when he left for Rome. I am not aware of any other copy of the *Epistle* that gives the date of the original work. 'Bernardos' version was probably written within twelve years or so of the original, for another work copied by him in the same MS. bears the date 18th October 1473.

Within a very short time of its first appearance, Pius's *Letter to Mahomet* was circulating throughout Europe*. Although there is nothing to suggest that the Muslims took any notice of its precepts, the letter had profound influence upon the Christian outlook. It would not be true to say that the Pope had wasted his time in writing it, for undoubtedly the letter provided Christian leaders with food for thought and animated discussion. It is a very clear and admirable exposition of the western point of view; that it did not appeal to the Turkish mind demonstrated how very far the author was from recognizing the gulf that lay between Mahomedan and Christian. To later readers it is interesting, not only as a literary exercise of the highest quality[19], but also as an instance of Pius's indomitable faith in the powers of persuasion.

* A number of copies are still extant and are widely distributed.

CHAPTER XII

The City of Rome

The condition of this city thou must have heard from others, so I shall be brief. There are many splendid palaces, houses, tombs, and temples, and other edifices in infinite number, but all are in ruins; much porphyry and marble from ancient buildings, and every day these marbles are destroyed by being burnt for lime in scandalous fashion. What is modern is poor stuff, that is to say the buildings; the beauty of Rome lies in what is in ruins. The men of the present day, who call themselves Romans, are very different in bearing and in conduct from the ancient inhabitants. *Breviter loquendo,* they all look like cowherds. – *Letter of Alberto de'Alberti,* 22nd March 1444[1]

I

News of disturbances in Rome, of lawlessness, and a confusion amounting to governmental chaos, had been brought to the Pope while he was still at Siena. He knew then what a serious situation he would have to face when he brought the Curia back to Rome after the long absence, but he would not hasten his progress unduly and continued to take stock of the places he passed through, talking with the citizens while he formed his own opinion of their needs and problems. Meanwhile the summer was wearing on; soon there seemed no excuse for Pius to postpone his entry to Rome. He finally reached the city on 6th October[2], to the joy of all those citizens who were tired of discord and only wished for peace.

Peace, however, could not come until order had been restored. The trouble in Rome was of long standing, dating in its acute form from the pontificate of Nicholas V but deriving its inspiration from much earlier times. A Roman named Stefano Porcaro had had delusions of grandeur in the mid-fifteenth century: he saw himself as another and more successful Cola di Rienzo, exalting the Roman Republic to its ancient fame and himself winning renown as Tribune. With none of Rienzo's genius, Porcaro had an even higher degree of arrogance. For a time his energies were turned to useful ends, for he served as podestà successively in Bologna, Siena, and Orvieto. These three years (1434–6) were the quietest of his career; thereafter his ideas became increasingly fantastic—antiquarianism cloaking a kind of disordered democracy. Thus he was led to seek revolution for its own sake and an outlawry that was self-imposed. Nicholas V had tried to buy Porcaro off by making him Rector of the Campagna and Marittima[3], but he returned to Rome after a year's absence and had to be sent away again, first to Germany as ambassador, and finally to Bologna where he was required to report his presence daily to Bessarion. The Pope gave Porcaro an allowance of 25 golden florins a month as long as he remained in that city[4]. This expedient could never satisfy Porcaro's desires; he still burned with ambition that would not let him rest. He made a dash for Rome, bent upon raising revolt with the help of his relatives and friends. Bessarion, however, was able to send the Pope warning, so that the conspiracy had no time to develop before measures were taken to suppress it. Porcaro's sister hid him in a wooden coffer but —less fortunate than Aeneas's hero Euryalus[5]—he was found, imprisoned, and executed within a few days.

Nicholas V showed little magnanimity; not only did he order the execution of many of Porcaro's followers, he tried to erase all memory of the conspirators and had Porcaro's dwelling demolished. His severity to some extent recoiled upon the Papacy, for before the end of the century the house had been rebuilt and was again inhabited by the Porcari, while Stefano was extolled as a democratic hero by later generations. Even in the nineteenth century his name was still being used as a rallying cry: in 1866 a pamphlet demanding the secularization of Rome was issued in his name[6]. The reputation was greater than the man.

One of Porcaro's strongest supporters had been Angelo de Maso[7]; when he and his eldest son were executed in company with their leader, Angelo's two younger boys were profoundly distressed and mortified. In their desire to avenge their father and brother, Tiburzio and Valeriano formed a gang, about three hundred strong, vowed to every kind of lawlessness. Insolence, robbery, rape, and even murder were their weapons; since many of them belonged to patrician families who protected them it was very difficult to bring them to justice. When the young gangsters found that their earliest petty thefts ('of hens and things of little value') went unpunished they became increasingly daring and their conduct from scandalous passed to insupportable. One of Tiburzio's friends was a youth named Bonanno Specchio, who quickly became a leading spirit. The Senator of Rome, finding himself unable to check the violence and fearing, indeed, for his own safety, left his 'magnificent house' in the Campo de' Fiori and took refuge in the Vatican palace[8]. One of the young men, suitably nicknamed 'L'innamorato', kidnapped a maiden of Trastevere as she was on the way to her wedding: this was too much for the citizens, who forced the Governor into taking action. Some of the gang fled to sanctuary in the Pantheon, but before long Tiburzio and Bonanno were again swaggering about the city. They 'planned the rapes and adulteries they should commit, and feasted together, robbing by night and amusing themselves by day.' At last Tiburzio was persuaded to leave the city, though he walked 'like some great prince through the city to the gate', where he mounted and rode off to stay with his kinsmen the Savelli in one of their castles, Palombara, mocking and saluting the crowd of citizens who had come to see him depart.

All these doings had been reported to the Pope, who considered the matter very carefully and came to a just conclusion. The crimes of these young men were different in kind as well as in degree from riotous hooliganism, or the destructiveness of the 'pernicious' young Sienese who had broken up Pius's fountain.* The lawlessness must be stopped and the wrong-doers punished; nevertheless Pope Pius had a true understanding and sympathy with youthful exuberance and it grieved him deeply that retribution must come to Tiburzio, whose excesses had now gone beyond all bounds.

When he made it known that he was about to leave for Rome, Pius threw all the Curia into a turmoil. 'Some were filled with joy, others with trepidation', as the party took the southward road, over the summit of Monte Cimino and down through the dark chestnut woods that clothed its flanks. Pius spent that night in a tiny wooden

* See p. 151.

hut on the mountainside: next day he reached Nepi but would not stay there overnight. It was expected that the Pope would dine at Campagnano, as on his outward progress nine months earlier. The wife of Napoleone Orsini had prepared a festive supper for him but he preferred to push on to Formello. Here no one expected visitors: 'No food, no drink, no beds could be discovered'. However, bread and some onions were procured from the peasants' huts; washed down with water (since the wine was too bad to drink), these kept the party from starvation. Pius cared so little for creature comforts that the meal satisfied him—not so the Cardinals. Prospero Colonna made the excuse that he did not care to stay in an Orsini stronghold; he went off to dine with the Savelli. Alain of Avignon 'who could endure no discomfort' fared better still, for he went to Campagnano and consumed the supper intended for the Pope.

Next morning, before it was light, Pius was again on the road. Rome was only fourteen miles distant, but he chose to pause for dinner on the way in order to compensate for the sketchy meal of the previous evening. A charming place was found for the picnic, a shady grove beside 'a clear perennial spring'. Here it was that the deputation from Rome found the Pope and all dined together in perfect amity. Not only the Senator, Cardinal Tebaldo, who had roused the Pope's ire by his disloyalty during the Congress, had come, there were nobles too, and leading citizens, and—surprisingly enough—a company of young men on foot, with a litter on which they proposed to carry the Pope. These youths were part of Tiburzio's gang: 'For this reason the Pope's friends urged him not to trust himself to such wicked young men, but to be carried rather by his own cavalry. The Pope laughed at their counsel and, bidding the Romans draw near and take his litter, said: Thou shalt tread upon the lion and adder: the young lion and the dragon shalt thou trample under thy feet[9]. This prophecy has often been fulfilled elsewhere and it shall be fulfilled today. For what animal is more cruel than man? But man is an inconstant animal and the fiercest hearts are often tamed. These young men were prepared to rob us of the City and of our life, had they been able. They were not able, they recognized their error. They have been tamed and will carry upon their shoulders him whom they desired to trample underfoot. Nor was the Pope wrong. The young men eagerly received his litter and carried their Lord rejoicing to the Flaminian Gate.'

While his followers bore the Pope on their shoulders through the cheering crowds who had come to meet him, Tiburzio was conspiring with Pius's enemies outside the city walls. His hosts, the Savelli, were on terms of close friendship with Piccinino*, who had now made up his mind to throw in his lot with the French in Naples and to oppose the Pope's candidate, Ferrante. The Colonna family too were dissatisfied; even though they had received favours from Pius they acted as the agents who brought Piccinino and his forces into the Campagna[10] and the Pope had good reason to believe that they were also associated with the anti-papal party in Tivoli. It was high time for him to take up the reins of government: Pius had no intention of emulating the nine years' exile suffered by Eugenius IV.

The first thing to do was to break up Tiburzio's gang and to establish firm government in Rome itself. It so happened that Tiburzio's 'strong man', his friend Bonanno, ventured into the city at this time. He was caught and held prisoner: there seems little doubt that he was tortured to make him reveal the conspirators' plans, for he and Tiburzio were now caught up in a much wider and more dangerous plot and Piccinino had found them very useful tools. Tiburzio followed Bonanno to Rome, thinking that he might rescue his friend as on a former occasion, but he had misjudged both the resolution and the resources of the government now that it was stiffened by the Pope's presence in the Vatican. He, too, was captured by the Pope's men where he lay hiding in a bed of reeds among long grass and brambles, just outside the city walls. Valeriano, his young brother, had already escaped into voluntary exile, but several of his companions were taken with Tiburzio and all were led through the streets 'with downcast eyes' to imprisonment, trial, and death.

Cardinal Tebaldo, as Senator, planned a vindictive sentence— 'worthy of such atrocious crimes'—for Tiburzio, de Maso, Bonanno Specchio and the other six misguided youths. The Pope, however, intervened and ordered that, although they must be hanged, they should not be tortured and priests were to be allowed to attend them upon the scaffold. While the execution was being carried out Pius wept from pity and compassion. He prayed devoutly for the victims who were, he felt, more foolish than wicked although they

---

* Jacopo Savelli arranged quarters in his own estate for the condottiere's troops.

were guilty of so many and such odious offences. It was a sad home-coming for Pope Pius, one of whose strongest characteristics was a love for exuberant youth, but he believed that he must not flinch from the sternest measures in trying to restore to Rome the peace and good government she so sorely needed.

II

It has been necessary to describe Porcaro's conspiracy, and its sequel under the de Maso brothers and their lieutenants, in some detail in order to illustrate the chaotic condition of Rome at this time. The lack of governance was reflected, too, in the ruinous state of the city walls, the defacement of public buildings, and the cynical neglect that allowed ancient monuments to moulder into decay or to be ground down for lime. Moss-grown statues and indecipherable inscriptions were a commonplace, while great blocks of stone were dug from the ancient roads and carried into the city for new house-building without protest or even comment. On one of his progresses Pius saw with his own eyes a man digging stones out of the Appian Way—'smashing up large boulders into small pieces with which to build a house at Genzano'. Rage overcame the Pope; he 'reproved the man angrily' and gave orders that never again should the road be touched for such a purpose[11]. When Tiburzio returned to Rome, for the last time, he had made his way through a gap near the Baths of Diocletian 'where a part of the wall had collapsed'[12]: it was impossible to guard against the entry of such marauders either by day or by night—the condition of the defences was as conducive to lawlessness as was the apathy of the defenders.

Some fourteen years earlier a Spanish traveller[13] had complained that Rome was as desolate as when she had been plundered by the barbarians, that there were 'parts within the walls that look like thick woods', deep caves where forest animals were wont to breed and the lairs of wolves and foxes. Hares and deer could be caught in the streets and were welcome in many household kitchens, for the general incompetence of corrupt officials led to sudden and inexplicable crises when the Romans were near starvation and granaries that should have been full were found to contain only mouldy husks and a full complement of rats. The outlying estates and farms owned by the Romans were threatened by the ravages of

Piccinino's troops: their produce was either wasted or hidden away. This meant a heavy loss of provisions for Rome at a time when her need was greatest.

The threat of famine was accentuated when Rome was thronged with strangers, as at times of Jubilee or when conferences were held or deputations came to visit the Pope. Extra supplies of grain from the wheat-growing districts of the papal states—oil, cheese and figs from the March of Ancona[14], wines from the March and from Campagna, extra quantities of salted meat—all these should have been stored in readiness for the Jubilee of 1450, when more than a thousand inns were reaping a golden harvest from their tourist trade[15]. In practice, supplies were intermittent, prices rose steeply, pilgrims had to tighten their belts and even to leave Rome before their devotions were completed. The crowds were as unregulated as the supplies of provisions. Many were pushed into the Tiber or trampled underfoot when they tried to cross the bridge of S. Angelo: to the Florentine Vespasiano da Bisticci the throng of people seemed 'like ants'[16], but to the Romans they must have seemed more like locusts.

Under Calixtus III Rome had become very Spanish; his Borgia relations maintained this tradition not only in the Curia but also in the city, where Don Pedro Luis—elder brother of Cardinal Rodrigo Borgia and at one time Prefect of Rome—as Duke of Spoleto retained control of the fortresses. He it was who sold Castel San Angelo to the Cardinals for 20,000 ducats[17], and had he not died of fever at Civitavecchia a few months after the election of Aeneas to the Papacy Don Pedro and his friends might have caused the new Pope much embarrassment. The old Roman families resented the presence of the foreigners and felt envious of their power and riches. Even a peasant like Giovanni Campano, who raised himself from shepherd boy to Bishop, was moved to the defence of the old aristocracy. To his friend Matteo Ubaldo he wrote: 'few of the citizens have retained the stamp of ancient nobility. For they despise the glory of arms, the greatness of empire, simplicity of manners and integrity as something antiquated and foreign.'[18] Campano further stated that the foreigners in Rome were mainly cooks, sausage-makers, panders and jesters and that they were responsible for the squalor and filth of the city in his time.

Although Tiburzio's revolt had been successfully put down, there were still some of his supporters at large in the Campagna and

Sabina. Jacopo Savelli was still at large, also the more formidable Count Everso of Anguillara. Pius was not able to concern himself with reforms and rebuilding until his position was entirely secure. In March 1461, eleven disaffected nobles ventured out from their stronghold at Palombara and made for Rome in order to stir up strife. By this time, however, Piccinino had had to yield to the skilful strategy of Federigo of Urbino, who had pushed his forces back and had subdued almost the whole of the Sabine. The eleven trouble-makers were caught and hanged; their protector Jacopo Savelli was isolated, and rendered harmless*. At last Pius was free to follow his instincts. He was never a builder, patron, or collector on the scale of Nicholas V, but in an unspectacular way he carried on the works of repair and reconstruction that Nicholas had initiated. On 28th April 1462, Pope Pius published a Bull forbidding further destruction or damage of ancient monuments in Rome and the Campagna, even extending the ban to those situated on private property—a daring innovation. This was a beginning; thereafter he concerned himself first with structural repairs, to the roofs of the Pantheon, St Peter's, St John Lateran and other churches. Next came the mending of the city walls and bridges; only then was he able to turn to em-bellishment and new building in the Vatican and St Peter's. Pius did not confine his works to Rome; it was he who at his own expense repaired churches within the States—Assisi, Narni, Viterbo and Orvieto all owed him gratitude for his help in their maintenance. Perhaps his most famous legacy to Rome was the rebuilding of the terrace leading to St Peter's, with a tribune for Papal Benediction on the restored staircase. These steps were 133 feet wide; Pius adorned them with bold statues of St Peter and St Paul[19].

Among the Pope's most agreeable traits was one that endeared him greatly to his friends. This was his constancy. He remembered old acquaintances and was always delighted to recall shared ex-periences whether the connection was an important one or merely personal. It was typical of him that he sought out the old priest in Corsignano who had given him his first lessons, and no less so that one of his first actions after his return to Rome from Mantua was to send a splendid gift to the city of Basel, where he had served his

* Pius treated him generously, granting him forgiveness and peace on moder-ate terms.

apprenticeship as a man of letters. This present was a handsome disc-shaped monstrance; on one side there was an embossed figure of the Pope at prayer, on the other an Agnus Dei. It bore an inscription stating that Pius had given the monstrance to Basel 'in token of ancient friendship'[20].

Nevertheless, Pius would not use his new position to deal out rewards and favours to his friends unless there was good reason for exalting them. Those who thought that they had only to dedicate their verses to him, or fabricate graceful compliments, were quickly disillusioned. The election of Pius II had seemed to the mob of poets and literary adventurers who thronged the Roman court a signal for rejoicing. They were wrong, very wrong. Pius himself, as Aeneas Sylvius, had made many bids for favour from influential patrons: he knew just how they should be valued, and he was the last man to hand out pensions or lavish gifts in return for idle flattery. In his freelance days he himself had written many graceful verses, better than most of the genteel exercises he now received. Yet he would not discourage genuine talent; he was a generous if a shrewd critic.

It would be unprofitable, and very difficult, to make a full catalogue of the works that were at one time or another dedicated to Pius II. It was common practice to rededicate a poem or translation if the first patron was found to be unappreciative; sometimes as many as three or even four prefaces are associated with a single work. There do exist, however, several dedicatory letters to Pope Pius that have a special interest and these must be listed briefly. First, there is the very personal one written by Giovanni Matteo de Ferrariis that has already been noticed. This commentary on Avicenna most certainly was composed for Pius: that is established beyond doubt by the remarks about the Pope's 'unfortunate trouble' in his feet. De Ferrariis when he wrote this work was the medical attendant of Francesco Sforza; it may be that the *Commentary* was a bid to change his employment although there is no sign that he ever did enter the papal household—or, indeed, that he received the hoped-for reward.

Several humanists accompanied the Pope to Mantua, most of them his own friends and companions from earlier days. One of these was Francesco Griffolini of Arezzo[21], who inscribed to Pius his translations from Homer[22] and also his Latin version of the *Epistles* of Diogenes[23].

For many years Biondo Flavio of Forlì accompanied Pius wherever he went, exploring with him archaeological sites and sharing his delight in the beauties of the countryside. It was while he was in Mantua that Biondo completed his great work *Roma Triumphans:* it was inevitable that he should dedicate it to Pius neither as patron nor as Pope but as a fellow student of the antiquities of Rome. His work was, as Pius wrote, 'truly a laborious and useful undertaking'. Like some other archaeologists Biondo was more interested in his historical material than in the manner in which he set down his conclusions. 'He cared less', as Pius pointed out, 'how correctly he wrote than how much. If some time a man of learning and with experience of writing would undertake to correct and adorn Biondo's works, he would bestow no small benefit upon posterity and make himself famous; and he would also bring back to the light the deeds of many ages which have been almost buried.'

Pius added to his criticism of his friend's work the shrewd forecast: 'Someone will perhaps say the same about us, and with good reason. For though we write the truth, yet we mingle the paltry with the important and, lacking elegance, have woven a rough and formless story. Perhaps one day someone else will bring to this light Biondo's inventions and our own, and so earn the fruit of another's labour.'[24] Biondo died at Rome, poor, 'as a philosopher should', in the spring of 1463. Pius sent his own confessor to Biondo's deathbed and paid for his burial. Nor did he forget his friend easily; he provided a worthy post for his son Gasparo and he showed his appreciation of Biondo's work by making an abstract of the first twenty books of his *Decades*[25].

Another colleague of the Pope at Mantua, who was closely connected with his schemes for reforming the Curia and who undertook on his behalf a highly confidential mission to the Emperor, was Domenico de' Domenichi, the learned Bishop of Torcello. Two of his books were written for Pope Pius: the tract concerning the reform of the Curia that was printed at Brescia in 1495, and another that exists in manuscript[26].

Campano, of course, wrote many poems for Pius; they are to be found in his collected works printed at Rome in the same year as Domenichi's *Tractatus*. Orazio Romano, too, addressed to the Pope

nine Latin epigrams and three poems[27], as did the Neapolitan
Porcellio and a number of minor poets of whom little is known except their names. Among these was Leonardo Montagna who inscribed to him the metrical life of St Symeon of Armenia[28]. This
saint died (in 1016) at the Abbey of S. Benedetto in Polirone where
Pius had spent a vacation from the Congress. The *Life* of St Symeon
might have been expected to have a topical interest for the Pope,
though the connection was tenuous. A subject closer to his heart
was the *Epistola* from Constantinople to Rome (followed by another
from Rome to Constantinople), written by a young Roman of pre-
cocious talent named Niccolò della Valle. At the age of eighteen
this young scholar made some notable translations from the Greek;
he presented his version of Hesiod to Pius II together with a graceful
introductory letter in elegiac couplets[29]. Pius was ready to encourage a brilliant scholar like della Valle at the outset of his career:
what he would not do was to reward the professional scribblers
and hangers-on who attempted to live at his expense. He neither
sought nor needed their praises. Although the humanists were bitterly disappointed, even mortified, by Pius's attitude, they dared
not revile him or accuse him openly of meanness, for he was still
a formidable opponent and excelled most of them both in speech
and writing. Their weapons were his weapons: the difference was
that he could use them with more skill and subtlety.

Now that he was in a position to indulge his personal tastes, to
buy the books he had always longed to own but had been unable to
afford, it might have been expected that Pius would build up one
of the great Renaissance libraries, or at least continue the splendid
collection begun by Pope Nicholas V. He did neither of these things.
The books he bought were carefully chosen, beautiful without magnificence, few in number, and in no way to be compared with the
'crimson and silver' library of Frederick of Urbino. Pius was as frugal
in this matter as he was abstemious in eating and drinking, not because he was parsimonious but because he knew other and better
ways of finding value for money. The cause of his crusade came first,
and next to it his creation of Pienza—his private charities and presents to his friends and relations were lower on the list though they
were still important. Books for his own delight made a small item in
his expenditure. Nevertheless, their appearance as well as their content was important to him. Four of Pius's MSS. are among those

presented to the Bodleian Library by Sir Kenelm Digby in the sev-
enteenth century[30]. They illustrate his tastes both in form and subject. Besides his presentation copy of the *Commentary on Avicenna*
(MS. Digby 135) there is an Italian version of Livy's *History*, written in the previous century[31]; this has initial letters of fastidious
beauty and at the foot of the first page a charming landscape—a
lake where ducks and cranes swim and dive, surrounded by trees
with exquisite foliage. There can be little doubt that Pius chose this
book largely on account of the rare quality of its miniatures; it is
significant, too, of the elasticity of his mind that he should have
shown interest in a vernacular rendering of a classical text.

In MS. Digby 141 Pius has again selected an Italian text—the *Son-
netti e Trionfi* of Francesco Petrarch. Here also there is lively and
attractive decoration. Birds (parrots and finches) and a rabbit and
an antelope can be discerned on the border, together with two pairs
of putti adorned with coral necklaces. The hand is large and clear,
the initials are all in burnished gold. Pius II also owned, and perhaps had specially written for him*, MS. Digby 231. Here are the
Orationes of Cicero, in Latin, with magnificent illumination in the
Florentine style[32]. The full border of white branchwork on a blue,
green, and maroon background, has portraits enclosed in medallions
and wild animals and birds sporting among the tendrils. There are
wild boar, bears, a monkey and an antelope, all exquisitely drawn,
and in other borders the same quiet colours are found with occasional paintings of flowers and butterflies. More gorgeous manuscripts of this time do exist, but it would be hard indeed to find one
that is more attractive.

Yet another charming book is Pliny's *Natural History*[33]—more
than five hundred pages with some thirty-five miniatures that
closely illustrate the text. The illumination was probably the work of
Gioacchino Bemboli[34], a Sienese miniaturist who ornamented many
books for Pius in a style derived from the best Florentine models. It
is particularly interesting to find the coat of arms—enclosed as usual
in a wreath—Piccolomini impaling Lolli. The close friendship between the cousins Aeneas and Goro could not be better illustrated.
It is possible that the book was written for Gregorio Lolli with the

---

* This is impossible to prove, for the arms at the foot of fo. 1 have been cut
out.

Pope's encouragement; more likely that he had it made and presented it to his cousin as a graceful acknowledgment of their kinship.

The works dedicated to Pius II, and his selection of texts for his
own library, illustrate very clearly the catholicity of his tastes and
interests. Of material rewards to the writers there is little evidence,
although he inspired in some of them—Biondo of Forlì for one—a
really devoted friendship. Pius was, however, a discriminating patron who knew well how to pay for the works he had commissioned.
The scribes and artists who worked for him in the creation of Pienza
and its cathedral and library had no cause to complain of the Pope's
stinginess: the papal expenses recorded by his chamberlain for the
years 1461-2 are studded with payments for time, skill, and materials[35]. Pius was quick to see the merits of his friends' work, even
when it seemed to be in competition with his own. When Bartolomeo Fazio—who had already dedicated a small work[36] to Pius
before he became Pope—wrote a series of biographies, *De Viris Illustribus,* using the same title and imitating the form that he himself
had used, Pius showed no annoyance. Indeed, he wrote Fazio a
graceful letter of congratulation, thanking him simply and warmly
for the complimentary things he had said about his patron[37].

Pius gave praise sparingly, but with a warm generosity in keeping
with his emotional temperament. A striking instance of this quality
is seen in Pius's reception of an oration delivered to him by John
Tiptoft, Earl of Worcester. He had hitherto held no high opinion of
English culture: when Pius heard honeyed Latin phrases on the lips
of this talented Englishman he wept for joy, exclaiming, 'You alone,
of all the Princes of our age, we may compare in character and eloquence with the most illustrious Emperors of Greece and Rome'[38].
This was hyperbole in the grand manner: it was neither hypocrisy
nor calculated diplomacy, merely the tribute—wrung from him by
pleasure and surprise—of an impulsive and warm-hearted artist.
Vain, Pius may have been, but never pompous: as Aeneas Sylvius
he may have had moments of pettiness, but when he became Pope
his personality mellowed and his exaltation as head of Christendom
in no way interfered with his acceptance of his fellows as friends
and equals. In this fact lay his greatest strength.

CHAPTER XIII

Pius II in Italy and Europe

If we have not succeeded as we hoped, yet do we not regret our plan and our labour. The whole world has understood that it was strength, not spirit, that we lacked. None now can say that we have spent our time amid the pleasures of Rome while we allowed the orthodox faith to perish, since in our old age and infirmity we feared neither frost nor rain nor snow. We have gone a long way through foreign parts, we have called the princes, admonished the peoples . . . And what can now be imputed against us? – AENEAS SYLVIUS PICCOLOMINI, *Commentaries*

I

When Pope Martin V came to take up residence in Rome, determined as he was to heal the wounds caused by schism and lack of leadership, he faced a crisis that differed only in degree from the problem that awaited Pius II on his return from Mantua. Pope Martin's difficulties were far more formidable; his methods had to be ruthless but they set the pattern followed three decades later by his gentler and less single-minded successor*. Like Pius II Pope Martin found in the Lord of Milan 'a sympathetic spirit'[1] with whom he could combine to direct the destinies of Italy and to some extent those of Europe too. Martin's colleague, however, was the cunning and secretive Filippo Maria Visconti whose ambitions were centred upon survival, whereas Francesco Sforza, the contemporary of Pius, was a benevolent ruler with every reason to suppose that his position was secure. This made possible a relationship based less upon

---

* Martin V (Oddo Colonna) died of apoplexy, 20th February 1431: Pius II was not, of course, his immediate successor.

common fear of treachery than upon hopes for the future, bound together by a joint policy concerning the Kingdom of Naples.

All the *signori* of the Papal States, where their powers were not circumscribed by faction and strife within their own city walls, though potential sowers of discord might also be upholders of the Pope's authority through their military resources. But their support had to be won, their loyalty courted. Martin V had discovered that the *signori* of his domain were all for sale; he had bought and used their services with signal success. He himself had considerable military skill; had he not been Pope he might well have been one of the most notable condottieri of his age. By spending enormous sums on buying lands for his own family he was able to place his Colonna nephews in control of the most important strategic points; it has been estimated that he spent no less than 135,000 florins in this way. Even this large sum seems insignificant when compared with the half million laid out by Pope Boniface VIII for his family—the Gaetani—a century earlier. The mild nepotism exercised by Pius II, in advancing the fortunes of his sister's boys, was in no way comparable with this deliberate exaltation of the Colonna. Nor was it as effective, although it must be credited to Pius that his system of installing Piccolomini kinsmen as officials and castellans made for the strength rather than the ultimate weakness of the Papacy. He was not granting them church property as a possession, but merely as a trust. Or so he explained the matter to himself. In Book IV of the *Commentaries* he wrote: 'The Pope gave Castiglione with its citadels and the island of Giglio to his nephew Antonio, less for his benefit than that of his country, whose seaward places and the granaries of the state are protected by this place.' Even so, if Pius had not had the good judgement to secure the services of Federigo of Montefeltro, Lord of Urbino, he would have had small chance of checking the ravages of Piccinino in the papal lands.

In many ways Federigo was a man after the Pope's own heart. 'He had every characteristic of *virtù*,' wrote Vespasiano; 'there was no one like him . . . and he conquered his enemies as much by prudence and foresight as through force of arms.'[2] Even when his troops were in retreat, as from the battle of San Fabiano on 22nd July 1460, Federigo knew how to turn defeat into victory: in the end he subdued the whole of the Sabina, forced Jacopo Savelli to surrender his fortress, at Palombara, where Tiburzio had found refuge, and negotiated peace in this very vulnerable district of the Papal States. Pius had respect for Federigo as a soldier and affection for him as a man. Once, riding together before dawn 'a pleasant and lively conversation about ancient histories was carried on' and as they rode towards Tivoli they discussed the Trojan war. Federigo, 'who had read much, questioned the Pope whether the generals of old had been as well armed as our own': they argued too about the geography of Asia Minor and Pius drew from their talk the inspiration for his *Asia* that he was to write a few weeks later.

Not only did Pius find it difficult to engage men to fight for him: it was even harder for him to pay their wages. The papal income had been severely reduced by the reform decrees of the Council of Constance[3]: indeed, in the middle years of the fifteenth century the revenues were scarcely more than a third of those enjoyed before the Schism. The communes of Rome provided the salary of their podestà, but the papal camera had to find money to pay not only the host of officials and all expenses of the household but also the mercenaries. 'The money which can reach our treasury every year,' Pius wrote in the *Commentaries*[4] towards the end of his pontificate, 'does not amount in all to three hundred thousand ducats. Half of that is consumed by the custodians of our citadels, the captains of our provinces, and by our court officials; nor can the Apostolate be maintained without these expenses.' Whether from direct taxes— such as the annual subsidy on the Jews—or the constantly diminishing salt tax and hearth taxes (*focaticum,* or *fumantaria*), the estimated revenue nearly always exceeded what actually came to hand. Tallage levied on the towns of the March, the Patrimony of St Peter, and the Duchy of Spoleto, was sometimes assigned to mercenaries to collect for themselves. Profits of justice might or might not pay the judges' salaries. Pasture was taxed in the Patrimony, also the cattle, sheep and goats that fed upon it, but in practice this tax was disappointing for it was difficult and expensive to collect. It is easy to see that the papal income was uncertain, insecure, generally overestimated and always insufficient.

If Pius II had not lived so frugally and spent so little on his pleasures—apart from his buildings at Pienza—his financial position would have been grim. As it was, had not the fortuitous discovery of the alum mines come at exactly the right moment he could never have hoped to finance his crusading host. This stroke of good fortune could not, indeed, have been better timed! Pius was extremely quick to appreciate its implications. In the *Commentaries* he attributed the discovery of this valuable substance to Giovanni de Castro*, a distant kinsman of the Piccolomini. Instead of becoming a lawyer like his famous father and elder brother, Giovanni went into trade and worked in a business house at Basel, where he met Aeneas Sylvius at the time of the Council. Later, Giovanni went to Constantinople to act as manager of a large dye-works; it was here that he learned the properties of alum and became accustomed to identifying it in its natural state. When Giovanni's commercial venture turned out badly, partly to escape from his creditors and partly to persuade Pius to help him, he came to Rome. The Pope's generosity to an old friend and kinsman kept Giovanni from starvation and gave him leisure to ramble through the desolate countryside of the Campagna. One day, when he was walking in the hills near Civitavecchia, at a place called Tolfa, Giovanni noticed a herb that he had seen growing near the alum mines in Asia Minor. Near it were some white stones. Then, as Pius tersely put it: 'He bit one and it tasted salt. He baked it, made an experiment, and produced alum. Then going to the Pope he said: This day I bring you victory over the Turk.'[5]

Hitherto, the only alum found in western Europe came from a small mine in the island of Ischia and a cave in Lipari; for dyeing their wool all the Christian countries had to buy from the Turks to the tune of three hundred thousand gold ducats a year. Now, Giovanni's discovery meant that the Pope would be able to supply alum to all Europe, at great financial gain[6], and the Turkish trade would be correspondingly diminished. After careful inquiries had confirmed the truth of Giovanni's claim, Pius established the industry, paying a royalty to two brothers, lords of the land at Tolfa, and importing experienced artisans from Genoa to work the mineral. Some Genoese merchants were the Pope's first customers, then Cosimo dei Medici took seventy-five thousand golden ducats' worth. The enterprise was duly launched, the Pope established his monopoly, and a profit of a hundred thousand ducats came rolling in to the papal treasury each year. Giovanni was given his share and

---

* Although the biographer of Pope Paul II (*Muratori*, vol. III) gave this credit to a Paduan astrologer, Giovanni's claim seems established.

a statue was erected to him in his native city. Campano wrote an epigram on Pius's mineral wealth that must be quoted in full:

Who says the heavens alone are thine
Knows not, Pope Pius, thy power divine.
The very earth has given her treasure
And all herself in generous measure;
Here sounding copper, alum there,
And from a third vein silver fair.
All these for many years concealed
To their sole lord the mountains yield.
Now, richest earth, if you have gold in store,
Lest you be called a thief, to Pius give it o'er.[7]

In Romagna, the northern part of the papal state, Bologna remained aloof and taciturn[8]. Pius knew that a friendly relationship was most improbable, so he concentrated his efforts upon avoiding any action or utterance that could lead to friction. With Sigismondo Malatesta of Rimini, however, it was another matter. Sigismondo had come to Mantua less to help the project of the crusade than to further his own cause, for he was hard pressed by Federigo of Urbino, at that time in alliance with Piccinino. He deferred to the Pope because he hoped Pius would arrange a favourable peace. The Pope, however, had his own ideas as to what the terms of the settlement should be. He did arrange a peace, and warned Federigo against exploiting too far the advantages he was given[9], but he consented to the transfer of several Malatesta fortresses to the Duke of Urbino. Sigismondo accepted these terms most reluctantly; he only waited for a favourable moment, when the Pope's attention should be occupied elsewhere, before starting a campaign to win back his patrimony. For many months he met with little success, then, at sunrise on 2nd July 1461, he attacked and defeated the papal forces at Nidastore, capturing three hundred horsemen and much baggage belonging to the papal army. 'A shameless soldier found the mitre and vestments belonging to the Bishop of Corneto'[10] and 'at Sigismondo's command he donned the linen robe and episcopal pallium, and setting the mitre on his head he mounted a horse and rode this way and that with outstretched hand as though blessing the people, in scorn and mocking of the ecclesiastical order.'

The gesture was a trivial one, but significant of Sigismondo's deep antagonism to the Church and his personal animosity towards the

Pope. Pius was no less violently opposed to the Lord of Rimini. Early in the previous year, while the war dragged on its murderous and vindictive course, Pius brought to a climax the condemnation of Sigismondo Malatesta that had been begun on Christmas Day 1460. His effigy, created by no less an artist than Paolo Romano, was ceremonially burned on a pyre in front of St Peter's as a symbol of the Pope's detestation of his crimes. These, it is true, were heinous and manifest[11]: Sigismondo blended wickedness with enlightenment and a genuine love of poetry and architecture with unnatural and horrible behaviour. Nevertheless, among his own subjects he was popular to the last, for Malatesta rule in Rimini was comparatively benign and—despot as he was—Sigismondo had succeeded in inspiring loyalty and even affection in his native town[12]. To Pius, however, he appeared as a monster with no redeeming feature. The Pope, who had set himself to curb the impetuous judgements of Aeneas, in this one instance was implacable. The struggle with Sigismondo, resulting as it did in the humiliation of 'that perverse and evil man' when at last Fano was obliged to surrender after a gallant resistance[13], did not show the Pope at his most generous. His victory was applauded by many of his contemporaries, but everyone was aware that for Pius it was shaded by selfish ambition.

The spoils of Rimini were his to distribute. They were divided mainly between Federigo of Urbino and Pius's own nephew Antonio. This condottiere was the most military-minded of Pius's sister's[14] sons and had already won a measure of fame in the Neapolitan war. As a boy Antonio was the greatest possible contrast to his studious brother Francesco, who graduated at Perugia at his uncle's expense and diligently followed the course laid out for him. At twenty-one Francesco became Archbishop of Siena, then Cardinal, and two months before he died (in 1503) he was elected Pope. Antonio's career never took him to such heights, but he lived an exciting life and must have been an attractive person to have won such strong affection from Pius. Long before Antonio's triumph over Sigismondo Malatesta, and six years before he had been given his first assignment as Castellan of San Angelo, Pius had written to his brother-in-law commenting on the boy's 'execrable' handwriting and remarking 'we understand that Antonio is no scholar'[15]. Nevertheless, this was his favourite nephew. In the end Antonio fulfilled his uncle's hopes, organizing attack or defence as each became necessary and contributing substantially to the stability of the Papal States. Ferrante created him Duke of Amalfi and gave him his own natural daughter in marriage; in 1463 Antonio was also made Count of Celano.

The same year Piccinino took the opportunity to change sides— not through treachery or any feeling of disloyalty to his late employers, but simply as a new professional contract. The effect upon the Neapolitan-Angevin war was to bring it to an almost immediate end. Ferrante of Naples had been deeply concerned in the difficulties of the Papal State—indeed, it was his personal rashness that had led to the Angevin victory at Sarno. Now, however, his star was in the ascendant. The young son and heir of René of Anjou, John of Calabria, was the French claimant; Pontano said of him that he was 'graver and more circumspect than most Frenchmen'[16]; thus it was only to be expected that he would take a realistic view of the situation and withdraw from an impossible position. Early in 1464 John sailed back to Provence, taking with him the twenty-four ships that had been built for war against the Turks, whose only service had been in the Neapolitan adventure, now ended.

Although his instinct to protect Italy from invasion across the Alps, by resisting to the utmost French ambitions, was sound, and although his policy gave Italy thirty years' respite before the troops of Charles VIII came pouring down to the Lombardy plain, Pius could not claim much credit for the settlement of the Neapolitan succession. When all seemed lost after the battle of Sarno, and when news was brought that the Duke of Milan was seriously ill, perhaps dying, Pius certainly wavered, and again after the defeat of his forces at Nidastore he for a time lost heart. The Milanese ambassador wrote to Sforza a long account of his conversations with the Pope, when Pius voiced his fears lest France should become so antagonistic—through his support of Ferrante—as to resort to a General Council. The ambassador, Otto de Carretto, took the Pope's fears very seriously but did his utmost to prove them groundless. 'My most anxious endeavour will be,' he concluded, 'to keep his Holiness firm in this matter, and to take care that no one should know of his vacillations.'[17] When better news began to arrive, and particularly when Ferrante won a small but important victory at Troja six months after the ambassador had sent Sforza his gloomy dispatch, Pius's native courage reasserted itself. He had seen from the first that although opposition might revive in France ideas of summoning the Council he so greatly dreaded, yet submission could lead to a renewal of the humiliations of the 'Babylonish Captivity' at Avignon. As always, Pius tried to steer a middle course: if his prudence were mistaken for cowardice, that would be unfortunate but not disastrous.

II

Otto de Carretto had underestimated not only the Pope's resolution but also his intelligence. He was now about to perform one of the most difficult feats of his career in completing the process begun at Mantua. On 16th March 1462, Pius received the French ambassadors in solemn audience. It was a deliberately contrived state occasion; the Pope, robed in full pontificals, was seated upon his throne in the great hall of the Consistory, with the Cardinals ranged opposite him, and a great throng of spectators—bishops, officials, and lay-men—completely filled the chamber. The first speaker was Jean Jouffroy, Bishop of Arras; he 'made a long oration about the great-ness of the French'[18], boasting that King Louis XI was preparing to send 70,000 men to fight the Turks, although he had no evidence to show that this force existed outside his imagination. More realistic and of far more immediate importance was his announcement of the abrogation of the Pragmatic Sanction of Bourges initiated twenty-four years earlier. The very use of the term 'Pragmatic' de-fines the specialized character of this decree, issued by the assem-bled majesty of the French church at the ancient city of Bourges on 7th January 1438. In its antique meaning it was 'a solemn settle-ment of ecclesiastical affairs by the civil government'; it was in this sense that the French monarchy set up a national church, whose first action was to abolish most of the sources of papal revenue from France and its second to limit severely the Pope's right to nominate French Bishops. It is not surprising that Popes Eugenius IV and Nicholas V resisted the Pragmatic Sanction with such strength as they could muster, nor that the French King felt himself powerful enough to reaffirm it in 1450 and again two years later. It was not until the papal armoury was reinforced by the weapons of persuasion and diplomacy that there was any hope of an effective answer to the Sanction.

For nearly a quarter of a century this had been a source of contention and great bitterness. At its inception there had been some justification for the French King's adoption of its provisions, for in 1438 the quarrel between the Papacy and the whole idea of a Council had been at its height. It became expedient therefore to make a practical application of those decrees from Basel that seemed relevant to the situation in France, and to reject such Papal rights as the Council had already denied. When, however, Pope Eugenius IV accepted reconciliation—and still more when Pius II issued his bull *Execrabilis*—the whole situation changed. The French King, Charles VII[19], intended to cling to the Pragmatic Sanction, although many Frenchmen felt that it had outlived its usefulness. In July 1461, however, the Dauphin became King as Louis XI: at once he reversed his father's policy[20]. Louis believed the Sanction to have lost all practical value and so was willing to exchange it for the more substantial advantages and favours he expected from the Pope. Pius had been working for abolition of the Sanction with all his heart and soul: now that success had come far more quickly and easily than he had hoped, he rose splendidly to the occasion. His oration was magnanimous; his references to the splendour of France and the virtue of the King in revoking the Pragmatic Sanction, no less than his ignoring of what he privately termed the 'imaginary, fictitious, and meaningless' offer of men for his army, were models of diplomacy and tact. 'All listened to the Pope with close attention, as though they were being refreshed after the boredom they had suffered while listening to Arras.'[21]

Bishop Jouffroy of Arras was more intent upon the Cardinal's hat that he so greatly coveted than upon the implications of the surrender that had been made through his mouth. He gained his reward within two months; so did his companion Louis d'Albret, for both were among the Cardinals created in December. In Rome there was great rejoicing when news of the repeal was brought: Goro Lolli wrote a jubilant letter to the Signoria at Siena in which he declared that this was the most solemn and important event that had occurred for many years. 'Praise be to God,' he said, 'that during the reign of a Sienese Pope Holy Church should be so exalted!'[22] Pius himself wept tears of joy. He sent to Louis XI a sword that had

been blessed on Christmas Eve. Engraved upon it were lines that
he had written in the hope of stirring the French King into action:

> Against the furious Turks, Louis, may thy right hand
> Draw me: I shall avenge the bloodshed of the Greeks.
> Mohammed's power will crash and, glorious once again,
> Under thy leadership French courage seek the stars.[23]

There still remained, however, a deep rift between France and
the Papacy in the matter of the Neapolitan succession. Both King
and Pope were masters of persuasion and each believed himself
capable of outwitting the other. Pius, however, had not only oratori-
cal but also literary weapons in his armoury. His letters, that seemed
so reasonable, conceded nothing. Louis, prepared to grant his inch
in the hope of securing his ell, found himself echoing the words of
the French envoys: 'The Pope had uttered many words but had
accomplished no good deeds.'[24] He began to send Pius threatening
messages; if he would not reverse his policy of supporting Ferrante
against the French candidate in Naples Louis would recall the
French Cardinals. He did not say that he would intrigue against the
Pope with his enemies in Germany, but Pius knew that it was all too
likely. He continued to keep up appearances, but privately he wrote
in the *Commentaries* that the envoys were 'like dogs vomiting and
barking against the apostolic see, because they could not bite her'.

Despite his worry and disappointment, coupled with exaspera-
tion, Pius was able to take an objective view of the struggle between
England and France. The passages describing the course of the war,
the brilliant sketches of French history and the part played by the
Maid of Orleans, are some of the best he ever wrote. Not nearly
enough attention has been paid to his account of Joan of Arc, for he
is almost alone among contemporary writers in assessing her quality
as an individual and her importance to her country in an estimate
uncoloured by personal prejudice. Concerning her supernatural powers he kept an open mind. 'Whether she was the work of God or a
human invention we would not like to say.'[25]

In his analysis of the later stages of the Hundred Years' War, Pius
showed only a perfunctory interest in English affairs, though he
remarked in passing that Henry V had been 'easily the greatest of
the kings of his day'. His journey through England, after the chilly
sojourn in Scotland, had left him only superficial impressions—and
mostly unfavourable—of English customs and institutions[26]. Nor

had the information supplied by his Legate Francesco Coppini[27] improved the Pope's opinion of England and the English. Coppini had become involved in the tangled web of English politics and Pius had good reason to believe that he had gone far beyond his instructions. The French naturally supported Queen Margaret of Anjou. They declared that the Legate had been sent to the English 'to implore their help against the Turks and instead of making peace, had roused them to revolt, had marched with them to war and raised the standard of the Church, had excommunicated the King's party and promised eternal life and given his blessing to those on the other side' (i.e. Yorkists). Pius was obliged to admit that 'there was some truth in the rumour. Ambition and vast promises had led Francesco astray.' In the end he was recalled, deprived of his bishopric and—instead of receiving the hoped-for red hat—he was confined for the rest of his life in the monastery of S. Paolo on the Aventine[28]. There did not seem to the Pope to be much prospect of aid for his plans from this quarter: he expected neither men nor ships for his crusade from a king whose ability he probably underrated, but whose preoccupation with island affairs was evident to everyone.

III

As relations between France and the Papacy grew increasingly tense, and in France herself a considerable body of opinion[29] came to believe that the abolition of the Pragmatic Sanction had been not only a blunder but a betrayal, further clouds loomed beyond the Alps. His early travels and his familiarity with all parts of Germany were of inestimable value to Pius II in his dealings with the amorphous Empire. He could assess the character and ambitions of Bishops and princelings, he knew the fundamental weakness of the Emperor's position, and he could guess with great accuracy in what quarter and in what circumstances trouble might occur. In sending Cardinal Bessarion to Germany from Mantua Pius cannot have had very high hope of persuading the Princes to give active help to the crusade, but in many ways it was a good choice of ambassador. There could be no possible doubt of Bessarion's loyalty and sincerity; the Greek Cardinal made no secret of the fact that the recovery of Constantinople was the ruling passion of his life. To be at liberty to campaign for this cause, and in the course of it to promote peace within the Empire, outweighed the fact that he was a frail old man (he was in his sixty-sixth year) and that—despite his powerful intellect—as an orator he was notably inept.

At first there seemed a prospect of success, then early in 1460 open war broke out between the houses of Wittelsbach and Hohenzollern[30]. A Diet at Nuremberg was succeeded by another at Vienna: neither could achieve its object, for everyone was preoccupied with private warfare and personal ambitions. The impartiality of Pius was called in question, for during his long years in Germany he had been identified with Imperial interests and so inherited the enemies of Frederick III to add to his own detractors. Chief among these was Diether, Archbishop of Mainz, as strongly anti-papal as he was anti-imperialist, and above all anti-Italian. 'The Italians are true to their proverb,' he declared, 'which says that cunning can extract money from barbarians. And it is we that they call barbarians. And what is the meaning of those tithes they ask or those indulgences they offer, think you? They say that it is to make war upon the Turks that they need the money. But in truth it is on us they have declared war when they rob us of our substance, it is for our wealth that they lay their snares. The Italians do not hate the Turks so much as they hate us.'

The grain of truth that lay in Diether's fulminations was that Pius did indeed regard the Germans as barbarians. Individuals he could respect and admire, but generally speaking he felt a distaste for their civilization that the more intelligent were quick to appreciate. In the map of Germany that illustrates Pius's *De Europa*[31] the whole area is dominated by barrels of beer, wolves in the forest, dogs hunting bears, and a drawing of a ship with a mast as thick as a tree trunk and a square sail most untidily reefed. This was printed more than a hundred years after his death, but in a sense the picture typifies Pius's view of the country and its inhabitants. When Diether's election was found to be invalid, and he was excommunicated, he threatened to appeal to a General Council: this made his quarrel with the Papacy irreconcilable and he added personal rancour to the quarrel by joining forces with Pius's old enemy Gregory Heimburg.

Another bitter dispute, that had dragged on for more than a decade, concerned the claim of Cardinal Nicholas of Cusa to the

Bishopric of Brixen. The chapter's right to elect their chosen candidate had been overruled in favour of the upright and saintly but implacable Nicholas. He outraged public opinion in his diocese by the harshness of his reforms, completely alienated the chapter that he might have placated, and quarrelled with Count Sigismund of the Tyrol. The original trouble had nothing to do with Pius, but it was clearly his business to solve the problem if he could. As a young man Sigismund had been his friend, and he had long had a deep regard for Nicholas of Cusa. Since both protagonists genuinely wished for peace the matter should not have been difficult to arrange when it was brought before the Pope at Mantua. Had it not been for the spiteful interference of Gregory Heimburg a happy solution might well have been found. As it was, violent controversy was matched by violent action: in April 1460 Sigismund took the Bishop prisoner and compelled him to sign a renunciation of his claims. Nicholas of Cusa returned to Italy, discredited and disillusioned, and a few months later Bessarion also left for Rome to report his failure to the Pope. Not surprisingly, Sigismund was excommunicated for his flagrant disrespect. The Brixen dispute lingered on until at last peace was made on 25th August 1464: Rome then won a hollow victory, for Nicholas of Cusa died a fortnight before this date and the Pope himself only three days later than his friend.

The Emperor's own position had also been in jeopardy, but for once he had stirred himself to action in time. In his moment of triumph Heimburg was suddenly cast down, when Pope and Emperor combined to summon a Diet at Mainz in the early summer of 1461. 'It is difficult to overthrow the apostolic see and the Roman Empire at the same time. Their roots are planted too deep for the wind to prevail against them,' wrote Pius to the Emperor at the beginning of May. He was right, for at this Diet Heimburg—now excommunicate—found that blasphemy and invective were not enough. The papal envoy, Rudolf of Rüdesheim—briefed, it is thought, by the Pope himself—argued the case for Rome with great ability. Diether recognized defeat and made submission, although he afterwards resisted the appointment of his successor[32]. Heimburg, still truculent and unrepentant, left Mainz for the Tyrol. Pius could see no good qualities in this man, although by his own standards he was a patriot fiercely resisting exactions that he believed to

be unjust. The Pope was less than fair in this instance, for he felt so
strongly that papal policy must be beyond criticism that he allowed
his emotions to outweigh his judgement.

IV

In the course of his European wanderings Pius II had spent enough
time in Bohemia to acquire first-hand knowledge of the peculiar
and equivocal position of the Church in that domain. Indeed, he
was something of a specialist on the Compacts that promised reconciliation with the Papacy, and had made an oration on this subject
in 1455 before Calixtus III[33]. These Compacts had been concluded
at Basel in 1433, before Aeneas Sylvius had begun to take any part
at the Council, but in 1451 he had been Nuncio in Bohemia and
had seen for himself that the document was evasively worded and
capable of several kinds of misinterpretation. He had, however, high
hopes that peace and reconciliation could be brought about through
its medium between heretical Bohemia and the restored Papacy.
That is, if both parties would exercise understanding and tolerance.
It seemed that Pius II, of all people, should be the peacemaker[34].
This, however, was not to be. The failure of his Bohemian policy
was the deepest disappointment of his career, and due as much to
his misunderstanding of the forces behind Bohemian discontent[35]
as to his preoccupation with church doctrine.

At first, all had seemed set fair. After the death of Ladislas Postumus a new king of Bohemia had been chosen. He was George
Podiebrad, a curious man, a supple diplomat, a patriot, unpredicta-
ble, and fantastically ambitious. It was not until March 1462 that
his embassy reached Rome with the intention of completing the
reconciliation begun at Mantua. One of the principals, Prokop von
Rabenstein, a devout Catholic, was a close friend of Pius who was
delighted to welcome him—'embraced him warmly and showered
him with rare gifts'. The other chief delegates were the Hussite
Sdenko Kostka and two priests. One of these 'in a sounding voice
and with headlong delivery' demanded that the Compacts should
immediately be confirmed by the Holy See. A few days later Pius
had a private conversation with Kostka, attempting to explain to
him that the Compacts were really no longer valid since their provisions had repeatedly been broken in Bohemia and that the Church
could not allow the continuance of heresy. Then, in an open Con-

sistory, with four thousand people present, Pius announced that he must annul the Compacts, for 'As a faithful shepherd guards his sheep that they may not stray, so are we bound to watch that the nations do not wander from the way of salvation'[36]. It was a bitter decision that he had to make, but he felt no doubt at all that he was acting rightly.

George Podiebrad now showed himself in his true colours. As soon as Prokop and Sdenko brought the Pope's message to Prague he repudiated his coronation oath and took his stand with the Hussites. At the same time he put forward his plan for an independent crusade with the object of gaining the throne of Constantinople for himself. This alone would have been enough to alienate Pius II, but George went a step further and announced the reform of the Church through a General Council of European princes. He had now outraged all the Pope's susceptibilities; it is not surprising that Pius abandoned all hope of bringing Bohemia within the fold while George Podiebrad remained in control of her destiny. In the very last Consistory that Pius held in Rome, on 16th June 1464, he was saddened by having to issue a Bull declaring George a heretic and summoning him to answer the charges it contained. Reconciliation with Bohemia had been the Pope's strongest intention: now the problem must be left to the future for settlement. The Pope, in his zeal for unity through the extirpation of heresy[37], had been compelled to destroy the instrument that might have brought peace had both sides shown the requisite tolerance, good will, and good faith.

With his apparently implacable attitude towards heresy Pius had in his character strongly liberal traits that were not really contradictory although they might seem so at first sight. He himself cared nothing for astrology and was ready—against the opinion of his time —to make fun of ridiculous predictions. Yet he did not condemn interpreters of dreams, as he showed in his own De Somnio. In his attitude to the slave trade with West Africa he was uncompromising in his opposition—here he was centuries ahead of his contemporaries. At the same time Pius showed his deep love of justice in protecting the Jews against oppression, detailing the Bishop of Spoleto to examine their complaints and forbidding the baptism of children under twelve against the wishes of their parents[38]. A strong principle can be seen in all these opinions, quite strong enough to refute those of Pius's detractors who accuse him of expediency.

CHAPTER XIV

Summer at Tivoli

The Pope stayed here a little over three months, with much delight to his spirit, the place was so beautiful, despite the fact that ceaseless cares weighed on him on account of his wars as well as those that even a peaceful pontificate must bring. — AENEAS SYLVIUS PICCOLOMINI, *Commentaries*

Although it has only been possible to indicate in the broadest way the problems that beset Pius throughout his pontificate[1], enough has been said to show that the year 1461 was the most critical of his whole reign. By July, however, he was beginning to see his way more clearly; his thoughts began to turn away from Rome and towards the centres of disaffection that still remained to be reduced or pacified. Chief among these was Tivoli, a Colonna stronghold where the chief families were on friendly terms with Jacopo Savelli, Count Everso of Anguillara, and others strongly opposed to the Papacy. It seemed to Pius an excellent plan to spend the rest of the summer there so that he could make friends with the townspeople, build a strong citadel to defend Tivoli from attack, and escape from Rome during the unhealthy and enervating months of August and September. It had been an exceptionally hot July; many of the Cardinals and the nobles and courtiers had already left for higher ground and mountain air. When they heard of the Pope's plan, however, they were alarmed and sent word to Federigo of Urbino that he should come to Rome to dissuade the Pope from his project.

Federigo needed no second bidding. With his usual directness he came straight to the Curia. 'If what I hear is true, Pope Pius,' he is reported to have said[2], 'I cannot but be surprised. It is rumoured that you are going to Tivoli. Who gave you this advice? Have you forgotten the treachery of that people? They belong to the

Colonna and are your enemies. They have conspired with Savelli, they give ear to Piccinino's counsels and are friends of Everso's. There is nothing they hate so much as you. Will you commit yourself to men who several times this year have shut their gates against your forces and opened them to your enemies? Come, Pope, take thought for your own safety.'[3] Both courtiers and Cardinals supported Federigo's argument, but in the end Pius talked them all round to his point of view. 'The mob is easily swayed,' he told them, 'and no people is ever of one mind for long. They hate for one moment, love the next. What the multitude wants depends upon convenience. And what greater benefits can be offered to any people than those which the Roman Curia brings with it? Houses are let, food is sold, wine and cattle are turned into money. Even the women benefit by washing clothes. The people of Tivoli know this and that is why they ask us to visit them. It is an opportunity that ought not to be missed.'

The Pope's practical realism conquered all objections, though there were still some who thought he should be guarded from his own temerity. Federigo himself proposed to give him an armed escort for the journey; early on the appointed day he met the papal cavalcade on the far bank of the Aniene and rode with ten companies of horse towards the gates of Tivoli. Pius took infinite delight in the glittering array of men and horses, the rising sun reflected in their shields and touching their crests and helmets in 'marvellous splendour'. The young men brandished their swords and made their horses prance and curvet for the pleasure of the Pope. The people of Tivoli had come out from the city two miles to meet him, and as Federigo's forces wheeled away and made for home, the citizens hoisted the Pope into a litter and 'with fear and love' carried him into the city.

As Pius had foretold, discordant elements—'more conscious of their own sin than of the Pope's mercy'—had gone into voluntary exile. Immediately upon arrival he called a gathering of the citizens, spoke gently to those who had feared his coming, and outlined his design of building a fortress for the city's defence. It seemed good to Pius to build his citadel on the foundation of the ancient fortress, now crumbled into ruin. With his customary enthusiasm he gave orders for the work to be begun at once and incited all the citizens to give their services, so that the new walls and towers soon began to rise.

'Two towers were raised, the walls of which were twenty feet thick, while one was a hundred and thirty feet high, the other a hundred. The other walls were in due proportion. A broad, deep moat was dug all round, two wells were dug, and the whole was adorned with a marble gate on which the Pope had these lines engraved:

'Friend of the good, foe of the bad, enemy of the haughty,
Thine am I, Tivoli, for so has Pius commanded.'⁴

All the building, except the double wall leading from the citadel to the gate of the city, was completed within a year. Its construction would have cost the papal treasury more than 20,000 golden ducats if the people of Tivoli had not given their services without charge. The fortress seemed to them, as the Pope said, both splendid and necessary.

In one of the most vivid passages he ever wrote, Pius describes the situation of Tivoli, with its olive groves and pinewoods, the placid course of the Aniene until it tumbles down the crags below the monastery of Subiaco, and again beneath the walls of Tivoli, where the river runs 'foamy and complaining'. He notes that 'the water of this river is very clear and cold, and many trout are found in it'. When he is describing the ancient aqueducts that carried this water to Hadrian's villa, the ruins, and the sunny landscape of his day, Pius paints a scene as no one else could: the passage may be quoted as an outstanding example of his style⁵.

'About three miles outside the city the Emperor Hadrian built a very fine villa, like a great town. The wide and lofty arches of its temples stand to this day, and the half-ruined buildings may be seen that once were halls and chambers. The columns of peristyles and great porticoes are also visible and traces of fish-ponds and baths to which at one time part of the Aniene was diverted to cool the heat of summer. Age has spoilt all. The walls that once were hung with painted cloths and gold-enwoven curtains are now clothed with ivy. Thistles and brambles have sprung up where once the tribunes sat together in their purple; serpents dwell in the chambers of queens. So fleeting is our mortal state. Between this villa and Tivoli are very lovely vineyards and olive-groves, and among the vines you will find every sort of tree, with a vast number of pome-granates that bear fruit of peculiar size and sweetness. On every side about the city there are in summer most delightful greenswards, where to relieve his spirit the Pope often went with his Cardinals, and sometimes he would sit on some grassy spot under the olives, sometimes in a green meadow on the bank of the Aniene where he could look on its pellucid waters. . . . In these meadows Pius often rested by babbling springs or by shady trees, discussing affairs of state with the Cardinals or receiving the delegations which followed him wherever he went.'

Together with the Cardinals Pius made a number of expeditions to neighbouring villages and abbeys. On 7th September they were invited to accompany him on an excursion to the cloister of S. Caterina sul monte S. Angelo[6]. The greatest heat of summer was now past and leaving as they did at first dawn ('between night and day') the outward journey was delightful. The Pope, however, desired to return to Tivoli by another route, directing the party to travel over ground so rough and broken that all had to dismount and make their way on foot down a narrow chine, perspiring and complaining. This was particularly awkward for the stouter prelates, the largest of whom was Giovanni Chinugi of Siena, lately appointed the first Bishop of Pius's new diocese of Pienza and Montalcino[7]. Biondo made an amusing story of it in a letter to Pius's cousin Goro Lolli, but it cannot be denied that Pius on this occasion showed little consideration for his fellows in the heat of the day. He himself rode, as usual, in a litter, but he too must have suffered in his arthritic limbs from the jolting progress.

While he stayed in Tivoli Pius made his headquarters with the Minorites who had a convent perched on a spur of the mountain, whence there were pleasant views of the plain below but where the rickety and ruinous old house was exposed to wind and rain from every quarter. Mice too, which the Pope thought were 'as large as rabbits', infested the building and scurried about so noisily that they kept him awake all night. Pius had not much sympathy with the conventual Franciscans; his associations with S. Bernardino had made him a supporter of the reformed branch of the Order, the Observantists. On finding that his hosts 'lacked piety' and that their discipline was poor, Pius turned out the Conventuals in favour of Observant Franciscans, whom he ordered to repair the buildings and to remedy all abuses.

The weeks slipped by, till summer was nearly over. Before returning to Rome Pius was invited by Cardinal Carvajal to visit the monastery of Subiaco[8]. Taking four Cardinals with him he made a leisurely journey along the left bank of the Aniene, spending the night at Vicovaro. Here he was lodged in a house which provided a wonderful view across the Aniene to vineyards and groves of oak trees with high mountains beyond. People from the villages around came crowding to receive the Pope's blessing, many of them bringing him presents of wine and food. Pius bade his servants prepare dinner in the open air beside a clear spring. Near by was a pool, crystal clear with a shining gravel bottom: the water was ice-cold. Pope and Cardinals drank it with their wine 'and took less pleasure in the sweetness of the wine than the coolness of the water'. All the country people dined with them; when the meal was over they waded into the river and caught trout for the Pope's servants with their bare hands. 'And they at every fish they caught raised a shout and saluted him.' As the party progressed along the valley, still accompanied by the villagers, the vineyards of Subiaco came in sight. Within living memory no Pope had visited the town, so the people there were honoured by Pius's visit and received him with great joy. As he climbed the steep ascent his mind was full of thoughts of St Benedict, the founder of the convent. Pius admired the asceticism of the twenty brethren dwelling in this remote monastery that appeared to hang 'on the lofty cliff, from which often fragments fall and kill the monks or make a ruin of their buildings'. Some of them were eighty years old; all lived on a very low diet, slept little, and prayed with great devotion. 'We may well believe,' Pius wrote, 'that they are dear to God.'[9]

Between Subiaco and Palestrina more and more villagers gathered to watch the Pope pass and to gain his blessing. When he came to Passerano they brought him fish from Lake Nemi for his dinner, since it was a Friday; these were cooked and eaten by a wayside spring under the shade of leafy branches hastily set up as shelters for the Pope and Cardinals. The expedition was now nearly at an end. So, indeed, was the sojourn at Tivoli for, a few days after their return there, the Curia left for Rome. This was on the sixth of October. Pius took the precaution of inviting to accompany him those citizens whose loyalty he doubted, whom he did not wish to leave behind to conspire with his enemies. On reaching Rome the Pope was met by certain of the Cardinals, Thomas Palaeologus the Despot of Morea (see Chapter XVI) and various foreign delegates. But, just as his chief interest throughout his vacation had been in simple, natural people and things, now the attention of Pius was caught by a party of young men from Poland, 'elegant of appearance with yellow wavy hair streaming behind them in the breeze and dressed in green. Seated on tall and well-fed horses they carried, as is the custom of their nation, at one side bows and at the other a sword and a quiver of Libyan bearskin filled with arrows. On their hair they wore either a light feathered cap of green or wreaths of flowers. The beauty of these young men seemed superhuman. As they approached the Pope they leaped from their horses and falling upon the ground did reverence with the leaders of their delegation to the Saviour's vicar, whom they had never seen before. He himself entered the City where he was received with great favour by the citizens, went to salute the blessed apostles in the basilica of St Peter, and so returned to the apostolic palace after an absence of not quite three months.'[10]

CHAPTER XV

The Pope and the Cardinals

The Cardinals listened to the Pope's words not without admiration and great astonishment. — AENEAS SYLVIUS PICCOLOMINI, *Commentaries*

I

On the very first day of his pontificate Pius II confirmed his friend Jacopo Ammanati as apostolic secretary—an office to which Calixtus III had appointed him—but he did not take advantage of his new position to promote Ammanati's fortunes when he selected six new Cardinals on Wednesday, 5th March 1460. None of the new men had overwhelming personality, but all proved themselves satisfactory and loyal members of the Curia. Five were Italians by birth. The last to be chosen, Alessandro Oliva of Sassoferrato*, was the most pious and learned of them all: a poor man of excellent character who had served as General of the Augustinians. His appointment—solely on his merits—caused some surprise, both within the Curia and in the world outside. The other five Cardinals,[1] the German Burchard, Archbishop of Salzburg, Angelo Capranica, Bishop of Rieti, Bernardo Eroli, Bishop of Spoleto, Niccolò Fortiguerri of Pistoja, Bishop of Teano, and young Francesco Todeschini Piccolomini were more conventional selections. The last two were Pius's own kinsmen, his cousin and his nephew. Both were men of good character and some ability; Francesco was too young to have proved himself fully, but Niccolò was known to be skilled in military matters and he did in fact become Pius's most reliable adviser and go-

---

* He died in 1463, at the age of fifty-five; Pius II personally performed the rites at his burial.

between in organizing the papal armies. His gifts were diplomatic as well as military, the inheritance of many generations, for the Fortiguerri had taken a prominent part in Tuscan affairs for several centuries until their power was eclipsed as was that of the Piccolomini.

There was little scope for criticism in this first creation of Cardinals, except from the ultramontanes—especially the French—who felt they should have been represented. In Advent, 1461, Pius again decided that the time had come to increase the number in the Sacred College. This time he felt a moral obligation to select one or more Frenchmen in return for the revocation of the Pragmatic Sanction. The idea of including Bishop Jouffroy of Arras in the Curia was as repugnant to him as to the Cardinals themselves, but he realized that he might be even more dangerous and turbulent were he left outside. Both Louis XI and Philip Duke of Burgundy were strongly pressing his claims; Pius considered it advisable to call the Cardinals together in a Consistory and put the matter before them. As he expected, the proposal was 'most unpopular and quite contrary to the wishes of the College'². They 'shuddered at the Pope's words and shut their ears like asps and would not be persuaded'. Pius, however, was not afraid of the Cardinals, even when they behaved like asps. He talked with them individually, 'arguing, flattering, promising, using threats or menaces, as he thought suited to the character of his hearer'. To the formidable Cardinal of Rouen he promised the Bishopric of Ostia in return for his support. The Cardinals Carvajal and Bessarion were easily won to his side, also his old friend Calandrini of Bologna, but there were still some who were implacable. Sternest of all was Jouffroy's countryman, Alain of Avignon. He warned the College against this 'daring and pernicious man' and his bigotry, for 'He thinks that he understands human and divine law as though he had invented them . . . he is always teaching and will never learn . . . Do you suppose that he will hold his peace or allow anyone else to speak? You will bring fire into the senate and a worm that will forever gnaw you . . . For myself I see perpetual warfare with this man if he receive the red hat . . . often will you say: Oh that I had listened to Alain.'

In some ways this was the most difficult situation that ever confronted Pius, for he could not but agree with every word spoken against his proposition. Yet, in one short speech he set the dilemma

before the Cardinals so clearly and persuasively that Avignon himself came to his way of thinking and only Cardinal Orsini remained
obdurate. Pius's old friend Nicholas of Cusa, however, listened 'with
angry eyes' to the Pope's words, and Pius had to speak to Nicholas
so severely that he burst into tears and drew 'painful groans from
the bottom of his breast'. In the end, however, he accepted the
Pope's reproof and at the second Consistory called for the election
of the six new Cardinals, neither he nor any others opposed the
Pope's wishes. As well as Jouffroy and the other Frenchman, Louis
d'Albret, Pius promoted a Spaniard, Don Jaime of Cordova, Bishop
of Urgel. The fourth new Cardinal was the Papal Legate who
had done such good service in the Neapolitan war—Bartolomeo
Roverella, Archbishop of Ravenna. Another strong supporter of the
Pope was the young son of the Marquis of Mantua; his elevation
to the Cardinalate gave rise to great rejoicing in Mantua and set a
seal upon Pius's friendship with the Gonzaga family. The young
Francesco—he was only seventeen—was a student at Padua, where
he had shown a greater interest in the arts than in theology. He
was, nevertheless, a thoughtful and intelligent boy, as Mantegna
showed in the charming portrait of him that he painted at this time.
Lastly there was the faithful Ammanati, a most admirable man who
served the Church and the Papacy with unswerving devotion[3] until
his death in 1479. To show his gratitude and affection to Pius II
Jacopo Ammanati added 'Piccolomini' to his surname; although
there was no tie of kinship there was very strong community of
aims and interests. At the time of his election Jacopo was still a
youngish man (he was born at Lucca in 1423); he had attracted
Pius's attention by 'the dexterity of his wits' several years earlier
and he was given the Bishopric of Pavia, on the death of Giovanni
Castiglione, soon after Pius's accession.

With characteristic thoroughness Nicholas of Cusa had spent
years working out a comprehensive scheme for reforming the
Church. A similar, perhaps less doctrinaire, plan had been put forward by the Bishop of Torcello[4]. Pius had the utmost respect for
the wisdom of these two men, despite his occasional differences of
opinion with both of them. He was conscious, too, of the implications of the Capitulations he had signed at his election[5], in which
he had promised to reform the Curia. That his intention was to start
action immediately is clear from the fact that he asked the advice

and help of S. Antonino, Archbishop of Florence. This shrewd and saintly man died on 2nd May 1459, so Pius can have wasted no time at the beginning of his pontificate before taking up the matter of reform. His respect for the judgement of S. Antonino was profound. Pius says of him: 'He shone with theological learning and wrote many books which the learned praise . . . He reformed the morals both of clerics and laity, was diligent in settling disputes, drove enmity as far as he could out of the city, distributed the revenues of his church among Christ's poor, and gave nothing to his kinsmen or connections unless they were really in want.'[6]

After Antonino's death Pius could refer to his written precepts, but for practical details he had to rely upon Nicholas of Cusa and Domenichi. Pius did draw up a Bull containing his project of reforms, but for some reason it was never issued[7]. It may be that Pius thought the time was not yet ripe for such sweeping and far-reaching changes before Christendom should be united and men's minds prepared for a new discipline. The reforms that he did introduce were on points of detail, and piecemeal at that; they show very clearly his realism and his desire to check licentiousness and arrogance. Had the Bull of 1460 been enforced the Cardinals would have found their households rigidly reduced, their goods would have been confiscated and given to the poor, and they would not have been allowed to hunt or to keep hounds. The religious congregations, however, Pius helped to put their own affairs in order: this he did with great sympathy and understanding. The Benedictines, Dominicans, and Carmelites in particular owed him thanks for his solicitude in restoring discipline and harmony among their ranks.

Pius himself was not particularly interested in theological controversy. Discussions upon the interpretation of difficult passages of Scripture or points of logic, that had been meat and drink to medieval scholars, were not in his line. This personal trait, far more than practical diplomacy, was at the root of the coolness he showed in academic strife. He gives many pages of his *Commentaries* to the famous debate between Franciscans and Dominicans that was staged in Rome during his pontificate, but he himself remains aloof and uncommitted. The background of this dispute was a sermon delivered at Brescia by a Franciscan named Giacomo della Marca, 'once a companion of S. Bernardino and a popular preacher of the

Word of God, but now decrepit with age'. He, 'falling into an error common to all who speak rhetorically in churches', Pius said, 'made many statements to display his learning which it had been better to have left unsaid.'[8] The point at issue was not new, but Fra Giacomo brought up once again the declaration that the Blood of Christ shed during His Passion was not, as it lay upon the ground, worthy of adoration since it was separated from the Lord's body. The Dominicans ('whether filled with zeal for the Faith or pricked by the goad of emulation') swooped in with a charge of heresy. Both parties referred their quarrel to the Pope, who arranged a three days' debate when some excellent speeches were heard on both sides. The Bishop of Torcello (Domenichi) and most of the Cardinals supported the Dominicans; privately Pius agreed with them but he feared to alienate the Franciscans who were so admirably supporting the cause of the crusade. 'So it was resolved to postpone a decision until some other time.' All parties, apparently, found this a satisfactory conclusion.

On occasion Pius could administer rebukes that were all the more effective because they were rare. When some of the Cardinals objected to forming an honourable escort for the Burgundian envoys, as they approached Mantua for the Congress, he spoke very sharply of the virtue of humility[9]. 'Men did not like the haughtiness of the Cardinals,' he told them, for they 'looked upon themselves as gods and had no respect for ordinary mortals. They must purge themselves of this sin of pride.' The Pope nominated two of the most aristocratic members of the Curia for this mission and for good measure sent all the rest to greet the delegation outside the city gates. The Cardinals murmured, but they obeyed. It was sometimes necessary to point out his faults to an individual. Although Pius liked Rodrigo Borgia personally, and had a high opinion of his talents, he could not approve his behaviour. When the Curia was at Siena on the way home from Mantua, while the Pope was absent at the baths of Petriolo, Rodrigo took the opportunity to give a series of wild parties. He invited the notoriously merry Sienese ladies, telling them to leave their husbands and brothers at home. Reports of scandal reached Pius at Petriolo; on 11th June 1460 he sent Rodrigo a stern letter. 'We leave it to you to judge', he wrote, 'if it is becoming in one of your position to toy with girls, to pelt them with fruits . . . and, neglecting study, to spend the whole day in every kind of pleasure.' Pius added that although he was a young man Rodrigo was quite old enough to know better. 'Your years,' he concluded, 'which give hope of reformation, induce us to admonish you as a father.'

II

Not only did Pius exercise authority without apparent effort, he also attracted loyalty and devotion in an uncommonly high degree. He made friends easily and he kept them all his life. This tight-lipped little man, constantly in pain though seldom drawing attention to his infirmities, had a warmth and generosity that won him the regard even of his former enemies. It is hard to imagine a fiercer rivalry than had existed between Aeneas and Estouteville, the Cardinals of Siena and of Rouen, at the time of the Conclave in 1458. Yet, within a few months all was forgotten, for Estouteville also was a strong and generous man and he put his conspicuous talents into serving the new Pope whose place he had hoped to fill. When Pius made Estouteville Bishop of Ostia both men recognized it as a gesture of friendship as well as of expediency. Soon after his appointment the new Bishop invited Pius to visit Ostia, which he had never seen. This proved an expedition as delightful as it was adventurous. Accompanied by members of his household, Goro Lolli, and four Cardinals, the Pope boarded a ship below the Aventine and sailed down the Tiber towards its mouth. His own words bring the scene vividly to mind:

'On either side the river banks were green, for May was clothing all in fresh grass and a variety of flowers, except where stood traces of the ancient ruins which at many points, like parapets, compress the bed of the river. When he reached Ostia he was offered seven large fish on the shore. Our generation calls them sturgeon and sets a high value on them. We have not discovered the ancient name unless anyone would have it that these were the fish called *Lupi Tibertini*[10]. The weight of one of these was said to be two hundred and fifty pounds. The city of Ostia was built by Ancus, third of the ancient kings of Rome. That it was once great is proved by its ruins which cover much ground. It stood about a mile from the sea. Fallen porticoes, prostrate columns, fragments of statues are still visible, and there are the walls of an ancient temple which, though stripped of their marble, show that once it was a noble building. One can see also part of the aqueduct which carried wholesome water to the city from a long way off. The older and more ample walls of the city fell down long ago . . . Such then is Ostia today . . . On the bank and among the reeds of the lagoon swans lay their eggs and bring up their young, and it is delightful to watch and listen to the flocks of cygnets . . . At its broadest the lagoon is a furlong across and never deeper than a man's height. As it approaches the sea it becomes narrower and has the appearance of a canal, hedged in on either side by trees in which sweet birds sing. It never joins the sea except in rough weather. Then the strand that forms a beach between the lagoon and the sea is covered over with waves, and the lagoon is swollen till it forms one whole with the sea. All the peninsula is green with grass and useful for pasturing flocks, although on some parts and especially near the sea there is a lot of sand.'[11]

While Pius lingered in Ostia Antica, examining the remains and visiting the spot where the body of St Monica, mother of Aurelius Augustine, had been discovered*, he received a further invitation. This came from Cardinal Juan Carvajal, who was Bishop of Porto. He asked the Pope to visit his church also, and persuaded him to embark in a ship with all the Cardinals to prolong his expedition. Almost immediately an argument broke out as to the exact site of a certain palace—whether it was in Ostia or had stood on an island opposite this city. From an academic wrangle between archaeologists the field widened to include the sailors and other passengers. Goro Lolli, who sided with Pius, made a bet with Cardinal Borgia, 'and he who lost was to be fined as large a sturgeon as could be got'. Some grew so excited that they leaped ashore, took horses and rode overland to prove their point. They returned with the news that Lolli had won his bet. The party then proceeded amicably up the western arm of the Tiber that led them to a flat and grassy island where stood the ruined church of Porto. Pius was particularly interested to find here great blocks of marble that had been brought from the Ligurian mountains for sale to the Romans, each piece inscribed with its weight and serial number. Cardinal Juan had set

---

* During the pontificate of Eugenius IV. It was brought to Rome and buried in the church of the Augustinians. 'The poet Maffeo Vegio founded a marble shrine in her honour and adorned it with verses.' *Commentaries*, Book XI.

up tents and shelters built of branches for the papal party 'and here he received Pope Pius with a joyful face and pleasant conversation, speaking much about Trajan the Spaniard, the Emperor who had built the city of Porto, whom he, another Spaniard, had succeeded.'

On his return to Ostia Pius found that the local fishermen had caught a huge dolphin, which the French servants of Cardinal Guillaume d'Estouteville had cooked and were greedily devouring. This catch was thought to presage a storm, and, sure enough, the following night there was a furious tempest. 'Huge waves beat on the shores, you could hear the sea as if it were moaning and lamenting, and such was the violence of the winds that it seemed nothing could resist it.' Thunder and lightning were incessant and a thunderbolt struck the ancient watch-tower, bringing to earth a turret and a bell. Terrified cattle in their stables close by added their bellows to the clamour. Not all the members of the Pope's household had been able to find quarters in the Bishop's palace; some were sleeping under canvas and others had gone to rest in the ships. In the darkness, lit only by lightning flashes, soaked to the skin by rain and waves, they huddled together in their misery, but the plight of those in the tents was even worse. Pius describes the experiences of Cardinal Borgia's household with his usual felicity.

'All the tents had been torn down by the wind . . . the violence of the hurricane carried these off, bursting the ropes, breaking the posts, and tearing the canvas absolutely to ribbons . . . Everybody fled from the dismembered tents, but in the dark they could not see their way. The force of the rain drove them naked among the thistles that grew thick in that place and they were wounded by the sharp spikes. A wretched sight! Covered with blood, stiff and almost stupefied by the cold, they at last reached [Cardinal Borgia] who was lying in the palace, terrified by the storm. And when he saw that his people had abandoned the tents and arrived naked, he inquired not whether they were safe, but where they had put his money.'[12]

In contrast to this turmoil, those who had drunk deeply at supper were still snoring on their couches. The Pope himself lay quietly in bed, dictating to his secretary[13], until the clatter of falling tiles suggested that the whole roof might blow away. 'And looking at the partitions and the ceilings he noticed how old they all were and was afraid lest, being rotten, they should collapse.' Pius had no intention of venturing out naked among the thistles, even to save his life, so he sent his secretary to fetch his clothes and made a careful toilet. When he was half-dressed, 'suddenly the storm subsided and all the winds were silent, as though they feared to cause inconvenience to a Pope. Nothing was heard but the rain. And Pius changed his mind and went back to bed.' A few miles away at Porto, Cardinal Carvajal had tucked his head under the bedclothes when his tent was blown away, and so escaped injury. Next day the bedraggled party returned to Rome, where the people welcomed the Pope most warmly, for they had thought he would spend the summer at Tivoli. So ended this extraordinary May-morning picnic.

III

An expedition with a happier outcome was the fruit of an invitation from the Papal Chamberlain, Cardinal Luigi Scarampo, who as well as the Patriarchate of Aquileia held rich lands and possessions. Indeed, he was said to be the richest man in Italy except Cosimo dei Medici. Scarampo had built himself a magnificent country house, near the ruined monastery of S. Paolo in Albano that he had restored and rebuilt. Pius set out to visit him, accompanied by his household and three Cardinals, along the Appian Way. This was soon after the feast of the Ascension in 1463. Where once there had been lairs of wolves and foxes Scarampo had planted a garden and filled it with exotic animals that he kept as pets. Peacocks displayed on his lawns, and among the other creatures were 'Indian hens, and goats from Syria with very long wide ears hanging on either side of their faces and covering both cheeks'[14]. Pius was delighted to explore the ancient ruins of Albano; he found that its walls enclosed a space as large as the city of Bologna, stretching from the shore of the lake as far as the castle that still dominated the surrounding country.

Next day the Pope journeyed further along the Appian Way until he reached Lake Nemi. 'Nature has made it a delightful road,' he exclaimed, 'though art has made it better.' The lake lay still as glass, surrounded by chestnut trees, apples, quinces, pears and medlars interspersed with nut-trees loaded with ripening filberts. The walks beneath the shade of these fruit trees were made, he thought, for poets, for 'the poet whose genius remains unmoved by Nemi will never be inspired'. With the utmost enthusiasm Pius described 'the ship which was discovered in our time at the bottom of the lake'. Cardinal Prospero Colonna had sent to Genoa for sailors who were used to working under water, in order to try to raise it to the surface. The ship was built of larch-wood, encrusted with bitumen; Pius thought it had a house or cabin built upon it 'like Borso of Ferrara's ship upon the Po or Lodovico of Mantua's on the Mincio, and like those used on the Rhine by the prince electors'. He had talked with the sailors who had dived down to the sunken ship; they told him that 'they saw in the bottom . . . a box of iron or copper fastened with four rings, and an earthen jug with a cover of gilded bronze'. Pius supposed 'that the ship was made by the Emperor Tiberius, because a great number of lead pipes have been found at the bottom of the lake, on which was inscribed in capital letters: TIBERIUS CAESAR'.

Near Genzano the country people flocked to see the Pope and to receive his blessing, crying out: 'Who would have thought that before we died we were to see a bishop of Rome in these parts?' Next he visited Cardinal Colonna's stronghold at Rocca di Papa: 'Here you are so high,' he noted, 'that, despite Monte Cimino which lies between, you can see Monte Amiata. The Pope sat down with his Cardinals for a little time and, looking towards the seashore, measured with his eyes all the coast belonging to the Church from Terracina to Monte Argentario. He saw the hills of Civitavecchia, which have enriched our age with new alum-mines, and as far as Porto Romano and the shores of Tuscany beyond it, then Ostia in Latium and the Tiber that slips through the flat country like a snake twisting this way and that . . . And he saw on the seashore Nettuno, built on the ruins of Antium, whose inhabitants live by fishing, hunting, and fowling. In early spring when the quails are returning from Africa, they are enticed by reed-pipes and caught in nets. The fowling lasts thirty days, and in one day's catch often more than a hundred thousand quails are killed. Then too they capture a great number of pigeons when these are getting ready to leave Italy and fly across the sea. The Pope also turned his eyes on the summit and fabulous ranges of Monte Circeo, the isle of Ponza ennobled by the capture of King Alfonso by the Genoese, 5th August 1435, and lastly Terracina which the Volscians called in their tongue Avuxur[15].

'In the same way from that mountain were seen the lakes of

Nemi and . . . Albano, as clearly as though you were sitting on their shores; and from this point one could learn correctly their size, and their shapes and the spaces between them, covered over at that time of the year with leafy woods and green grass, and picked out with many cheerful colours. That which gave most pleasure was the broom, which covered with its flowers a great part of the plain. Beyond, all Rome offered itself to the view, and Soracte and the country of the Sabines, the range of the Apennines white with snow, and Palombara, Tivoli, Palestrina, with many places in what is now called the Campagna . . . When the Pope had seen all this from the mountain he returned to the fortress and there spent the night.'[16]

As the Pope sat with his Cardinals upon the mountainside and cast his eyes over his temporal domain, he mused also on the problems and achievements of his pontificate, his relations with foreign powers and with the Sacred College, the high points of his career and 'the spaces between them'. Descending from the mountain top and laying aside his meditations, Pius returned to the ordinary affairs of his office. He rose at early dawn and went to visit an ancient monastery at Grottaferrata that was conducted according to the Greek rite, where the monks were bearded and sang their offices in Greek. Their Abbot—a Calabrian—was constantly at odds with the neighbouring Roman landowners; there was continual friction and litigation, and at times disorder and even bloodshed. With considerable tact Pius went to the root of the trouble—the alien character of the Abbot's rule—and at once found a solution that pleased everyone. The Abbot was transferred to Sicily where he was promoted Archimandrite, equivalent to 'Abbot General'; the monastery was put in the charge of Cardinal Bessarion who began his restoration 'with new and exquisite buildings'.

After dinner the papal party left Grottaferrata for Rome. Pius entered the city by way of the Lateran 'where he prayed for a little by the high altar, examined the roof, a great part of which he had restored, and gave orders for the rest to be done also'. Instead of approaching the Vatican in ceremonial parade, Pius made his way through the slummy quarters of Trastevere, to see for himself how the lesser people lived. Next day his excursion ended when he entered St Peter's to celebrate the Feast of Pentecost and bless the Roman people.

IV

The Sacred College in Pius II's time was far from complaisant. It held many discordant elements and the characters of the Cardinals ranged from worldly princelings like Borgia and Scarampo, through violent egotists like Jouffroy of Arras, to such simple-minded churchmen as Filippo Calandrini of Bologna. In promoting this half-brother of Pope Nicholas to hold the office of Grand Penitentiary Pius showed good judgement and good taste. He did not forget that at the first scrutiny of the papal Conclave that elected him Calandrini had had an equal number of votes, but had unselfishly withdrawn in favour of the more forceful candidate. It is doubtful if Calandrini would have filled the position well, for he was unsophisticated to the point of boorishness. Indeed, Pius once had occasion to reproach him for his lack of manners in not dismounting from his horse to show reverence to the Pope[17]. For Pius would not allow any disrespect to his office, however informal he might be in his private life. Not only was Pius quick to remember and reward such action as Calandrini's at the Conclave, he was magnanimous enough to forget the opposition of those who had then voted against him. Certainly neither Estouteville nor Bessarion had reason to complain of any lack of cordiality. Under the wise leadership of Pius II rivalries seldom became bitter—except, perhaps between Scarampo and the Cardinal of San Marco*, who added to warring personalities furious envy of each other's artistic treasures.

The varied tastes and characters of the Cardinals are nowhere better illustrated than in their choice of tableaux and decorations on the Feast of Corpus Christi, celebrated at Viterbo in 1462. The Pope was undergoing a course of treatment at the baths: the Cardinals had fled thither from Rome where plague had broken out. All decided that the festivities this year should outdo all others, and, because they had no preoccupations, members of the papal court were able to throw all their energies into preparations of great ingenuity and elaboration. The Pope was lodging in the citadel; he

* Pietro Barbo; Scarampo is said to have had a seizure caused by rage when he heard of Barbo's election as Pope Paul II. He died early the following year (1465).

was delighted by the urbanity and politeness of the people of Viterbo and by the efficiency with which they had organized supplies adequate for the whole Curia[18]. 'The various wines were as good as any at Florence or Siena. The bread was white and tasted delicious, as was the flesh of their animals, fed on thyme and fragrant grasses. There was abundance of fish, some from the Tyrrhenian Sea, some from the neighbouring Lake of Bolsena. Not even the horses were in want of fodder.'

As the festival drew near, Pius ordered that the road leading from the citadel to the cathedral should be cleared of all balconies, projections, and porticoes, so that the whole way could be decorated at will by the Cardinals, bishops, and courtiers. Each chose a section for which he would be responsible: each secretly planned to outdo all others in magnificence.

Pius himself arranged a temple before the church, hung with coloured cloths, 'and ancient stories woven in silk and wool and gold, with portraits of famous men and pictures of all kinds of wild animals'. The whole length of the route was surmounted by arches of flowering broom, myrtle and laurel, and the street was strewn with country flowers. The standards of the Pope, the Cardinals, and the princes were blowing in the wind. The French Cardinals had used the custom of their nation, covering the houses in their section with rich tapestries of Arras. As the Pope, carrying the Sacred Host, passed in procession Cardinal Carvajal had staged a drama: his decorations were centred round a mighty dragon 'with many shapes of evil spirits threatening horribly. But an armed knight representing the Archangel Michael cut off the dragon's head just as the Pope was passing and all the devils fell headlong, barking. A reddish cloth overspread the sky like a cloud, and leather studded with gold flowers in the Andalusian manner covered the walls of the houses.'[19] Bessarion's unambitious tableau was of an altar flanked by boys singing like angels, as was its neighbour. Then came seventy-four feet of gorgeousness devised by Borgia who outdid everyone in elaboration and allegory against a rich and sombre background of gold and purple. The Cardinal of Santa Susanna went to nature for his inspiration; his contribution Pius found particularly charming, with its flower decorations and a fountain of white wine, the aromatic herbs and the orchestra giving great pleasure to the whole crowd. The soldier Cardinal, Niccolò Fortiguerri, 'to please the Pope's passion of strange things, had brought from his native city of Pistoja players and boys with melodious voices', who played scenes from the Resurrection in the great Piazza of the Commune. Most of the other scenes were less elaborate; those Cardinals who could not afford to provide painted cloths and gold and silver ornaments made equally charming decorations from flowers and leaves. The Pope was amused to notice that the unpopular Cardinal of Arras had frugally used lengths of Florentine cloth—made of English wool, in colour 'between red and grey'—that he had ordered for making new uniforms for his household. The night before the festival 'a great gale had sprung up, which, beating and driving the ropes this way and that, had torn most of the cloth, diminishing the purposed garments with no small loss to his household'.[20]

At last Pope Pius finished his course, after feasting his eyes on the treasures and marvels that had been displayed before him. He came to the broad piazza in front of the cathedral, but large as it was it could not hold all the people who wanted to receive his blessing. After a High Mass had been celebrated by the Cardinal of S. Marco, the Pope went to a high window in the bishop's palace and from that vantage point he blessed all those who had gathered in the meadows behind the palace. Afterwards he attended a dinner party in surroundings of the greatest magnificence. The food was 'exquisitely elegant and delicious . . . Nothing you could wish for was lacking to that feast. Pleasant conversation and wit tempered with decency made the hours pass quickly.' This banquet brought the festivities to a close. The pageantry had been a tremendous success; the Festival of Corpus Christi in this year was the most colourful episode in the whole of Pius's pontificate. But the rejoicing was brought to an end abruptly, for the hangings and scaffoldings had hardly been taken down when news came of an outbreak of plague. Almost all the Cardinals exclaimed that they must depart forthwith. The Pope himself stayed on in Viterbo for a time, taking the opportunity to visit an ancient monastery on Monte Cimino, there to meditate on human vanity. This foundation, high on the hillside among chestnut woods, watered by clear streams, had fallen into decay. 'Once many monks sang God's praises here; now crows dwell here and pigeons, and sometimes the owl with ill-omened song intones his lamentation.'[21] Pius's thoughts were sombre, as he pondered the crumbling of human achievement, but as usual he had a constructive plan. He committed this cenoby of St Martin to the care of his nephew, charging him to restore it to its former purpose. Then, refreshed by the mountain air, Pius returned to the stricken city of Viterbo.

The Cardinals were gone to healthier refuges: Pius too made his way to a resort near the Lake of Bolsena where he could spend the rest of the hot summer. Here, among the vines and limestone crags he found peace enjoying the lakeside scenery and, in the cool of the day, exploring all the neighbourhood. Some of the Cardinals were lodging near by and came by road or by ship on stated days to attend the Signature*. Pius took a deep interest in all that went on, inspecting the eel-traps and visiting the islands of the lake. He decided to go to the chapel of the Friars Minor on Bisentina to celebrate the birthday of St John the Baptist, 24th June, and afterwards the Pope dined with the Friars 'not disdaining' the poor fare they had to offer.

Meanwhile, the Lord of Bisentina had made arrangements for a regatta. The Cardinals of Spoleto and Teano, Bernardo Eroli and Niccolò Fortiguerri, were with Pius, also Estouteville and others who were lodging not too far away. Pius took a deep interest in the races, appointing his own major-domo and the captain of his body-guard to act as umpires and to award the prize, eight ells of the best Florentine yellow cloth, to the winning crew. The signal to start was given by the Bishop of Corneto. Five ships were entered for the main race, four oarsmen and a coxswain or 'pilot' to each boat. All the contestants, especially those from Bolsena, were boasting of their skill and scorning their rivals. 'The pilots sitting at the helm bound their hair with white cotton and poplar leaves. So did the oarsmen, who were naked but for their privy parts and glittering with oil.' Pope and Cardinals sat watching 'with no little pleasure and refresh-ment of spirit', though they pretended to be discussing affairs of state. Pius recounted the race in Book VIII of the *Commentaries*, modelling his description closely upon Virgil[22]. A nobleman named Guicciardo Fortiguerri, a kinsman both of Pius and of the Cardinal of Teano, led the cheers for Bolsena, for he was captain of that city. At first the Bolsena crew led, elated as they were by local wine, but,

---

* *Segnatura di Grazia e Giustizia,* supreme ecclesiastical court of the Church of Rome.

as their rivals said, 'it is not so easy to pull upon the oar as to drain the cup'. The men of Marta came from behind to win easily and to the Pope's pleasure secured the trophy. The spectators from Bolsena scowled as their boat came in last, the crew sweating and short of breath.

It had been a pleasant holiday and, like Pius's other excursions, did much to encourage good relations between the common people and the Curia. Too often the Cardinals had seemed remote beings, yet here was a bishop starting the boat-race and the Pope and Cardinals applauding the contestants as though made of the same clay. Although he insisted upon deference to his great office, Pius II remained a man supremely conscious of the needs and desires of his fellows. Moreover, he succeeded in instilling into at least some members of the Curia something of his spirit.

CHAPTER XVI

St Andrew and St Catherine

To master Francesco dal Borgo, for a tabernacle to hold the head of St Andrew in the church of St Peter . . . 100 ducats. – *27th February 1462/3, Papal expenses, 1461–2*[1]

For four quires of parchment, bought for writing out the Oration on St Andrew. – *Ibid.*

Rewards to six religious women that attended the canonization of St Catherine. – *Ibid.*

While Hungary struggled heroically to keep the Turks at bay, and Cardinal Carvajal used all his arts of persuasion and diplomacy to keep the King of Bosnia in the struggle, the Sultan increased his pressure till it became unbearable. In Bosnia the position was especially dangerous. There was a disloyal element here, in the supporters of the Manichean heresy, that made it easy for Mahomet to swoop into the country, capture and kill King Stephan, and use Bosnia as a base for further attacks upon Hungary*. Stephan's widow and some of his household fled to Rome, there to swell the number of refugees all seeking the Pope's support and clemency. Pius felt the tragedy of Bosnia very keenly; in his impulsive way he was anxious to help those who had been obliged to flee from their homes, particularly when they were the victims of the hated Turks. Sometimes he was imposed upon, and his customary shrewdness deserted him, when he was confronted by threadbare foreigners with a plausible story to tell. Even before Pius reached Rome on his return from Mantua he had been importuned by one Moses Giblet who

---

* This did not happen until May 1463, but Carvajal had given repeated warnings that such an invasion was imminent.

claimed to be Archdeacon of Antioch; disregarding the warnings
of his household he accepted Moses at his face value and rewarded
him with money and hospitality until his visitor disappeared as
mysteriously as he had come.

A still more outlandish embassy arrived towards the end of the
same year (1460). This was composed of representatives from
Trebizond, Armenia, and Persia, under the charge of a Franciscan
missionary named Lodovico of Bologna. This friar had conducted
the party through the court of Frederick III and had even beguiled
the Venetian Senate into giving hospitality to these exotic envoys.
When they arrived in Rome the Pope received them with every courtesy and provided food and lodging for everyone. 'Their
clothes,' he noted, 'were as diversified as their manners, so that . . .
wherever they went people stared at them and they drew a crowd
of children in their wake.'[2] The envoys asked for more and more
money for their expenses; since some of them were said to have
eaten as much as twenty pounds of meat a day, Pius remarked to
Campano, if only the contest were over a banquet these men would
be marvellous allies in the Turkish war[3]. At last suspicions were
beginning to form in the Pope's mind that all was not well with the
delegation. He wondered whether the letters of introduction were
forged and came to the opinion that Fra Lodovico was 'a liar and
a deceiver'. It was impossible to verify the references offered; the
best course seemed to be to pass the visitors on to other courts if
they could not be persuaded to return home. The Venetians also
had begun to probe the character of Fra Lodovico and would have
imprisoned him had he not made off with all speed. Nothing more
was heard of the delegation or its leader, but the visit had the effect
of damping down the Pope's credulity. 'From that time all news
from the east and across the sea was looked on with suspicion by
the Pope, and especially such as was brought by needy and obscure
men.'[4]

It was another matter when genuine suppliants arrived in Rome
to lay their distress before the Pope and to ask his advice and help.
Charlotte of Lusignan, dispossessed Queen of Cyprus, had no cause
to regret her visit: no one could have been kinder than Pius[5] in
comforting the luckless woman and in arranging for her journey
to her father-in-law, the Duke of Savoy, in search of material aid.
As for Thomas Palaeologus, the Despot of the Morea, Pius gave him

a pension of three hundred ducats a month[6], with permanent lodging for himself, his wife, his four children, and his seventy horses (of which sixty-seven were borrowed) in the Hospital of Santo Spirito. After the fall of Constantinople the Emperor's two brothers, Demetrius and Thomas, had been allowed to rule the Morea while paying tribute to the Sultan, but at the time of the Congress of Mantua Thomas had to appeal for an army to repel Turkish infiltration into his province. The small force sent to help him proved useless: a few months later Thomas reached Rome dismayed and penniless. Demetrius had less spirit and more worldly wisdom. He retired with a pension to Adrianople where he lived very comfortably. His daughter entered the Sultan's harem.

Thomas Palaeologus was not able to accommodate himself happily to the life of an exile. He was a melancholy and disappointed man: neither he nor his wife survived long enough to see the disintegration of his family life[7], but neither the generosity of the Pope nor the devoted attentions of Cardinal Bessarion could compensate him for the loss of his domain. Nevertheless, Thomas felt deep gratitude to Pius for all he had done. The only return he could make was to offer the Pope the treasures that he had brought from the Morea. First, there was a singularly beautiful cope, of English workmanship, dating from the fourteenth century. This is now known as the 'Pienza cope', for Pius gave it to his new cathedral there and it is still to be seen in the little museum founded to preserve his most precious belongings. The material is of linen, so finely stitched that none of the fabric is visible. The threads of green and blue and gold have kept their lustrous colour; the delicacy of the hands and faces —embroidered, not painted as in lesser examples of this craft—is in no way marred by six centuries of exposure. The borders of foliage, birds, and animals enclose scenes of the life of Christ: in the centre is a particularly beautiful Nativity, with figures 28 centimetres tall. There are scenes too of the lives of the saints, with particular emphasis on St Catherine (of Alexandria) disputing with the philosophers, her martyrdom, and her reception into heaven[8]. The effect is of subdued magnificence. It is hard to imagine Pope Pius making personal use of the cope, for its dimensions are gigantic, it is 3.5 metres wide and 1.63 high, but there can be no doubt that he was delighted by a present that he was well able to appreciate.

Even more precious to the Pope than the cope and the jewels

that Thomas Palaeologus gave him were the relics of St John the Baptist and St Andrew. The right arm of St John the Baptist was presented to the Pope only three months before his death: the Milanese ambassador[9] wrote from Siena a dispatch to Francesco Sforza in which he described the reception of this sacred relic. The Despot, he said, had brought it from Constantinople, and on 6th May 1464 the ambassador had accompanied the stately procession that conveyed the relic to its resting place in Siena—'con gran divotione'. Still greater devotion and far more pomp marked the reception of the most precious of all the Despot's gifts: the head of St Andrew the Apostle, snatched from the site of his martyrdom at Patras to save it from falling into infidel hands.

The Corpus Christi festival at Viterbo had been exciting and colourful; the splendour of the procession on Palm Sunday, 1462, was on a grander and more solemn plane. In many ways it was the supreme moment of Pius's pontificate, when his genuine emotion and piety were reflected in the gorgeous ceremonial. Cardinal Oliva was chosen to meet the relic when it was brought to Ancona. From this port Oliva conducted it with all reverence to the papal fortress at Narni: here Pius ordered it to be guarded until arrangements could be made for its interment in a proper resting place*. 'He held that, now that it had left its home and could not easily be restored, nowhere would it find a worthier refuge than at Rome, near the bones of its brother St Peter, prince of the apostles.'[10] There was no time to build a special chapel to receive St Andrew's head—this Pius did subsequently, erecting a great statue of the saint that still stands at the south-west corner of the framework of the dome. This marks only the site of the tomb, for Pius's chapel was demolished when that part of St Peter's was rebuilt.

As Palm Sunday[11] drew near, final arrangements for the journey took shape. Pius had selected three Cardinals to fetch the sacred head from Narni and to bring it to Ponte Milvio, the bridge over the Tiber close to the Flaminian Gate. Bessarion was one, Oliva again, and the third Cardinal was Francesco Piccolomini. All along the route people were gathered to do reverence as the relic was carried by, for St Andrew has always been one of the most popular

---

* St Andrew's body, all but the head, had been buried with great honour at Amalfi. Pius had visited this shrine during his sojourn at Naples, see p. 105.

saints, particularly in the Middle Ages. Great crowds had gathered, too, in Rome, undeterred by the fearful storms that raged nearly every night that month, and on many days as well, threatening to ruin the ceremony. The sun shone through the clouds during the journey from Narni, but that night there was such torrential rain that it seemed the decorations would all be washed away and the roads would be impassable. At dawn the Pope looked out anxiously, to find a watery sun and the meadows outside the Flaminian Gate 'shining with grass and flowers'. In procession with the clergy, all bearing their palms in their hands, Pius went to receive the sacred casket from the three Cardinals. 'And Bessarion, taking the holy head, offered it weeping to the weeping Pope.'

Pius made a brief but very moving oration, recorded in his *Commentaries*. Unlike some of his more ambitious speeches it bears no sign of rewriting or retouching. Then a hymn was sung that had been specially composed by Agapito di Cenci de' Rustici, a Sienese poet who was a friend of the Pope from his student days. That night the head was deposited in the church of S. Maria del Popolo, and there the Pope and the Cardinals rested. Again there came storm and rain, again sunrise brought promise of a fine day. Pius celebrated Mass and read the Passion according to St Luke before setting out on the procession to St Peter's. Some of his advisers suggested that the Cardinals and prelates should ride the two-mile course, 'for priests carrying the Sacraments and wearing their sacred vestments to walk through thick mud did not seem advisable'. This, however, Pius would not allow. He bade them all go on foot to show their devotion and humility. Only those who 'by age or bad health could not endure the effort' would be allowed to ride, and they must travel to St Peter's by another route, through back streets. Only Prospero Colonna ('illustrious for his learning and his rank but suffering from gout') and one other ancient Cardinal availed themselves of this permission. Two or three had to be excused on grounds of ill health, Nicholas of Cusa among them, also Calandrini, but Bessarion struggled for most of the way, despite his infirmities.

'It was a splendid spectacle,' Pius observed, as he rode in his golden litter, 'to see those old men walk on foot through the mud, holding palms in their hands and wearing white mitres on their white heads . . . And some who till then had lived delicately and could hardly move a hundred paces except on horseback, on that day walked two miles through mud and water with ease, though burdened by their sacred vestments.' The two stout French Cardinals, Estouteville and Alain of Avignon, went cheerfully on their way despite their corpulence. Carvajal was commended by everyone for his dogged perseverance, 'for though he was an old man and in bad health, yet he walked all the way in prayer, with joyful countenance and spirit'. The younger men, Barbo of S. Marco, Rodrigo Borgia, and Francesco Piccolomini made light of the ordeal.

Certain noblemen held a gilded canopy over the relic, till Estouteville and two other Cardinals carried it to the Pope's hands. Great crowds thronged about his litter, to catch a glimpse of the relic and to gain a blessing. The number of lighted candles was estimated at thirty thousand. 'And so numerous were the priests that those who went in front had reached St Peter's before the Pope had started. And yet they were walking one behind another treading close on the heels of those ahead of them.' All the road was strewn with flowers and aromatic herbs, charming when first cast down but soon trampled in the mud. Those who dwelt in the houses that lined the route knelt at prayer; some exhibited their treasures, boys were singing, organs playing, 'every instrument known to music was heard and from all the praises of the apostle filled the air'. The Cardinals had decorated their houses with cloths and tableaux: as usual Cardinal Borgia far surpassed all others. His house reminded Pius of Nero's dwelling, with its lavishness of gold and marvels.

Once arrived at St Peter's, Bessarion made one of his wordy speeches; the Pope followed it with a briefer one, for he knew how greatly everyone needed rest after such physical and spiritual exertions. Pius's oration had, however, been very carefully prepared for copying and distribution throughout Christendom; he intended it to be one of the most important of his utterances. Indeed, four quires of parchment were needed for making copies of it to be handed out officially[12]. After the relic had been laid upon the altar Pius left the Cardinals and bishops still singing praises, while he went to bless the multitude. Afterwards he withdrew to the Vatican and the rest of Holy Week passed in the usual observances. On Easter Day, however, the Pope himself celebrated Mass in St Peter's; this he was only able to do through a 'device' that enabled him to celebrate from a sitting position, for his arthritis was so bad that he could scarcely move his limbs and was unable to walk or even to

stand. After Mass there followed the usual exhibition of the hand-
kerchief of St Veronica imprinted with the face of Christ. Then 'the
Pope departed to his house and taking with him the holy relic of
the apostle put it for safe-keeping in the Castel Sant'Angelo, until a
suitable casket could be prepared for it'[13].

Another project very dear to the Pope's heart was the canonization of Caterina Benincasa of Siena. His local patriotism is easy to
understand, but his veneration of St Catherine was based primarily
upon his admiration of her ascetic and dynamic character. That she
was born in Siena was only one more jewel in her crown of virtues.
The redoubtable Catherine dominated her twenty-four brothers and
sisters, all her associates and even the Pope himself—in fact, everyone with whom she came in contact except her gentle little confessor, Raymond of Capua. Her utter disregard of bodily ills found
an echo in Pius's stoicism in the face of physical pain, and her single-
minded devotion to the cause of unity in the Church gave him a
shining example to follow. The Latin hymns that Pius composed in
her honour found a wide circulation, as did the saint's own letters[14].
Her impact upon her own times was strong indeed; a hundred years
later it had scarcely diminished. She was only thirty-three at the
time of her death, a simple nun who had turned the whole course
of European history. It is not surprising that her fellow townsmen
should have converted the house where she was born, in the quarter of Fontebranda, into an oratory.

As early as 19th May 1459 the process of canonization had been
begun. But Pius did not hurry the matter through; he appointed
three Cardinals to examine her life and miracles and patiently
awaited their report. He followed the teaching of the Blessed Raymond of Capua: 'in the prudent view of the learned, marvels and
miracles have to be scrutinized most carefully, since of themselves
they do not . . . prove that the person performing them has necessarily been predestined and admitted to eternal beatitude. But this
does not mean that miracles are not a great sign of holiness, especially if they are performed after death.'[15] There was no dearth of
miracles connected with St Catherine; the process passed smoothly
to its conclusion. At last, on the Feast of St Peter and St Paul[16], 1461,
'with the full consent of all the Cardinals, bishops, abbots, and other
prelates that were present and with all the usual ceremony'[17], Pius

announced the canonization and appointed a day for St Catherine's commemoration, 30th April.

There can be small doubt that, had not Nicholas V already done so, Pius would have arranged for the canonization of S. Bernardino, also of Siena. This great and good man had a stronger and more lasting influence upon the lively student at Siena than is sometimes recognized. Pius had an admiration too for the great St Bernard of Clairvaux and recalled that one of his kinsmen, Bernardo Tolomei, had also held a deep veneration for this saint whose name he bore. Together with Ambrogio Piccolomini and another Sienese of noble family, Bernardo Tolomei in the year 1313[18] had founded the order of Monte Oliveto. The three companions went to live on this austere mountainside fifteen miles from Siena, abandoning their birthright for a life of privation and extreme poverty. With their bare hands they hollowed out grottoes in the rock, gathered wild berries for their food, and slept on withered chestnut leaves. In time the monks by ceaseless labour made the ground fertile. They planted olive trees and almonds on the hillside, they built a church and furnished it with taste and grandeur. Bernardo lay buried there, and many of the Tolomei and Piccolomini sought to leave their bones on Monte Oliveto. The new order increased and multiplied so that by the mid-fifteenth century it had many branches.

Pius felt a strong desire to visit this monastery that for so long had been associated with his family. In the summer of 1463, as he travelled from Pienza to the baths of Petriolo, the Pope turned aside and made his way along the steep path that could only be trodden at that time of year, skirting the jagged rocks and precipices and fearing at every step that the bearers of his litter might lose their footing on the slippery white clay. In Book x of the *Commentaries* Pius describes Monte Oliveto and his feelings as he approached the monastery so dear to his ancestors. Close to the buildings the ground was cultivated and there were delightful groves and orchards. 'There are figs, almonds, and many kinds of pear and apple,' he wrote. 'There are shady cypresses among which in summer sweet breezes may be caught, and also vineyards with their shadowy tendrils, vegetable gardens, baths, a perennial spring, cisterns, walls, and on the face of the cliff oak-woods and junipers.' The community had developed far beyond the aims of its founder, but there was still austerity in their manner of living. The Pope arrived on a

Thursday, so that the Cardinals and all his household expected meat for their dinner, but Pius would have none of it and insisted on sharing the monks' simple fare. He dined with them in the common refectory, 'and brought his cantors who, while the company ate, sang a new hymn to Saint Catherine of Siena with such sweet harmony that all the monks shed tears of joy'. Pius granted indulgences and privileges to the Order to mark his approval and sense of kinship. The life was not for him but it was an ideal that he understood. As he looked at the vines, roses, and rosemary in the gardens he saw them as 'delightful solaces for the monks but better still for those who may look on them and then depart'[19].

CHAPTER XVII

The Creation of Pienza

Pius . . . took an extraordinary pleasure in the buildings that were arising on his native soil, and which seemed likely to be second to none in the whole of Italy. – AENEAS SYLVIUS PICCOLOMINI, *Commentaries*

Some men who have triumphed over poverty and won their way to fame are ready to forget their origins while they bask in new-found splendour: others turn back to their childhood surroundings and do everything they can to improve the fortunes of their families and friends. There can be no doubt as to which class Pius II represented. Not only did he arrange careers for his sisters' boys, he also contrived to find official positions for a large number of distant kinsmen, so that the names Tolomei and Piccolomini are constantly cropping up in the treasurer's department and administrative grades of the papal household. Giacomo Tolomei is typical of many; he was a young cousin of Pius II who was appointed vice-castellan of S. Angelo in Rome. Giacomo's success excited envy and dislike; he was accused of cruelty and imprisoned in his own castle as soon as Pius's death robbed him of his patron. He was, however, a man of some ability, so that King Ferrante was pleased to make him his personal secretary after securing his release from S. Angelo. Later, when Giacomo was serving as *capitano del popolo* in his native Siena, Ferrante pressed him to return to Naples on the ground that he still needed his services. Giacomo certainly seems to have been worth his place, although it would be too much to claim that every 'papal relative' given a position by Pius II was promoted solely on his merits. It does, however, seem that this Pope showed good judgement and it is not possible to point to any glaring instances of the kind of nepotism that disfigured the appointments made by Martin V and Calixtus III.

Not only did Pius feel strong affection for his kin, he also loved the countryside on which he had first opened his eyes. The Val d'Orcia, the mountains, the dusty volcanic soil of his father's farm, the familiar cottages of Corsignano, the little church where he had been baptized—all these were constantly in his mind. Early in his pontificate[1], Pius had taken the first steps to translate into fact his dream of a new and beautiful little town rising upon the foundations of the poverty-stricken village. It was not, however, until the early spring of 1462 that Corsignano became Pienza, by a decree of the Consistory that met to raise the status of the church to a cathedral and to create the new bishopric of Pienza with Montalcino*. Between these two dates Pius had visited the site whenever he was able; for the most part he stayed at Abbadia San Salvatore on the flank of Monte Amiata and watched from there his buildings rising stone by stone. His scheme was by no means grandiose; Pius never forgot that his miniature city must be kept to scale, that it must harmonize with its bleak position, that it must depend essentially for its beauty upon elegance and proportion, and that superfluous ornament would be entirely out of place. It is the unity of the design that gives Pienza its special quality, a unity that came from the mind of its founder though it may have owed something to the archaeological enthusiasm of Biondo Flavio, who spent four months staying in near-by Asciano in order to watch over the progress of the work. Biondo wrote a full description of the operations in the additions to his *Italia illustrata*[2]; this, together with Pius's own account given in Book IX of the *Commentaries*, is the chief authority for the founder's plans. So much of the original design, however, is still to be seen and the recent restorations have been made with such tact and insight, that it would be a very dull spectator who could stand in the little piazza today and fail to realize what was Pius's intention or how completely it has been fulfilled.

Some critics have held that the buildings are set too closely—John Addington Symonds maintained that they are 'huddled together in close quarters on a square too small for their effect'[3]. He found

---

* Pienza was taken from the diocese of Chiusi, Montalcino from that of Arezzo.

Pienza 'disappointing', but it must be remembered that Symonds visited the place in the early eighteen-eighties, when sordid accretions had been allowed to obscure the beauty of the buildings and the palace was being used as 'a granary for country produce in a starveling land'. To others the compactness is right and satisfying. All the building is centred upon the little square—the cathedral that so unexpectedly runs counter to tradition by presenting the high altar at the southern instead of the eastern end, opposite it the municipal buildings, and on either flank the new Bishop's and the Pope's own palace. The precipitous hillside, falling away to the southward, and the exigencies of the levels made it necessary to plan the buildings in this economical rectangular way: Pienza is equally a triumph of architect, engineers, and patron.

While he stayed in the monastery at Abbadia, Pius suffered acutely from arthritic pains that gave him no rest. He could no longer make the expeditions through the woods and meadows, to Pian Castajano or to Santa Fiora, nor could he hold the Signature 'in a grove beneath this tree or that', nor give audience in the shade of sweet chestnut trees while his dogs started a hare or a deer in a near-by thicket. Pius resolved to move on to Pienza, despite his racking pains, and ordered his litter to be made ready at sunset. Late at night on 8th August Pius was carried across the valley, past the Pieve and up the steep track that zigzagged to the piazza. It was too dark to see the buildings then, and next day he was disappointed to find he could not stir from his bed. When he had recovered a little Pius spent many happy hours examining the work, 'nor did he regret the expenditure, although he had spent on this undertaking more than fifty thousand gold ducats. The beauty and dignity of the architecture more than compensated for the expense.'[4]

The external appearance of the Piccolomini palace was everything that Pius could desire. It stood four-square, ninety feet high to the top of the rain-water tank on the roof. The masons had cut and bevelled every stone 'to the thickness of a finger'; the cornices were beautifully wrought beneath the two rows of twenty-three windows with little columns between. The squared pilasters were neatly fitted with base and capital. 'And at the corners of the palace and at many points between the windows he hung stone shields on which glittered in gold, silver, and other colours, the arms of the house of Piccolomini, with all the skill of sculptor and painter. In addition to these were many iron rings and implements which would hold burning torches at night and could at times carry banners . . . And round the palace were seats raised on two and, in some places, on three steps, of the same stone as the cornice.' The stone seats were for the people of Pienza, that they might feel at one with their fellow-townsman within the great palace; to this day they congregate in the piazza and recline in sun or shade as the mood takes them, while the Lord of Pienza* dwells in the great hall that Pius built, and looks out over the gardens laid out to the Pope's design. The people speak of Pius as though he had left the town only yesterday and would return tomorrow. The family who keep the café at the western gate seem to expect the arrival at any moment of the papal household from Siena or Petriolo; the road-mender's wife is happy in her cramped cottage because she has 'our Pope's view of Monte Amiata—the most beautiful in the world either at dawn or sunset'.

Pius, the most practical of men, had insisted upon great cisterns for water storage to give an abundant supply, running through iron pipes and purified by gravel. Had he not already worked out a plan for diverting a stream on Monte Amiata to feed the Orcia when that river shrank and wasted away in the hot summer months? He was at pains to provide good water for the citizens and built a special well (or *pozzo*) in the piazza whence all could help themselves at will. Characteristically, the design of this well-head has rare beauty, for it is the work of the Pope's own architect.

The palace is conventional in plan, in that it is built round a central court, as are those in Florence or Siena[5], but Pius gave his architect instructions to make the rooms light, airy, and comfortable, with a fireplace in every room. The staircase has forty easy steps leading to the first floor, where Pius had his own apartments. There is a great hall with a richly carved chimney-piece of white stone; the room opens onto the loggia where Pius liked to spend long hours watching the cloud shadows on the face of his beloved mountain. The hall was, he said, 'a place delightful in all seasons, never ex-

---

* Conte Silvio Piccolomini della Triana. It was by his kind invitation that I was able to explore the private apartments in the palace. Since this book was written, news has come of the Conte's death (in May 1962), news that grieves all citizens and friends of Pienza.

periencing extremes of heat or cold'. Three kitchens were made, one for each floor, at a corner of the palace, special attention being paid to make sure the chimneys would draw properly and that cooking smells could not penetrate the rooms. Pius's own bedroom had an eastern window, looking towards Montepulciano, for he welcomed the early morning sun. His bed is still to be seen there, and a fresco upon the wall that is said to be a portrait[6].

Unlike most of his contemporaries, Pope Pius loved to have a bedroom at a great height above the ground with windows that he could fling wide open. Once, this habit brought a minor tragedy. Pius had a little bitch puppy called Musetta, who was his constant companion, climbing upon his knee to 'make lamentation' when anything displeased her, and sitting upon his window sill when Pius was resting in his bedroom. One day, a sudden gust of wind struck the puppy and hurled her to her death in the garden below. The little Musetta, 'white . . . not very lovely, but elegant and charming and knowing very well how to insinuate herself and win affection', had survived two other accidents: once she had fallen down a well and cried for help but 'all supposed she was barking at cats, as usual'. At the last moment she was 'snatched from her peril and taken to the Pope. To him she complained with a long lamentation.' The very next day Musetta was bitten by 'an immense long-tailed monkey who happened to be loose'. To posterity as well as to the Pope, these incidents are 'of small importance but not quite without value', for they illustrate the extraordinary freedom and casualness with which Pius conducted affairs of state. When the monkey was at large the Pope was merely having an informal discussion with the Cardinals over supper in the garden, but the search for the puppy when she fell into the well interrupted an audience that was being given to important delegates.

At Pius's own suggestion his bedroom was panelled with ash, so that he should not suffer from the dampness of the masonry before the walls had dried out. For his special convenience, too, there were no steps or changes of level in either of the upper floors, so that he was able to walk about easily when his arthritic condition allowed. As he roamed the palace Pius took pleasure in the paint and gold leaf that embellished beams and rafters of the ceilings, the colours reflected in the polished surface of the floors. 'And if, as some think,' he said, 'the principal charm of a house is light, then surely no house was ever to be preferred to this. For it receives without impediment the four quarters of the heavens, and light is admitted in abundance not only by the external windows but by those that look into the hollow of the building, and it reaches down into the lowest store-house.'[7] The three porticoes looked southward across gardens that were laid out with a deceptive simplicity. The ground was trenched and levelled, built up on columns of stone and brick; the vaulted space beneath furnished stabling for a hundred horses and a black-smith's forge for attending to their needs. Thyme and rosemary and other aromatic herbs scented the air; vines and shrubs shaded the stone benches where one could sit at ease and admire the incom-parable view.

The same preoccupation with light is found in the design of the cathedral—tiny in size but of such perfect proportions that it seems far larger than it really is. Sunlight streams in through the three large windows of the apse, and opposite them, above the central doorway on the north side, is the single large round window that reminded Pius of a cyclop's eye. When new the stonework of walls and pillars gleamed white, untouched with painted decoration; there were no frescoes and only the four altars and the roof and capitals showed gold and colour. The azure of the roof, with its golden stars, simulated the heavens; the capitals were painted in imitation of porphyry and precious stones. Pius recalled a church with three naves that he had seen in Austria; he charged his archi-tect to follow the same plan. 'As you enter through the middle door,' he wrote, 'all the church with its chapels and altars lies before your eyes, made striking by the great clarity of the light and the splendour of the workmanship.' He was so determined that no one should in-terfere with his original scheme that by a Bull dated 16th Septem-ber 1462 he forbade any additions or modifications upon pain of excommunication. This could, of course, be revoked by papal au-thority, should such action subsequently become necessary.

The architect chosen by Pius was a Florentine named Bernardo; he is generally thought to have been Bernardo Rossellino[8] though it is possible that Bernardo Mattei had a hand in the design of the cupola. Certainly Rossellino was responsible for the palace; there was some criticism and grumbling on the part of the Sienese who thought an architect from that city should have been entrusted with the work[9]. Pius, however, believed that he had made a good choice

and supported Bernardo most loyally. Indeed, the relationship between client and architect was so unusual that Pius's words must be
quoted in full. 'You did well, Bernardo,' he exclaimed after he had
made a full inspection of the works, 'to lie to us about what this
undertaking would cost us. Had you spoken the truth, you had
never persuaded us to spend so much money, and this fair palace,
this church the loveliest in all Italy, would never have existed. Your
deception has created these most glorious buildings which all praise,
except a few eaten up by envy. We thank you, and we consider you
of all the architects of our day deserving especial honour. And he
bade them pay the man his full price and also give him as a gift a
hundred gold pieces and a scarlet robe. He also granted the favours
which Bernardo asked on behalf of his son, and put him in charge
of fresh undertakings. He, when he heard the Pope, shed tears of
joy.'[10]

Nevertheless, Pius showed a better appraisal of the technical
problems presented by building on the face of a crumbling hillside
than did the professional architect. From the first excavations, that
went down to a depth of 108 feet, it had not been possible to find
satisfactory foundations. The builders were seeking for rock: they
found only 'continuous clefts and sulphurous exhalations'. At last it
was decided to build wide arches to bridge the points where solid
rock was found, and to pile the weight of the church upon them. In
the course of the digging some labourers were killed when a trench
collapsed upon them: throughout, the operations were as dangerous
as they were difficult. 'We are not sure,' Pius wrote, 'how firmly the
works are established, and certain little cracks which have since
appeared in the building and run from top to bottom make one
suspect that the foundations are not secure. The architect believes
that the lime has sunk while hardening, that this is the cause of the
cracks and there is no cause for anxiety. Time will reveal the truth.'
That Pius's forebodings were well justified has been proved by the
five hundred years' history of the cathedral. Underpinning, constantly renewed, has kept the walls standing, continual patching
has held them together, but the fundamental cause of all this trouble
remains. At the beginning of this century great efforts were made to
reinforce the structure; twenty-five years ago modern engineering
technique seemed to have conquered the problem[11]. But today, on
the eve of the fifth centenary of the dedication (on the Feast of St

Matthew, 21st September 1462) of the cathedral to Our Lady, feverish efforts are being made to fill the crevices and stop the cracks and to pump concrete into the cavities beneath the floor that is sinking so ominously. Even as these words are written the air is full of the jarring sounds of concrete-mixers working at full pressure on the piazza: the cathedral is roped off from the citizens, who may creep into one of the chapels to say their prayers, but must attend Mass, as did Pius himself, in the Church of S. Francesco close by.

Although the walls were left plain, Pius ordered exquisite altar-pieces for his chapels, painted by the Sienese masters he so much admired[12]. The choir-stalls were made by craftsmen particularly skilled in inlay-work, the service books by the best scribes and illuminators of the day. The finest work in these *corali* is by Sano di Pietro, the artist who had won distinction by his pictures of S. Bernardino and some very good *tavolette* or wooden book covers that he painted for the Sienese archives[13]. His very best work went into the miniatures of the *corali*, which outshine even those at Siena or Chiusi. In the illuminated border of a *Graduale* there is a caricature of the Pope, in profile; it is hard to resist the conclusion that it was put there at Pius's own suggestion[14]. The fourteen great service books or Graduals could not be completed in time for the consecration: in the list of expenses incurred by the Pope during 1463 that is preserved in the Archivio at Pienza a number of items can be found that refer to the buying of parchment and the reward of scribes. The account is made out by Niccolò Piccolomini who was still in charge of the Pope's personal expenses. Between 1st August and 23rd September considerable sums were paid out for vestments, altar frontals and so forth, for specially woven silken hangings (in pure white) from a Florentine craftsman, book-covers of cloth of silver and a pair of very tall candlesticks. Even the sacristan was to have a special book, costing three ducats, in which he was to write the inventory[15].

Pius had desired to have his piazza surrounded by 'four noble buildings'. On the west side stood his own palace, on the south the cathedral. The eastern side was intended for the Bishop and canons; Pius entrusted to Cardinal Borgia the task of constructing a Bishop's palace and house of residence for the canons from the 'old building which the podestà and other magistrates were wont to use'. Knowing full well Borgia's taste for sumptuous splendour Pius restrained him from setting up anything that would be out of keeping: it is, in fact, a very successful building, plain and of excellent proportions. To the north stood a row of private houses; these Pius bought and demolished so that he could erect the graceful town hall, with its portico, clock, and bell-tower that stands today almost exactly as the architect left it upon completion. For this building the Pope provided workmen and paid a large part of the price, but he invited the townsfolk to contribute something of the cost. When, however, he instructed the Cardinals to buy or build themselves houses in the city, Pius expected them to finance the whole operation themselves. Young Cardinal Gonzaga wrote home to his parents at Mantua, asking urgently for money, as he had already had to invest in a house at Rome. It was convenient that members of the Curia should have country-houses in Pienza, so that they would be near at hand for attending Consistories and Signature. Cardinal Jouffroy of Arras built himself 'a large and lofty house', so did the Papal Treasurer and Goro Lolli. Cardinal Gonzaga bought his site, awaiting his subsidy from home before starting to build, but Calandrini demolished some squalid old buildings and started at once to replace them by something more worthy of the Pope's city. Pius's close friend Ammanati, Cardinal of Pavia, imitated the Pope's tastes and erected a house that delighted everyone—'very suitable and charming, square and standing alone'[16]. Several of these palaces remain, though now converted to other uses. Pienza's one hotel, the Albergo Letizia, in the main street, a few yards west of the piazza, still retains the splendid hall where proud Cardinal Jouffroy used to dine, though now it is shorn of its elegance and occupied only by bagmen and the occasional tourist.

These palaces, modest by Roman and Florentine standards yet startling enough in the quiet little city, combined with Pius's buildings round the piazza to make a nucleus for the town. But in later years it grew very little; communications were too bad, trade by-passed Pienza, and there was little in its soil or its exposed position to attract new agriculture. No fortuitous discovery of alum, as at Tolfa, came to give the district new life. Even Montalcino, standing high on a hill-top on the far side of S. Quirico, flourished more than did Pienza, whose population dwindled as the centuries passed. Yet Pienza retained the individual character of Corsignano, and poor as its people have always been—doomed to the hardest of labour in the most unfruitful of soils—they still have the joy in simple pleasures and the dry wit that so strongly distinguished the township's most famous son.

In inviting the French Cardinal-Bishop of Ostia* to dedicate his church and its altars Pius was showing magnanimity to his one-time enemy. He himself anointed the front of the high altar and placed in it the holy relics. This ceremony took place on the Feast of the beheading of St John the Baptist (29th August); it coincided with the transference to Pienza of the Bishopric of Chiusi. The Cathedral was dedicated to Our Lady, to whom Pius had a whole-hearted devotion that he shared with the people of Siena. One of the altars was assigned to St Andrew, in memory of the great procession held so recently in Rome.

The townsfolk of Pienza had adopted St Matthew as their patron; every year on 21st September they celebrated his feast by holding a fair that drew great crowds from the neighbouring countryside. The Pope determined that he and the whole Curia would round off the Pienza celebrations by giving aid and patronage to this occasion. Word went round the neighbouring villages that this year there would be splendid prizes, for the Pope himself had promised to pay the expenses of the meeting and to give a new robe to each of the town officials. All the money, then, could be spent on the prizes— from the *palio* of eight ells of scarlet cloth for the winner of the horse-race, down to the live goose that would be offered to the boys. Tents were pitched outside the town, where cooks were preparing thirty great white oxen, taken from the plough, and many smaller beasts, for the great feast that would take place immediately after Mass.

Everyone attended Mass, celebrated at sunrise, as the natural beginning of their holiday. Pius noted the 'deep devotion' shown by all the townsmen. Afterwards they migrated to the fair-ground for trading and feasting. All the cooked meats were devoured at a single meal, then came the business of the day, the buying and selling, the bargaining 'and the cheating'17 that were hallowed by custom. By evening trade was over, it was now time for sport. The horse-race came first; this offered the best prize but aroused little interest as the favourite romped home and so 'this spectacle was

* Guillaume d'Estouteville: see Chapter IX.

spoilt'. The donkey race was much more exciting. In Pius's own words: 'The rivalry between the donkeys was intense, now one and now another leading, spurred on by frequent blows. At last Sacchino's ass, which had often won, flung off its rider and came first to the goal. The next man, who was still upon his donkey, argued that the prize[18] was due to him, and not to Sacchino who had been thrown from his steed. But the judges rejected his claim, because the prize had been offered to donkeys, not to men.'

Like Sacchino's ass, many of the human runners were seasoned veterans. The track was over four furlongs; since there had been some rain the surface was very muddy. The men ran naked but soon most of them were clothed in mud. The result seemed open, till one of the cooks slipped into the throng of runners and darted into the lead, grasping the winning-post and loudly claiming the prize. He had, however, forgotten to take off his doublet, and since he was scarcely splashed with mud, the fraud was soon exposed. The judges laughed and, in great good humour, the length of coloured cloth was given to the man from Sarteano who had truly won.

In the Pope's opinion, sympathetic as he was to youth, 'The boys' race was the best of all the shows. There was a large number of them on the course, children leaping about naked until the signal went, when they contended with amazing rivalry, each trying to surpass the other. They could not pull their feet out of the sticky clay, their spirits sometimes sank and they fell back, then recovering breath they surged forward again. And some had parents, some had brothers, who kept their courage up with many exhortations. They ran about a furlong to the gate of the town, and victory was wavering among many. But just then one of Alessandro's[19] servants, a very small man and without a beard so that he looked like a child, joined the race, flew to the front and, running swiftly across the town, laid his hand victoriously upon the winning-post and demanded the prize. Next came a boy of Pienza, with fair hair and a lovely body, though all bedaubed with mud. And as he knew he had been outdistanced by three or four paces, he bewailed his fortune and cursed himself for not having run faster. His mother was there, quite a handsome woman, comforting her child with gentle words, and wiping off the sweat with a towel. The judges seemed on the point of bestowing the prize on him who had come first when Alessandro, noticing this, exclaimed: "My servant is eighteen and it is by a trick that he is taken for a boy. Do not let him profit by his dishonesty." On hearing this they gave the prize to the boy of Pienza, who received the live goose, was carried home on the shoulders of his devoted parent followed by a vast crowd, and filled with rejoicing all the neighbourhood. All this the Pope and Cardinals watched from a high window with no small merriment, though in the intervals they were busy with affairs of state.'[20]

CHAPTER XVIII

Ancona: The End of the Road

There were assembled at Ancona many soldiers ready to embark when the Pope should come to lead them in person . . . But it was not God's will. – *Chronicle of the City of Fermo*[1]

In Pienza the golden days slipped by until autumn turned into winter, and the time came for the Pope to return to Rome. He left on 19th November, returning by way of Montichiello and Todi, and reaching Rome, 18th December. There he would have to face far sterner problems than the questions concerning decoration and design that had occupied his summer. On two further occasions—the last only three months before his death—Pius returned to his 'piccola città' for a few days' visit, but he was already gravely ill, tense and worried by the storm clouds over the Adriatic.

Before he went to Pienza in 1461 Pius had written to the Doge of Venice* to tell him in confidence of his proposal to lead the crusade in person; early in the New Year of 1463 he sent to Venice a sword that he had blessed, for he hoped that the Doge would accompany the papal host and so give a lead to all the rulers of Christendom. Those who imagined that the Pope had shelved his crusading project, in favour of political or personal enterprises, were confronted by zealous and realistic preparations for his campaign, coupled with pointed reminders concerning their own commitments. Pius himself had never lost hope that once the rulers of Europe had composed their differences, and home affairs had become stable within the Papal State, all would be able to unite together to destroy Turkish

---

* At that time Pasquale Malipiero. He died on 5th May 1462, and a week later Cristoforo Moro was elected to succeed him.

rule in Christian territory. He had enough insight to realize that commitments at home, as well as resources in arms and in manpower, must decide the contribution that each could make. It was clear that much more might be expected of some nations than of others, and that leadership is a rare as well as a precious quality. The Pope knew very well that he himself had neither the experience nor the special knowledge that make a good soldier: courage he had in plenty but he was no Julius II, nor was he even a Cardinal Fortiguerri. Pius was content to leave both tactics and strategy in the hands of the professionals. As to weapons, he showed only the same kind of interest in the new carbines[2] as he extended to any novelty. His acquaintance with artillery, too, was confined to naming the three new cannon that won victory for him in 1461 'Enea', 'Silvio', and 'Vittoria'[3] after himself, his father, and his mother.

It was manifest to everyone except to the Venetians themselves that they ought to declare war upon the Turks and, if only in their own interest, seek to turn them back from the Dalmatian coast. The Venetians were ready enough to shelter behind Sigismondo Malatesta during his war with the Papacy while they appropriated to their own use convenient tracts of papal territory lying on the shores of the Adriatic[4]. Yet they seemed unable to appreciate that the threat to Ragusa—now that they had by their neglect allowed Bosnia to become a Turkish province—was a very real danger to Venice herself. With the accession of the new Doge matters improved to some degree and the war party could at least make their voices heard in the Senate. Pius was greatly incensed at the dilatoriness of the Venetians—as Cardinal Francesco Gonzaga wrote to his parents on 22nd June 1463[5]. Pius had no illusions about the self-interest that prompted the policy of the Venetian Republic, nor did he doubt that the price of help from their navy was control of the Morea and all its valuable trading stations. What did exasperate him was that Venice seemed to be unable to understand how deeply vulnerable was her position. Nor could Pius think very highly of the members of the Senate from an ethical point of view—'What do fishes care for justice?' he asked scornfully.

Some of the most outspoken passages of the *Commentaries* are those concerning Venetian affairs at this time; these sections were pruned away by a discreet editor[6] for fear of offending that powerful state.

Cardinal Bessarion, after the Pope himself the most single-minded supporter of the crusade in the whole of the Sacred College, had been sent to Venice to reason with Doge and Senate. Unfortunately, the Greek Cardinal was more learned than shrewd, and far too ready to believe uncritically whatever he was told. Nevertheless, he wrote to the Pope in the late summer of 1463 that he could not understand why the Venetians should make such difficulties about making a formal break with the Turks, since they were already mobilized both by land and sea[7]. Within a month the Republic had at last begun to levy the tithes (decided upon at Mantua but not yet collected) to raise money for the crusade. Some four weeks later a still more important step was taken when on 12th September 1463 the Senate entered into a long overdue alliance with Hungary. At last Venice seemed ready to act. It only remained to unite the Christian forces behind her.

This unity was easier to promulgate than to achieve. Although towards the end of 1463 it really seemed that there was hope of co-operation and good will, there were still many quarrels and jealousies to be resolved. The Burgundian mission that had visited the Pope earlier in the summer while he was at Tivoli had brought glowing promises from Duke Philip that made Pius's volatile spirit leap to a new plane of optimism. The time had come, he felt, to lay his scheme before the Sacred College. In a secret Consistory on 23rd September he addressed the Cardinals in long and earnest speech[8]. 'We shall imitate our lord and master Jesus Christ,' he told them, 'the holy blessed Shepherd Who did not hesitate to lay down His life for His sheep. We too shall lay down our life for our flock, since otherwise we cannot help the Christian religion, that it be not trampled under foot by the Turks. We shall arm a fleet as great as the resources of the Church permit, we shall go on board ship; old man and broken by infirmities as we are, we shall spread our sails to the winds and be carried to Greece and Asia . . . We hear your murmurs: If you consider the war so difficult with what hope do you go on with it when you lack sufficient resources? We are coming to that. War with the Turk threatens us unavoidably. Unless we arm and go against the foe, we believe that our religion is done for. We shall be among the Turks as today we see the despised race of Jews among the Christians. Unless we make war we are disgraced . . . Our position is that of bankers who have lost their credit: nobody

trusts us. The priesthood is a laughing-stock, the very name of cleric
is an infamy. They say we live for pleasure, hoard up money, serve
ambition, sit on fat mules or pedigree horses, spread out the fringes
of our cloaks and go about the city with fat cheeks under our red
hats and ample hoods: that we breed dogs for hunting, spend freely
upon players and parasites, but nothing in defence of the faith. Nor
is it all a lie. Many of the Cardinals and other courtiers do all these
things and, to speak the truth, the luxury and extravagance of our
Curia is excessive. Because of this we are hateful to the people, so
much so that even when we speak the truth they will not hear us.
What in your opinion must we do amid such scorn? . . . We must
turn into paths abandoned long ago. We must find by what methods
our fore-runners created for us this vast dominion of the Church,
and use them. For power is easily retained by those methods which
first created it. Abstinence, chastity, innocence, zeal for the faith,
religious fervour, contempt for death, desire for martyrdom: these
things put the Church of Rome at the head of the whole world . . .
Nor is it enough to be confessors, preach to the people, fulminate
against vice, praise virtue to the sky. We must go back to those fore-
runners who gave their bodies for God's testament. There is nothing
we ought not to endure for the preservation of the flocks entrusted
to us, even though it means laying down our life . . . We know it is
a serious matter for a man of our age, and that we shall go to certain
death—in one way or another . . . We must die one day and we do
not mind where, provided we die well.'

These were brave words that Pius spoke to the Cardinals: they
realized that he meant every one of them. The speech was no rhetorical exercise, it was a confession of faith. The Cardinals sat with
downcast eyes, many of them weeping, while they pondered the
Pope's exhortation. It was hard for anyone to oppose him; Estouteville was heard to mutter that there was nothing he disliked more
than sailing, but the old Cardinal of Porto (Carvajal) wept copiously
as he declared: 'I have always thought you were a man, Pope, now I
say you are an angel . . . if you go through flames I shall not leave
you, since you go straight to Heaven.' Spoleto and Arras raised difficulties but in the end Pius won at least verbal support for his scheme
from everyone.

The Pope's great share in the crusade, following the lines laid
down by his predecessor Calixtus III, has not always been duly

acknowledged[9]. Had the other leaders supported him the movement would have gained the momentum it so sadly lacked. Although there were many good signs in 1463—Ferrante firmly established in Naples, Hungary freed from the fear of a stab in the back by the Emperor[10], a truce between Burgundians and Armagnacs in France, a splendid picaresque leader of almost superhuman strength and courage in George Skanderbeg of Albania—all was nullified by the myopic selfishness of states and nations.

No help was forthcoming from England, but at least her rulers did not make offers and then withdraw them when the time came to implement words with deeds, as did the French King and several more. Those who had warned Pius that he was nursing a viper in his bosom when he appointed Arras a Cardinal, were amply justified. Now Cardinal Jean Jouffroy showed himself in his true colours, making every attempt to impede Pius in his arrangements so that the Pope was compelled to recognize him as he really was. 'For till he was made Cardinal Arras took every care to conceal his perverse nature, and while his verbosity in dispute made him appear learned he wanted also to appear good by an imitation of the virtues. But when he obtained the red hat he could control himself no longer, but loosed his reins and flung himself into every kind of evil. Lying and perjury were so familiar to him that he often deceived himself and spoke the truth thinking that he lied. When he read to the Pope the letters of the King of France, he frequently altered the sense and affirmed that the King desired this or that thing which had never come into his head. Pius observed this and once, when he had caught him in a flagrant error, for he recited far more than the page could contain, said: Give us the letter that we may see whether you read it correctly.'[11] Jouffroy's personal animosity towards Pius was strengthened by the Pope's refusal to bestow on him simultaneously the famous churches of Besançon and Albi. Pius agreed that he might be eligible to hold one of the dioceses, but not both. Jouffroy then tried to bribe him with the offer of 12,000 ducats. Pius burst out: 'Go to the devil with your ducats and take your money with you to perdition'. Thereafter, 'Arras was never the Pope's friend, though he sometimes dissembled'.

Since he was in an excellent position to make matters difficult for the Pope, especially by betraying his secrets to the Duke of Anjou, Jouffroy did more than anyone to poison relations between France and the Papacy. In Rome, too, he caused trouble through his ungovernable temper; he was with good reason the most unpopular member of the Curia. Pius drew an amusing picture of the man and his relations with his household. 'He wanted to seem devout,' the Pope affirmed, 'and would often conduct divine service . . . in the basilica of St Peter . . . By face and gesture he would show how much he was carried away, drawing sighs from the very bottom of his chest, weeping and, as it were, conversing with God. But before he had taken off his sacred vestments and left the altar he had cuffed one or other of his servers who had made some slight mistake . . . and the Pope was told that he struck one of them such a box on the ear in front of the altar that he fell to the ground . . . At meals if he was annoyed by some trifling offence, as often happened, he would hurl silver goblets or loaves at his servants. Sometimes in his fury he would overturn the very table with everything that was on it, even when distinguished guests were sitting at it. For he was gluttonous and an immoderate drinker, and when he was heated with wine no one would stay in his service. For that reason his servants seldom remained with him longer than one month.'[12] Pius went on to accuse Arras of lust, also of aspiring to the Papacy when he himself should die. This is one of the most trenchant portraits that ever came from his pen, for he felt so strongly that this man was the greatest obstacle in the way of the crusade that for once his urbanity deserted him. The sharp touches of realism bring to life most vividly a singularly unlovable character.

From the time of the Diet of Mantua, when he had held such satisfactory conferences with Francesco Sforza, Pius had always looked upon the Duke of Milan as the ideal commander-in-chief of the papal forces. Thus it was the severest possible blow when Francesco began to offer excuses and to declare preoccupations that the Pope well knew existed only in his mind. Sforza's defection sprang from the enmity between Milan and Venice that was itself rooted in past treacheries and three generations of warfare between these states. Florence, too, refused to co-operate on the grounds that she would be fighting battles from which only Venice could profit. The cynicism of the Florentines and the evasiveness of the Milanese were matched by the cunning of Louis XI of France who baited the Pope with the threat of calling another Council. Only the Duke of Burgundy seemed to be holding firmly to the vow that he had taken. When at last he too defaulted, Pius was deprived of his last hope of genuine support. This did not occur until the early spring of 1464, when the Duke was physically exhausted by his excesses and so lacking in spirit that he welcomed the interference of his overlord, Louis XI, who forbade him to take any part in the enterprise. Had Philip really wished to set forth on the crusade, Louis XI was in no position to stop him: of all the excuses for non-co-operation his was perhaps the feeblest.

Burgundy's repudiation of his vow still lay in the future: long before the end of 1463 extensive preparations for the expedition had been begun. On 12th November the Sienese envoy[13] wrote to the Signoria that the Holy Father was 'indefatigable in his efforts . . . His Bull on the subject has been sent into all Christian countries, and will, I believe, lead many to take part in it. God has indeed sent this Pope for the salvation of His people, whose Princes have forsaken them, and left them a prey to the attacks of the Turks.' In this dispatch Benvoglienti put his finger upon the important point that the intentions and aspirations of ordinary men were of a far higher and purer quality than those of the men who should have given them leadership. The preaching of the Friars Minor, particularly in Germany, drew recruits from among the workers and lesser tradesmen. Pastor quotes the *Hamburg Chronicle* to illustrate their enthusiasm: 'the people forsook their waggons and ploughs to hasten to Rome to take arms against the Turks.'[14] Two thousand would-be crusaders came from Lübeck, three hundred from Ghent, and recruits too from such distant lands as Spain and even Scotland. To look after these volunteers, to house them, equip them, arm them, and interpret their uncouth speech, was itself a major problem. The Pope was always ready to encourage enterprising individuals who wanted to help his cause. Among many donations to friars, monks, and pilgrims in his account-book for 1462 is to be noted the sum of ten ducats[15] to a provincial cleric who proposed to raise his own company of crusaders. This was not likely to be of much practical use, but it was a gesture of goodwill; Pius recognized it as such and made his token acknowledgement in the same spirit. Supplies were trickling in, transport vessels were being chartered, the promised triremes were said to be in preparation, but everything moved slowly and reluctantly. Cities that had agreed to provide food, munitions, or ships sought loopholes whereby they might avoid their obligation. Bologna, the rich and self-sufficient, complained that she could not afford the allotted two galleys, while Perugia had to be threatened with an interdict before she would do her part.

Only the dynamic efforts of the Pope kept matters moving: had he flinched there can be no doubt that the whole project would have melted into nothingness. The Account Book, bound in red morocco and full of entries made by Niccolò Piccolomini (who had proved his worth as Treasurer at Pienza), still lies in the State Archives at Rome as witness to the seriousness of the Pope's intentions. Old and ill as he was, discouraged by the faithlessness of the Princes and the tepid enthusiasm of most of the Cardinals, in the teeth of hostility from the Romans who resented furiously the Pope's departure, Pius still maintained his course, defying his doctors and the Cassandra-like prophecies of his advisers.

On 18th June 1464, Pius took the Cross in the basilica of St Peter. Soon afterwards he left Rome for the last time. He was so infirm that the journey to Ancona had to be made very slowly and as far as possible by water in order to ease his pain. Sometimes only six or seven miles could be covered in the course of a day. The Pope could no longer continue his *Commentaries* in the old manner, writing or dictating during hours stolen from sleep. The thirteenth and last book totally lacks the sparkle and bite that make Pius's reflections upon his life and times incomparable. It is to Campano's very moving account of the Pope's last days[16] that we must turn for homely details; his restraint in describing his own bitter grief makes it the more poignant.

Few men in like condition, racked with pain and with all their energies bent upon a single aim, would have found compassion to spare for a young waterman who during the journey fell from his barge into deep water and was drowned. But Ammanati tells us[17] that the Pope lay silent for a long while, 'with tears in his eyes as he prayed for the departed'. After four days of leisurely progress, Pius staying on board each night while his companions slept ashore, the party reached Otricoli. On the bank of the Tiber a litter was waiting for the Pope; he was carried in it to the town of Terni, where he had received so tumultuous a welcome five years earlier on his way to Mantua. Then, the snows of winter were receding and the promise of spring showed in the fresh herbs strewn in his path. Now, it was high summer and a season of enervating heat. The Pope's servants drew the curtains closely round his litter, partly to exclude the sun but chiefly to shield their master from the sight of bands of dispirited crusaders homeward bound. With an instinct that all might not be well at Ancona, Pius sent Cardinal Carvajal ahead of the cavalcade, with instructions to organize the crowds of ill-disciplined and impatient soldiers gathered there, and to begin the work of embarkation. Three more Cardinals, Borgia, Estouteville, and Eroli of Spoleto, joined the Pope at Terni, but at Spoleto the party suffered temporary loss when Ammanati had to be left behind suffering from a high fever[18]. In the good air of Assisi the Pope recovered a little of his strength; on 7th July he reached Fabriano and gave audience to his old friend and colleague Frederick of Urbino. From a letter written by Goro Lolli next day[19] it seems that Frederick tried with all his eloquence to persuade the Pope to give up his purpose.

Pius was now crossing high ground: on a spur of the Apennines he came to the shrine of Our Lady's House at Loreto and turned aside to offer there a golden chalice. From this windswept vantage-point he could see the shimmering waters of the Adriatic. He was near his journey's end. By the time the Pope and his bearers had descended to the shore at Ancona, and climbed the little eminence where stood the Cathedral of S. Ciriaco, he was at the point of exhaustion. Arrangements had been made for him to lodge in the Bishop's Palace adjoining the Cathedral. Here there were no cheers or welcoming crowds, for all were absorbed in personal quarrels and where there should have been singleness of purpose there was only brawling and chaos. Estouteville was sent to help Carvajal quell the intransigence of the crusaders, especially the Frenchmen and the Spaniards, but little could be done to organize the armies until the promised transports should arrive. Neither the lamentable unpreparedness of the army nor the sparsity of supplies could be attributed to the Pope's negligence, for he had most explicitly stated that his summons was addressed to soldiers 'well-armed and fully provisioned for at least half a year'[20]. The well-meaning volunteers who had come to Rome in the first flush of enthusiasm had been equipped as far as possible at the Pope's expense and the rest sent home; most of those who were now gathered in Ancona were either unwilling mercenaries or simply adventurers in search of personal plunder.

It was a grim prospect, made the grimmer by rumours that raced

through the streets and whispers that hung in the sultry air. It was
said that pestilence had broken out, that the Venetian fleet would
never come, that the Turks were advancing on Ragusa, that the
Pope was already dead. In actual fact, things were bad enough.
Water was scarce, lodgings were over-crowded, the Venetian ships
had not yet arrived, and few if any of the promised troops could be
assembled. As July melted into August, and the heat became unbearable, pestilence did indeed sweep through the March of Ancona,
invading the crusading host and even the Cardinals' households.
Borgia took fright and left the city; the other Cardinals stayed on,
but the number of crusaders equipped and ready to embark dwindled till only a handful of soldiers remained.

When at last the Venetian transports arrived, on 11th August,
there were not enough crusaders left to fill them. The Doge had
sent no word of his movements: men doubted whether he would in
fact put in an appearance, for everyone knew of his reluctance to
take part in the crusade. The fleet, when it did come, was therefore
too late to be of any practical use. The Pope was obviously a dying
man. His servants lifted his fragile body and carried him to the window of his bed-chamber so that he might watch the arrival of the
twelve ships[21]. The sight gave him no joy. All this time he had
waited for the fleet for his expedition; now that the ships had come
the expedition had melted away. It was the end of his dream.

Racked with stone, exhausted by fever, unable to sleep, Pius was
sinking fast. His mind was still clear when he received Holy Communion on the morning of 13th August, and afterwards he was able
to address his household. With humility he told the Cardinals how
he had laboured for the Christian faith, and charged them to carry
on his work. In tears, and deeply moved, they stood by his bedside
while they listened to his admonition. At last Bessarion made in
their name a short reply. He, who had once opposed Pius's election
but had thereafter been his most loyal supporter, was the only Cardinal able to find words and voice. Then, all present knelt round his
bed to kiss the Pope's hand and to receive his last blessing.

On the eve of the Feast of the Assumption it was arranged that
next day Ammanati should bring him Holy Communion, but during
the night Pius fell into a peaceful sleep and his spirit quietly passed
away. His last words were a whispered request to Ammanati that he

should be remembered in his prayers. Pius died on 14th August*, just three days after his friend and colleague Nicholas of Cusa. He was only fifty-nine.

The Pope's body lay in state in the Cathedral of S. Ciriaco on the Feast of Our Lady that he had so longed to celebrate: two days later it was removed to Rome for splendid burial in the chapel of St Andrew that he had built. His viscera were buried in the choir of S. Ciriaco at Ancona and an inscription was carved there on a marble slab:

MCCCLXIIII. XIX kls. Sept.
PII II
Pont. Max. prae-
cordia tumu-
lantur.
Corpus Romam
translatum. Anco.
moritur dum
in Turcos bella parat.[22]

Cristoforo Moro, the Doge, was soon leading his ships back to Venice, with the 40,000 ducats collected for the crusade securely in his coffers. The money was to be transmitted to the King of Hungary for carrying on the Turkish war. The crusaders vanished overnight. The Cardinals rode hastily back to Rome to be in time for the next election. On the headland facing the sea, close to the Cathedral where once there had been a Temple of Venus, a memorial to Pope Pius and his crusade was set up. But it was shattered in World War II: there is little enough to remind the world of Pius's unselfish ideals and it is ironical that the best testimony of his life and work is to be found in the pages of his *Commentaries*, that he himself looked upon as a frivolous indulgence, reflections of his ingenious mind, written in midnight hours and in his few moments of leisure.

* On the very day of his death Skanderbeg won a resounding victory, but the news came too late to bring comfort to the Pope.

NOTES

INTRODUCTION

1. Professor E. F. Jacob in *Italian Renaissance Studies,* London, 1960, p. 24 ff.
2. *Commentaries,* Book III. (For the reader's convenience, all quotations are from Flora Grierson's translation. See Bibliography.) Aeneas stated that Francesco was sixty years old: actually he was 58.
3. For Ippolita Sforza, who married Alfonso, King of Naples, see p. 136–7.
4. F. C. Lane: *Venetian Ships and Shipbuilders of the Renaissance,* Baltimore, 1934, pp. 15, 16.
5. *Ibid.,* p. 16. This was a record voyage, the distance being about 2,500 miles.
6. Denis Hay: *The Italian Renaissance in its Historical Background,* Cambridge, 1961, p. 30. See also E. F. Jacob: *Italian Renaissance Studies,* p. 26.
7. See the introductory chapter of Hastings Rashdall: *The Universities of Europe in the Middle Ages,* ed. Powicke & Emden, Oxford, 1936.
8. *Vite di uomini illustri del secolo XV,* ed. Paolo d'Ancona & E. Aeschlimann, Milan, 1951, pp. 44–5.
9. 'Aeneas rejicite, Pius suscipite.' *Commentaries,* Book I.
10. Especially G. Toffanin in his introduction to the *Lettera a Maometto II,* Naples, 1952, p. lv. 'In effetti Pio II fu un atleta della fede e tra i grandi papi umanisti forse il più grande.' *Cf.* also G. Paparelli: *Enea Silvio Piccolomini (Pio II),* Bari, 1950, *passim.*
11. Ludwig von Pastor: *Geschichte der Päpste* (new edn.), Freiburg, 1926. As *The History of the Popes* it was translated by F. I. Antrobus, London, 1894, and this version is quoted for the reader's convenience. See vol. III, p. 3.

CHAPTER I

1. See *Dizionario enciclopedico italiano* (Roma, 1957), vol. 7: also *Enciclopedia italianica* (new edn., 1949) under Controriforma.
2. *Miscellanea storia senese,* vol. I, pp. 156 ff.
3. Paparelli: *Enea Silvio Piccolomini,* p. 17.
4. *Commentaries,* Book I.
5. *Vita Pii, II,* in Muratori: *Rerum Ital. Scriptores,* II, pt. ii, p. 974, Milan, 1734.
6. *Commentaries,* Book I.
7. See Chapter VII, §i. The Epistola is printed by R. Wolkan: *Der Briefwechsel des E. S. Piccolomini, Fontes Rerum Austriacarum,* ser. ii, vol. LXI, Ep. 166.

It has been translated into Italian by G. Paparelli (Lanciano, 1948) and into English by W. P. Mustard (Baltimore, 1928).

8. *Commentaries*, Book II.
9. *Commentaries*, Book VII.
10. *Commentaries*, Book VIII.
11. See Plutarch's *Life of Artaxerxes*.
12. *Commentaries*, Book IX.

CHAPTER II

1. *Epistolae et commentarii Jacobi Piccolomini Cardinalis Papiensis*. Printed in *Pii II Commentarii*, Frankfurt, 1614, Ep. XLVII.

2. This and the succeeding documents are printed by L. Zdekauer: *Lo studio di Siena nel rinascimento*, Milan, 1894, pp. 156–9.

3. On 18th September, 1420. Zdekauer, *op. cit.*, p. 158.

4. *Ibid.*, p. 159.

5. *Commentaries*, Book VII. He also lectured at Bologna from 1424–9. A. Sorbelli: *Storia dell'università di Bologna*, Bologna, 1940. Vol. I, p. 247.

6. R. J. Mitchell: *John Free*, London, 1954, p. 77.

7. Printed from Cod. A XI. 12, fo. 33^r, Bibl. Com. di Siena, by R. J. Mitchell in *Italian Studies*, vol. VIII (1952), p. 74. He was an Englishman named Edward.

8. *Epistolae . . . Cardinalis Papiensis*, Ep. XLVII.

9. *Commentaries*, Book I.

10. *Aliotti, Ep. et Opusc.*, ii, p. 349. Quoted by G. Lesca in his edition of the *Commentarii* (Pisa, 1893), p. 49. *Cf.* also Paparelli: *op. cit.*, p. 22, n. 15.

11. *Epistolae . . . Cardinalis Papiensis*, p. 494.

12. In August, 1460. He was John Gunthorp, later Dean of Wells. The MS. is now in the British Museum, MS. Harley 2485. See R. J. Mitchell: *John Free*, p. 65.

13. Now at Oxford, Balliol College, MS. 258. The copyist was Richard Bole.

14. Giulio Prunai: 'Lo studio senese dalla "migratio" bolognese alla fondazione dalla "Domus Sapientiae" (1321–1408)': *Bullettino Senese di Storia Patria*, ser. iii (1950). See also Rashdall: *op. cit.*, vol. II, pp. 32–4, and Zdekauer: *op. cit.*, Chapter I.

15. S. Domenico was a church without a parish. The obituary is Cod. c. III. 2, in the Bibl. Com. of Siena. See also Luschin von Ebengreuth: 'I sepolcri degli scolari tedeschi in Siena', *Bullettino Senese di Storia Patria*, Siena, 1896, pp. 9–21.

16. G. Prunai: *op. cit.*, p. 16 and n. 3.

17. *Epistolae . . . Cardinalis Papiensis*, Ep. XLVII.

18. In 1444. R. Wolkan: *Der Briefwechsel des Eneas Sylvius Piccolomini*, vol. I, pt. i, Ep. 153. Hereafter this work is quoted as Wolkan: *op. cit.*, with the number of the letter.

19. Ugo Fritelli: 'Le prediche volgari di San Bernardino da Siena', in *Bullettino Senese di Storia Patria*, new ser., anno 11 (1931), fasc. 1, pp. 35–44.

20. Aeneas Sylvius, *De Viris Illustribus*, Stuttgart, 1842, p. 25.

21. By Voigt, for instance. See his *Enea Silvio de' Piccolomini als Papst Pius II und sein Zeitalter*, 3 vols., Berlin, 1856–63, *passim*. Voigt calls Aeneas's conversion a 'Bordell-Comödie'.

22. *De Viris Illustribus*, p. 27.

23. *Lettera a Maometto II*, ed. G. Toffanin, Naples, 1952, cap. xviii. Bernardino was canonized during the pontificate of Nicholas V.

24. Leonardo Bruni of Arezzo and Johannes da Imola, I.U.D.

CHAPTER III

1. By Professor G. Zannoni: 'Per la storia di due amanti', in *Atti della R. Accademia dei Lincei*, ser. iv, vol. vi (Rome, 1890), pp. 126–7. See C. M. Ady: *Pius II*, London, 1913, p. 16, also Paparelli: *Enea Silvio Piccolomini*, pp. 23, n. 18; 93, n. 21.

2. R. J. Mitchell: 'Italian "nobiltà" & the English Idea of the Gentleman in the XVth Century' in *English Miscellany*, vol. ix, Rome, 1958, p. 23.

3. *De Natura et Cura Equorum*: Wolkan: *op. cit.*, Ep. 154. See p. 80.

4. *The Tale of the Two Lovers*, p. 13.

5. *Ibid.*, p. 4.

6. *Ibid.*, p. 41.

7. *Ibid.*, pp. 66–7.

8. *Ibid.*, p. 81.

9. The best known English translation is by W. Braunche: *The most excellent Historie of Euryalus and Lucretia*. London, 1596. The only fully critical text is that edited by I. Devay, Budapest, 1904. Miss Grierson's version (London, 1929) is, unfortunately, now out of print.

10. Voigt speaks of the novel as 'das gelesenste Werk'; *op. cit.*, vol. i, p. 287.

11. *The Tale of the Two Lovers*, p. 87.

12. It was completed in Vienna on 3rd July, 1444.

13. See pp. 81–3.

14. G. Paparelli: *Enea Silvio Piccolomini*, p. 20.

15. Socino Benzi. See the reference to this poem in Wolkan: *op. cit.*, Ep. 3.

16. Described by Gregorovius (*Hist. of the City of Rome*, vol. vii, pt. i, p. 161, etc.) as his 'erotic compositions'.

CHAPTER IV

1. As he wrote in a letter to Piero di Noceto: see Paparelli: *op. cit.*, pp. 18–19, n. 4.

2. It was addressed to 'Florida' and the others: 'ad Floridam ornatissimam et ceteras papienses puellas'. See Antonio Astesano: *De ejus vita et fortunae varietate Carmen*, ed. Armando Tallone. Printed in Muratori: *Rerum Ital. Scriptores* (new edn.), 1908, xiv, pt. i.

3. *Francisci Philelfi Epistolae*, Venice, 1502, Ep. 26.

4. *Epistolae . . . Cardinalis Papiensis*, Ep. xlvii.

5. *Francisci Philelfi Epistolae*, Ep. 8. See also C. Rosmini: *Vita di Francesco Filelfo*, Milano, 1808, vol. ii, pp. 104–9.

6. He lectured on both laws, 1410–34. See A. Sorbelli: *op. cit.*, i, pp. 244–5.

7. Aeneas quoted from Guarino's Latin translation of Strabo in his *La Germania:* see p. 31, n. 1, of G. Paparelli's edition (Florence, 1949).
8. *Commentaries,* Book v.
9. Wolkan: *op. cit.,* Ep. 2.
10. Commissioned by Aeneas's nephew Pope Pius III; see Corrado Ricci: *Pinturicchio,* trans. F. Symonds, London, 1902, and G. W. Kitchin: *Life of Pius II as illustrated by Pinturicchio's Frescoes,* London, 1881.
11. As Aeneas put it. *Commentaries,* Book I.
12. Tommaso della Gazzaia was podestà at this time. The letter was dated 28th February 1432; it is printed by Wolkan: *op. cit.,* Ep. 4. See also C. M. Ady: *Pius II,* p. 28.
13. Wolkan: *op. cit.,* Ep. 7.
14. *Commentaries,* Book I.
15. *De Viris Illustribus,* No. v.
16. C. M. Ady: *Pius II,* pp. 36-7.
17. Paparelli: *Enea Silvio Piccolomini,* p. 46.
18. *Commentaries,* Book VII.
19. *Commentaries,* Books I, VII.
20. *De Officiis,* i. 13. See C. M. Ady: *Pius II,* p. 39.
21. Written in 1457. *La Germania,* ed. G. Paparelli, Firenze (1949).

CHAPTER V

1. *Commentaries,* Book I.
2. *Vita Pii II,* in Muratori: *Rerum Ital. Scriptores,* III, pt. ii, Milan, 1734, p. 974 ff.
3. C. M. Ady: *Pius II,* p. 42, n. 2.
4. *Commentaries,* Book I.
5. From Vienna, 1st June 1451. Wolkan: *op. cit.,* Ep. 5, p. 11. '. . . vetus historia in manus venit, ante annos sexcentos ut signatum erat, conscripta, que si vera est et mee potest et aliorum satisfacere cupiditati.'
6. See authorities quoted by G. G. Coulton: *Life in the Middle Ages,* Cambridge, 1928, vol. I, p. 238 and note.
7. Oxford, Bodleian Library, MS. Digby 135, fo. 1^v.
8. *Ibid.,* ff. 105^v-107^v.
9. *De Viris Illustribus,* No. XXXII.
10. Printed in the *Opera quae extant omnia,* Basel, 1551, pp. 81-143.
11. 'Cuperent tam egregie Scotorum reges quam mediocres Nurnbergae cives abitare!' *La Germania,* ed. G. Paparelli, p. 60.
12. *Commentaries,* Book I. Cf. *Europa,* cap. XLVI.
13. *Commentaries,* Book I.
14. His itinerary has been worked out by Canon James Wilson in *Transactions of the Cumberland and Westmorland Antiq. and Arch. Society,* new ser. XXIII (1923), pp. 17-28.
15. Written 19th November 1444. The child, a boy, died soon after birth. Aeneas wrote philosophically: 'It does happen that more lambs die than sheep.' Wolkan: Ep. 162, p. 449.

16. *Commentaries*, Book II. See also *Europa*, cap. XLVI (*Opera*, p. 443).

17. Particularly by Dr. C. M. Ady: 'Pius II and his experiences of England, Scotland and the English', in *English Miscellany*, vol. IX, Rome, 1958.

18. Wolkan: *op. cit.*, vol. LXVIII, Ep. 133. Written from Graz, 3rd September, 1453. '. . . dentes in ultima Britanie parte, nunc appellant Scotiam, non sine cruciatu perdidi.'

19. The relations of the two countries are well summarized by Dr. C. M. Ady: 'Pius II and his experiences of England, Scotland and the English', pp. 39–49.

CHAPTER VI

1. Wolkan: *op. cit.*, Ep. 28.

2. As he wrote to the Republic of Siena, 1st November 1432. Wolkan: *op. cit.*, Ep. 8.

3. *I.e.* from January to December. Peter Partner in *Italian Renaissance Studies*, ed. Prof. E. F. Jacob, London, 1960, p. 260.

4. *Commentaries*, Book I.

5. The Council was held at Florence in 1438–9, and according to J. S. Gill: *The Council of Florence*, Cambridge, 1959, it had considerable importance in helping the Papacy to maintain its position and ultimately to overcome the Conciliar Movement.

6. *Commentaries*, Book I.

7. *Ibid.*

8. On 24th May 1437. Wolkan: *op. cit.*, Ep. 24.

9. Early in January 1438. C. M. Ady: *Pius II*, p. 61, n. 2.

10. *Commentaries*, Book I.

11. See A. Weiss: *Aeneas Sylvius Piccolomini als Papst Pius II. Sein Leben und Einfluss auf die literarische Kultur Deutschlands*, Graz, 1897, pp. 10 ff.

12. *Commentaries*, Book I.

13. *Commentaries*, Book VII.

14. *Libellus dialogorum de Generalis Concilii authoritate et gestis Basiliensium*, printed by A. F. Kollar in *Analecta monumentorum omnis aevi Vindobonensia*, vol. II (Vienna, 1762), coll., 691–790.

15. *Opera Omnia*, Basel, 1571, pp. 1–63.

CHAPTER VII

1. J. Chmel: Vienna, 1840, p. xxix.

2. Francesco Pizzolpasso. The letter is dated 5th December 1442. Wolkan: *op. cit.*, Ep. 41.

3. His name was Porcellio Pandone. See T. de Marinis: *La biblioteca dei re d'Aragona*, Milano, 1952, vol. I, p. 5.

4. *Cronache e statuti della città di Viterbo*, ed. I. Ciampi, Firenze, 1872, pp. 217–18.

5. Jean de Champdenier. Quoted by Du Fresne de Beaucourt: *Histoire de Charles VII*, tome V, Paris, 1890, p. 201.

6. Printed by B. Pez: *Thesaurus anecdotorum novissimus*, Vienna, 1721–9, tom. IV, iii, pp. 736–44.

7. *Commentaries*, Book I.

8. See Chapter III. In *La Germania* (ed. G. Paparelli, Firenze, 1949, p. 56) Aeneas describes his benefactor as: 'Gaspar Schlickius, . . . vir rarissimae laudis'.

9. *Commentaries*, Book I.

10. Act II, Sc. 1.

11. *Commentaries*, Book I. He was quoting Horace: *Satires*, 1, 9, 20.

12. Bibl. Lobkovitz, Cod. 462. See *Chrysis*, ed. I. Sanese, Florence, 1941, introduction.

13. To Count Johann von Lupfen; Wolkan: *op. cit.*, Ep. 135.

14. *Ibid.*, Ep. 158. On *Chrysis* see Paparelli: *E. S. Piccolomini*, p. 94, n. 23.

15. Wolkan: *op. cit.*, pp. 286–7.

16. *Commentaries*, Book I.

17. Act II, Sc. 7.

18. 'Britannicus' is often wrongly translated as 'English' at this period. (*E.g.* C. M. Ady: *Pius II*, p. 98, and other authorities.) On this whole question see the evidence collected by R. J. Mitchell in *Italian Studies*, VIII, p. 98 (1952).

19. 13th November 1442. For the place of birth see Wolkan: *op. cit.*, Ep. 162.

20. Wolkan: *op. cit.*, Ep. 78. This letter describes Aeneas's affair with 'Elizabeth' in some detail. It has been translated by Miss Flora Grierson and printed under the title 'Frank Confession' in *The London Magazine*, vol. I, no. 5 (June 1954), pp. 70–4.

21. At Todi, in 1462. *Commentaries*, Book X.

22. Wolkan: *op. cit.*, Ep. 162. On 19th November 1444. Aeneas's fortieth birthday was exactly eleven months later.

23. In the *Historia Friderici III*; A. F. Kollar: *op. cit.*, vol. II, p. 123.

24. Wolkan: *op. cit.*, Ep. 170. For Aeneas's reply, 18th February 1444, *ibid.*, Ep. 125.

25. Johann Tuschek, 31st October 1444. Wolkan: *op. cit.*, Ep. 159.

26. Voigt: *op. cit.*, vol. I, p. 367, says he was ordained in Rome, July 1446, but see C. M. Ady: *Pius II*, p. 100.

27. *Commentaries*, Book I.

28. *Ibid.*

29. *Ibid.*

30. They happened to meet at San Casciano, where they had a drink together 'and renewed their former understanding'. *Commentaries*, Book I.

31. Afterwards Cardinal. He had already acted as legate in the Imperial Court, where the foundations of his strong friendship with Aeneas were laid.

32. To Giovanni Campisio, September 1446. Wolkan: *op. cit.*, Ep. 185.

33. The Archbishop of Mainz needed a bribe. *Hist. Frid. III*, p. 127. See also Ady: *op. cit.*, p. 94. This was Archbishop Dietrich (d. 6th May 1459), of whom Aeneas afterwards wrote in the *Commentaries*, Book III: 'an ignorant man who had corrupted his virile nature with harlotry and feasting. The

one good thing by which he earned renown was that, during the Schism of the Council of Basel, he supported the apostolic see. And even this virtue he lost in his extreme old age, when he had become lacking in loyalty and eager for dissension.'

34. That is to say, four papal documents were issued, dated 5th and 7th February 1447, forming what is known as the Concordat of the Princes. See Pastor: *op. cit.*, vol. I, p. 349.

35. Kollar: *op. cit.*, p. 127. On Aeneas's passionate desire for the unity of the Church see I del Lungo: 'Umanista e pontefice' in *Rassegna nazionale*, 16th November 1905, 187.

CHAPTER VIII

1. Ed. L. Mehus; Florence, 1745, p. 26.
2. Cardinal of Santa Croce.
3. *Commentaries*, Book I.
4. On 19th March 1447, the fourth Sunday in Lent. See Pio Paschini: *Roma nel rinascimento*, Bologna, 1940, p. 171.
5. Printed by Wolkan: *op. cit.*, Ep. 44.
6. In 1446. *De ortu et authoritate Romani Imperii*. Wolkan: *op. cit.*, vol. II, Ep. 3 (pp. 6–24). The text, with German translation, is printed by G. Kallen: *Aen. Silv. Piccolomini als Publizist*, Cologne, 1939 (pp. 52–96).
7. *De Liberorum Educatione;* printed by Wolkan: *op. cit.*, vol. II, Ep. 40 (pp. 103–58). Text and translation by J. S. Nelson, Washington, 1940. (W. H. Woodward made a free translation in *Vittorino da Feltre and other Humanist Educators*, Cambridge, 1897, pp. 134–58.)
8. On 16th September 1443; Wolkan: *op. cit.*, Ep. 76. See also Ady: *op. cit.*, p. 110.
9. Woodward: *op. cit.*, p. 138.
10. On 13th November 1449. The letter is printed by Voigt: *op. cit.*, vol. III, pp. 394–7.
11. Cod. 1200 in the Bibl. Universitaria at Bologna, fo. 293 ff., has a very beautiful copy of the *Dialogus De Somnio*, written out by Goro Lolli. It was printed at Rome, 11th September 1475, by Johann Schurener. There is the copy in the Bodleian (Auct. 6.Q.5.30).
12. R. J. Mitchell: *John Free*, London 1955, pp. 128–9. The only known copy of this work (Cod. Vat. Lat. 1713) was discovered in the Vatican Library by Professor R. Weiss who kindly drew my attention to it.
13. R. Weiss: 'New light on Humanism in England in the XVth Century', in the *Journal of the Warburg and Courtauld Institutes*, XIV, pp. 30–1.
14. *Commentaries*, Book I.
15. *Commentaries*, Book I.
16. *I.e.* the Duomo. *Commentaries*, Book I.
17. He drafted in mercenaries, in case there should be trouble, and appointed thirteen regionary marshals to control them. Gregorovius: *History of the City of Rome*, etc., vol. VII, part i, p. 123.

18. L. Fumi & A. Lisini: *L'incontro di Federigo III imperatore con Eleanora di Portogallo . . . in Siena*. Siena, 1878.

19. *Ibid.*, pp. 47–8. The decree for its erection 'sul prato di Camollia' is dated 11th–13th March (1452). The column was in two pieces; special provision was made for a solid block of marble to form the base and a smooth tablet for incising the letters of the commemorative inscription.

20. *Hist. Frid. III*, p. 292. Charles IV was Emperor from 1346–78. The coronation is fully described, with long quotations from Infessura, in Pio Paschini: *Roma nel rinascimento*, pp. 177–8.

21. *Commentaries*, Book I.

22. On 12th July 1453. The letter is printed in *Pii II Opera*, Ep. 162. News of the disaster had been brought to Rome on July 7; it was announced next day to the people by the Franciscan preacher Roberto da Lecce. Paschini: *op. cit.*, p. 184.

23. See Aeneas's *History of the Diet of Ratisbon*, printed among his speeches in J. D. Mansi: *Pii II Pont. Max. Orationes politicae et ecclesiasticae*, Lucca, 1755–59, vol. III, pp. 1–85.

24. *Opera*, Ep. 405.

25. *Commentaries*, Book I.

26. Pastor: *op. cit.*, II, pp. 304–5.

27. *Commentaries*, Book I.

28. Dated 2nd December 1455. Now in the R. Bibl. Palatina at Parma. *Carteggio Lucca, 1° Supplemento*. I am indebted to the Direttore not only for permission to reproduce this MS. but also for his kindness in locating it for me.

29. Brit. Mus. Add. MS. 21517, fo. 2. It is not absolutely established that the earliest letter is autograph, but the probability is very strong that the explanation given is the true one.

30. *Ibid.*, ff. 5, 6. None of these letters to the Priori appears to have been printed, nor the autograph epistle that is in the Bibl. Laurenziana at Florence. Cod. 90, 44.

31. *Commentaries*, Book I.

32. Printed with an Italian translation by G. Paparelli, Florence, 1949.

33. Antonio Beccadelli, known as Il Panormita. See Paparelli: *E. S. Piccolomini*, pp. 162–3.

34. Pp. 37–40. Vespasiano da Biscicci says that Alfonso assigned 20,000 a year to the learned men in his court, paying a particularly handsome pension to the humanist Gianozzo Manetti. *Vite* etc., p. 52.

35. He said the bishopric of Siena was 'unfruitful as an elm tree'. A. Weiss, Ep. 130.

36. See J. Bayer: *Die 'Historia Friderici III' des E. S. Piccolomini*, Prague, 1872.

37. Printed in the *Opera Omnia*, pp. 387–471.

38. Some of the best of these are printed in part B of Berthe Widmer: *E. S. Piccolomini, Papst Pius II*, Basel/Stuttgart, 1960.

39. *Opera Omnia*, pp. 81–148.

40. *Commentaries*, Book I.

CHAPTER IX

1. *Cronache e statuti della città di Viterbo*, p. 71.
2. The issues at stake are well summarized by Dr C. M. Ady: *Pius II*, pp. 142–3. See also Gerhart Bürck: *Selbstdarstellung und Personenbildnis bei Enea Silvio Piccolomini*, Stuttgart, 1956.
3. The dispatch of Otto de Carretto is printed by Pastor, *op. cit.*, Appendix 1.
4. Pastor says that the first Capitulations were made at the election of Pope Boniface VIII (1294): *op. cit.*, I, p. 283. They were taken much more seriously, however, from the years following the death of Martin V (1431). See Mandell Creighton: *History of the Papacy* (new edn.), London, 1919, vol. III, p. 202.
5. *Commentaries*, Book I. The whole story is told here in such detail that the narrative in this chapter is taken directly from it and no further references need be given.
6. *Op. cit.* (Muratori, vol. III, pt. 2), p. 944.
7. News reached Siena the day after the election in a letter from Leonardo Benvoglienti, Sienese orator to Calixtus III. See Malavolti: *Historia di Siena*, Venice, 1599, Book III, part 3, p. 60ʳ.
8. *Cronache e statuti*, etc., p. 71.
9. John Free to William Grey, Bishop of Ely. Printed in an appendix to R. J. Mitchell: *John Free*, pp. 140–2.
10. Roberto da Sanseverino: *Viaggio in Terra Santa*, ed. G. Maruffi, Bologna, 1888, p. 189.

CHAPTER X

1. Dr E. Pellegrin: *La Bibliothèque des Visconti et des Sforza*, Paris, 1955, p. 338.
2. Art. v in Cod. Parm. 27, R. Bibl. Palatina, Parma. There is another MS. in the Bibl. Comunale at Savignano di Romagna (Cod. 33). The letters have not been printed.
3. In 1396. For this whole campaign see A. S. Atiya: *The Crusade of Nicopolis*, London, 1934, also the same author's article on *Nikopolis* in the *Enciclopedia italianica*.
4. Mostly from the Duke of Burgundy, who guaranteed with great magnanimity to finance the operation. A. S. Atiya: *The Crusade in the Later Middle Ages*, London, 1938, p. 460.
5. For a summary of the position see Atiya: *The Crusade in the Later Middle Ages*, pp. 466–8.
6. Atiya, *op. cit.*, p. 467. See also G. Schlumberger: *Siège, prise et sac de Constantinople par les Turcs en 1453*, Paris, 1926.
7. G. Toffanin, in his introduction to the *Lettera a Maometto II*, Napoli, 1952, p. xv.
8. Printed at Brussels in 1846. See Atiya: *op. cit.*, pp. 208–11.
9. *Opera*, Ep. 405.
10. It was printed in Rome without a date, probably by Stephan Plannck. There

is a copy in the Bibl. Univ. at Bologna, another in the British Museum (IA. 1869²). A slightly different version is to be found in the Bibl. Marciana at Venice. Neither is identical with the *Epistola* printed in the *Opera* (Basel, 1551), p. 678.

11. Printed with an Italian translation and introduction by G. Toffanin; Napoli, 1952.

12. The letters from Venice reached him at Spoleto. *Commentaries*, Book II.

13. G. B. Picotti: *La dieta di Mantova*, Venice, 1912, p. 400.

14. *The Papal State in the XIIIth Century*, London, 1961, pp. 80–1. Dr Waley is describing Rome two centuries earlier, but the basic economic facts were still the same.

15. *Commentaries*, Book II. On the relationship between Rome and Avignon see G. Mollat: *Les Papes d'Avignon* (9th edn.), Paris, 1949.

16. By a Bull dated 5th January 1459. F. Gregorovius: *History of the City of Rome in the Middle Ages*, trans. A. Hamilton, London, 1900. Vol. VII, part i, p. 175, n. 2.

17. *Commentaries*, Book II.

18. Francesco Cerasoli: 'Il viaggio di Pio II da Rome a Mantova', in *Il Buonar- roti*, serie iii, vol. IV, quaderno 6, Rome, 1891. (The MS. of Saracini's ac- count book is in the Arch. di Stato at Rome.)

19. *Commentaries*, Book II.

20. *Vita Pii II*, in Muratori: *Rerum Ital. Scriptores*, III, pt. ii, p. 975, Milano, 1734.

21. Cerasoli: *op. cit.*, p. 3.

22. *Ibid.*, p. 4.

23. *Commentaries*, Book II. See also Gasparo Zonta: 'Un conflitto tra la Repub- blica Veneta e la Curia Romana, per l'episcopato di Padova (1459–60)' in *Atti e Memorie della R. Accademia di Scienze, Lettere ed Arti in Padova*, vol. XI (1924).

24. *Commentaries*, Book II. The speech is printed in J. D. Mansi: *Orationes Pii II*, etc. Lucca, 1753, vol. II, pp. 1–4.

25. Cerasoli: *op. cit.*, pp. 4–5.

26. *Commentaries*, Book II.

27. *Cronache e statuti della città di Viterbo*, p. 258.

28. *Commentaries*, Book II. The chronicler Giovanni Cambi, in describing the event, said: 'The preparations had been great, and the expense large, but the pleasure given was small.' Quoted by Janet Ross: *Lives of the Early Medici*, London, 1910, pp. 61–2.

29. Gregorovius: *History of the City of Rome* etc. Vol. VII, part 1, p. 120, n. 1.

30. See Julia Cartwright: *Italian Gardens of the Renaissance*, London, 1914, pp. 13–14.

31. Cerasoli: *op. cit.*, p. 5.

32. Giulio Ricci: 'Il pontefice Pio II a Bologna' in *Il Comune di Bologna*, Febru- ary 1932.

33. C. M. Ady: *The Bentivoglio of Bologna*, Oxford, 1937, p. 53.

34. Cerasoli: *op. cit.*, p. 6.

35. *Commentaries*, Book II.

36. *Diario Ferrarese*, Muratori, new series, vol. XXIV, pp. 39–40; 41–2.

37. The book exists as a rare incunabule: it was printed at Rome in 1491 and at Messina eight years later. There is a copy in the University Library at Bologna (AVB.IX.32).

38. G. B. Manucci: 'Il viaggio di Pio II da Roma a Mantova', *Bulletino Senese di Storia Patria*, new series, 1941, fasc. i, p. 4.

39. He arrived at the Porta de la Pradela late in the evening. See Andrea Schivenoglia: *Cronaca di Mantova*, p. 135.

40. It is now in the British Museum—Add. MS. 21984. See E. Pellegrin: *op. cit.*, p. 367. Ippolita was only twelve years old in July 1458, the date of this MS, so she cannot have been as much as 14 on 28th May 1459, as is generally stated. She died in 1488.

41. See the excellent study of Vittorino by Mandell Creighton: *Historical Essays and Reviews*, London, 1902; also W. H. Woodward: *Vittorino da Feltre and other Humanist Educators*, Cambridge, 1907.

42. *Commentaries*, Book III.

43. *Op. cit.*, p. 183.

44. Bibl. de l'Arsenal 1222. For a description of this MS. see E. Pellegrin: *op. cit.*, p. 397.

45. Pastor: *op. cit.*, vol. III, p. 67.

46. A. B. Hind: *Calendar of State Papers and MSS. in Milan*, vol. I, London, 1922, p. 21.

47. Sir N. H. Nicolas: *Privy Council Proceedings*, vol. VI, London, 1937, p. 302.

48. R. J. Mitchell: *John Tiptoft*, London, 1938, p. 61.

49. *Ibid.*, p. 62.

50. *Commentaries*, Book III.

51. *Ibid.*

52. Schivenoglia: *Cronaca di Mantova*, pp. 140–1.

53. *Commentaries*, Book III.

54. Printed by Mansi: *op. cit.*, vol. II, pp. 9–29.

55. '. . . recita una dignissima e mirabile oratione'. *Cronaca di Veronese, 1448–1488*, ed. G. Soranzo, Venezia, 1915, p. 131.

56. In Pius's own hand there is a note written in the margin of the Vatican Manuscript Cod. Reg. 1995, p. 156, saying that the speech proved 'how far more eloquent he was in Greek than in Latin'. (See note on the *Commentaries*, Bibliography I.)

57. Quoted by Pastor: *op. cit.*, vol., III, appendix 27, p. 390.

58. *Commentaries*, Book III; cf. C. Roth: *A History of the Jews in Italy*, Philadelphia, 1946, pp. 177–8.

59. Pastor: *op. cit.*, p. 93: cf. also Voigt: *op. cit.*, vol. III, p. 85.

60. *Commentaries*, Book III.

61. *Commentaries*, Book III. Pius transcribes the full text of the Bull, which is printed by Mansi, *Orationes*, vol. II.

62. *Commentaries*, Book III (end).

CHAPTER XI

1. Schivenoglia: *Cronaca di Mantova*, etc., p. 144. The party boarded two barges and twenty-eight smaller boats—'2 bucentorij e 28 nave'. Several other Cardinals travelled to Revere by road.
2. *Ibid.*, p. 145.
3. *Commentaries*, Book IV.
4. S. Benedetto Po'. See G. B. Manucci: *Pienza: arte e storia*, 3rd edn., 1937, pp. 6–7. There is a terracotta replica of the bust of Pius II in the Bibl. Piccolomini at Pienza.
5. *Commentaries*, Book IV.
6. As Roberto Sanseverino and his companions found the previous year—*Viaggio in Terra Santa*, pp. 308–9.
7. *Commentaries*, Book IV.
8. *Lives of the Early Medici*, ed. Janet Ross, London, 1910, pp. 62–3. Giovanni responded to treatment on this occasion, but three years later he died from his disorders. These are described in detail by G. A. Pieraccini: *La stirpe de' Medici di Cafaggiolo*, Florence, 1925, vol. I, pp. 82–7, where he has much to say of the spas at Petriolo, Macereto, and Morba.
9. *Calendars of Papal Registers*, ed. J. A. Twemlow, vol. IX, London, 1921, p. 404.
10. L. Fumi: 'Pio II e la pace d'Orvieto', *Studi e Documenti*, vol. VI, pp. 249 ff.
11. Niccola della Tuccia: *Cronache e statuti della città di Viterbo*, pp. 81–2.
12. Mandell Creighton: *History of the Papacy*, new edn., London, 1919, vol. III, p. 311. The same author develops this theme in his article on Aeneas Sylvius in *Historical Essays and Reviews*, London, 1902, pp. 102–3.
13. Although there are many apocryphal replies—one of them written in Middle High German. Atiya: *op. cit.*, p. 228, n. 2.
14. I. del Lungo: *Umanista e pontefice*, Florence, 1905, p. 21.
15. *Lettera a Maometto II*, ed. G. Toffanin, Naples, 1952, cap. XIX.
16. Esp. Paparelli: *op. cit.*, pp. 317 ff. (quoting Toffanin's introduction to the *Lettera*); cf. also Gregorovius; *op. cit.*, vol. VII, pt. i, p. 204, n.
17. MS. Canonici Class. Lat. 151 ff. 52–85 (art. iii). 'Bernard' signs his name in Greek characters.
18. 'Data Senis Kalendis Quint, Millesimo quad, sexagesimo.'
19. Paparelli: *op. cit.*, pp. 318 ff.

CHAPTER XII

1. Translated and printed by Janet Ross: *Lives of the Early Medici*, London, 1910, p. 47.
2. Pastor: *op. cit.*, p. 111 and n.
3. For an excellent description of this papal province see Daniel Waley: *The Papal State in the Thirteenth Century*, London, 1961, pp. 81–3.
4. Gregorovius: *op. cit.*, p. 132.
5. In *The Tale of the Two Lovers*. See Chapter III.
6. Gregorovius: *op. cit.*, p. 139, n. 1.

7. He was brother-in-law to Porcaro, who had married his sister. *Commentaries*, Book IV.

8. *Ibid.*

9. Vulg. Psalm XC, 13.

10. C. M. Ady: *Pius II*, p. 197.

11. *Commentaries*, Book XI.

12. *Ibid.*, Book IV.

13. *Travels and Adventures of Pero Tafur;* ed. M. Letts. London, 1926, p. 43.

14. Waley: *op. cit.*, pp. 83, 87.

15. According to Giovanni Rucellai, quoted by Pio Paschini: *Roma nel Rinascimento*, Bologna, 1940, p. 175.

16. *Op. cit.*, p. 38. (From the Life of Pope Nicholas V.)

17. Gregorovius: *op. cit.*, p. 157.

18. Quoted *ibid.*, p. 187.

19. *Scritti inediti e rari di Biondo Flavio,* ed. B. Nogara, Rome, 1927, pp. 202–3.

20. Pastor: *op. cit.*, p. 301–2, n.

21. Not to be confused with the other Francesco Aretino, whose surname was Accolti. See G. Mancini: *Francesco Griffolini, cognominato Francesco Aretino*, Florence, 1890.

22. I am indebted to Professor Weiss for this information.

23. The dedication is found on fo. 1. of Cod. A. 914 in the Biblioteca Comunale at Bologna.

24. *Commentaries*, Book XI.

25. These notes are printed in the *Opera* of Pius II, pp. 144–281; see also 'The Decades of Flavio Biondo' by Prof. Denys Hay, *Proceedings of the British Academy* XLV (1959), pp. 97–128. Also pp. 34–8 of this author's *The Italian Renaissance*, etc. Cambridge, 1961.

26. Cod. A. 76. Inf. in the Bibl. Ambrosiana, Milan. See Pastor: *op. cit.*, p. 273 (notes).

27. Published in *Horatii Romani Porcaria:* ed. M. Lenerdt, Leipzig, 1907, pp. 42–53. I am indebted to Professor Weiss for this information.

28. R. Weiss: *Italian Studies* (1960).

29. It was printed by Sweynheym and Pannartz in Rome, 1471 (Proctor 3317). Tiraboschi (*Storia della lett. ital.*, vol. VI, pp. 833–4) says that Niccolò was twenty-two at the time of his death in 1473, but he must have been at least twenty-seven since he wrote his version of Hesiod not later than 1464 (*i.e.* during Pius's lifetime).

30. There were 238 in all. See E. W. Bligh: *Sir Kenelm Digby and his Venetia*, London, 1932, pp. 205 ff.

31. For Filippo Maria Visconti. MS. Digby 224. See F. Maggini: *I primi volgarizzamente dei classici latini*, Florence, 1952, pp. 54–70; also E. Pellegrin: *op. cit.*, p. 386; and Otto Pacht: *Catalogue of Italian Illum. MSS.*, Oxford, 1948, pp. 25–6.

32. Perhaps by Francesco d'Antonio del Cherico. See Pacht: *op. cit.*, p. 26. This is hardly likely to be the copy of Cicero's *Orationes* that Aeneas in his early

days had asked a friend to find for him (Wolkan: LXI, p. 162, Ep. 62) for it must have been very expensive.

33. London, V. & A. Museum, MS. K.R. Press D. 12.

34. According to an original letter, dated 1907, from Alessandro Lisini of the Archivio di Stato, Siena; this is attached to the MS.

35. See the instances in Eugenio Casanova: 'Un anno della vita privata di Pio II', *Bullettino Senese di Storia Patria*, new ser., anno II, 1931, fasc. I, pp. 19–34.

36. *De humanae vitae felicitate*.

37. The letter is dated from Rome, 25th March 1457 (i.e. when he was still Cardinal). It is printed by L. Mehus: *Bartholomaei Facii de Viris Illustribus*, Florence, 1745, pp. 82–3.

38. The words are reported by John Free in the dedication to John Tiptoft of his own translation of a minor work of Synesius of Cyrene (MS. Bodl: 80 in the Bodleian Library at Oxford).

Caxton in his prologue to Tiptoft's *Declamacion of Noblesse*, London, 1481, exclaims: 'What worship had he at Rome, in the presence of our holy fader the Pope!' He was probably mistaken: it is much more likely that Tiptoft's oration was made in Ferrara. See R. J. Mitchell: *John Free*, London, 1955, p. 106.

CHAPTER XIII

1. Peter Partner: *The Papal State under Martin V*, London, 1958, p. 196.

2. Vespasiano da Bisticci: *op. cit.*, p. 191.

3. In 1429. See Partner: *op. cit.*, p. 193, also in *Italian Renaissance Studies*, London, 1960, p. 256.

4. Book XII. In actual fact, the total recorded in the *Introitus et Exitus* for September 1461–August 1462 was 471,694 florins. Partner: 'The "Budget" of the Roman Church in the Renaissance Period' in *Italian Ren. Studies*, p. 260.

5. *Commentaries*, Book VII.

6. He lost no time in issuing a Bull (dated 7th April 1463) exhorting all Christians to buy alum only from the Papacy. By this time 8,000 workers were already employed in the industry.

7. *Op. cit.* The translation is by Flora Grierson. Voigt: *op. cit.*, III, p. 548, gives 1462 as the date of the discovery and, on balance, this is probably correct.

8. Giulio Ricci: 'Il pontefice Pio II a Bologna', *Il Comune di Bologna* No. 2 (February 1932).

9. C. M. Ady: *op. cit.*, p. 192.

10. Bartolomeo Vitelleschi, 'a man of great intelligence', who had been sent as legate to the army in the March (Pastor: *op. cit.*, vol. III, p. 120). *Commentaries*, Book v.

11. '. . . he was proved guilty of homicide, rape, adultery, incest, sacrilege, perjury, treachery, and an almost infinite number of most disgusting . . . crimes.' *Commentaries*, Book VII.

12. P. E. Jones: 'The end of Malatesta Rule in Rimini'; *Italian Renaissance Studies*, pp. 230–1.
13. The city fell on 25th September 1463. G. Soranzo: *Pio II e la politica italiana nella lotta contro i Malatesti (1457–1463)*, Padua, 1911, p. 461.
14. Laudomia, who married Nanni Todeschini. The other three boys were Andrea, Giacomo, and Francesco.
15. Wolkan: *op. cit.*, Ep. 37.
16. Quoted C. M. Ady: *op. cit.*, p. 191.
17. Pastor summarizes this report, *op. cit.*, pp. 142–8. Otto wrote it from Rome, 15th March 1462.
18. *Commentaries*, Book VII.
19. He was the more obstinate because he was mentally deranged, if not actually insane. According to Pius he imagined himself to be made of glass and insisted upon wearing iron bands under his clothes to protect his brittle frame. *Commentaries*, Book VII.
20. His letter to Pius II telling him of the abolition was dated 27th November 1461, but the formal announcement was reserved for the embassy planned for the following March.
21. *Commentaries*, Book VII. The speech is printed in Mansi: *op. cit.*, vol. II, pp. 103–14.
22. Printed by Pastor: *op. cit.* (appendix), pp. 406–7.
23. *Commentaries*, Book VII.
24. Nicodemus of Pontremoli to Francesco Sforza, from Florence, 31st May 1462. Quoted by Pastor: *op. cit.*, vol. III, p. 153, n.
25. *Commentaries*, Book VI.
26. The map in his *De Europa* notices no towns in the British Isles except London, 'Douer', and 'Edinburg'. *Opera*, Basel, 1571, p. 445.
27. Bishop of Terni until his disgrace in 1462.
28. C. M. Ady: 'Pius II and his experiences of England', in *English Miscellany* (Rome, 1958), vol. IX, pp. 48–9.
29. Students of the University of Paris performed a play in which the rats that gnawed the seals of the Pragmatic Sanction were awarded red hats. Pastor: *op. cit.*, p. 157, n. †.
30. For an able analysis of the issues at stake see Voigt: *Enea Silvio de' Piccolomini als Papst Pius II und sein Zeitalter*, vol. III, p. 213–19. In Pius's description of the affairs of Austria, *Commentaries*, Book XI, it may be noted that he refers to the revolting crimes of Count Dracula, who seems to have committed every imaginable offence except that he was not a vampire.
31. Printed at Basel, 1571 (*Opera*).
32. Adolphus of Nassau—'a man beloved alike by the clergy and the people' according to Pope Pius: *Commentaries*, Book VI. In the end Diether recognized Adolphus as Archbishop, in return for a grant of lands, and received absolution, but not until October 1463.
33. Printed by Mansi: *op. cit.*, I, p. 352. See also p. 103 above.
34. Howard Karminsky: 'Pius Aeneas among the Taborites' in *Church History* (American Society of Church History), September 1959.

35. A recent writer suggests that agrarian and economic forces were at work and were far more important than the religious question: though there is much to be said for this view it is not wholly acceptable. See Josef Macek: *The Hussite Movement in Bohemia*, Prague, 1958.

36. Quoted by Pastor: *op. cit.*, p. 229.

37. He had shown his hatred of heresy already in combating the Waldenses, and in a lesser degree by taking stern measures against Reginald Pecock in 1459 (when Pius deprived him of the Bishopric of Chichester). See Pastor: *op. cit.*, pp. 285–6.

38. C. Roth: *A History of the Jews in Italy*, Philadelphia, 1946, pp. 177–8.

CHAPTER XIV

1. See Chapter XIII. As stated on p. 7 the reader is referred to the profound and detailed works of Voigt and Pastor. Volume III of the latter's *Lives of the Popes* will be found particularly valuable for its very clear analysis.

2. The words are the Pope's, but the sentiments were certainly Federigo's.

3. *Commentaries*, Book V.

4. The words are still preserved on the gateway:

> 'Grata bonis, invisa malis, inimica superbis
> Sum tibi, Tybur, enim sic Pius instituit.'

5. *Op. cit.*

6. Letter from Biondo Flavio to Goro Lolli: *Scritti inediti e rari di Biondo Flavio*, ed. Bartolomeo Nogara, Rome, 1927, pp. 193–202 (letter no. 18).

7. *Ibid.*, pp. clxiii–clxiv.

8. Where Carvajal held the office of Administrator. *Commentaries*, Book VI.

9. *Commentaries*, Book VI.

10. *Commentaries*, (end of) Book VI.

CHAPTER XV

1. Burchard Weissbriach, whose appointment was not published until 31st May 1462 (at Viterbo). Pastor: *op. cit.*, p. 300; Bishop of Rieti, brother of Domenico, Cardinal Capranica, Bishop of Fermo, Aeneas's first employer.

2. *Commentaries*, Book VII.

3. There is a useful biography of Ammanati by G. Calamari: *Il confidente di Pio II*, preface by Albano Sorbelli, 2 vols., Rome, 1932.

4. Domenico de' Domenichi. For a detailed account of the two schemes see Pastor: *op. cit.*, p. 269 ff.

5. See Chapter IX.

6. *Commentaries*, Book II.

7. It exists in MS. in the Barberini library at Rome; Pastor prints an abstract of it, *op. cit.*, appendix no. 42; he dates it as written in Siena after the Congress of Mantua, *i.e.*, summer 1460.

8. *Commentaries*, Book XI.

9. *Ibid.*, Book III.

10. Horace: *Satires* II, ii, 31. But Lewis and Short say this is pike.

11. *Commentaries*, Book xi.
12. *Ibid.*
13. Agostino Patrizio. It may be presumed that Pius was dictating the *Commentaries;* this would account for the eye-witness character of his description.
14. *Commentaries*, Book xi.
15. Pliny, iii. 5.9.959.
16. *Commentaries*, Book xi.
17. *Commentaries*, Book viii.
18. See also Niccola della Tuccia: *Cronache . . . di Viterbo*, pp. 81–2. But the people of Viterbo objected very strongly to lodging without payment the troops that the Pope sent there the following year. *Ibid.*, p. 83.
19. *Commentaries*, Book viii.
20. *Ibid.*
21. Virgil: *Aeneid IV*, 462.
22. *Aeneid V*, 135 *et seq.*

CHAPTER XVI

1. Recorded by his chamberlain Niccolò Piccolomini. See Eugenio Casanova: 'Un anno della vita privata di Pio II' in *Bullettino Senese di Storia Patria*, new ser., anno II (1931), fasc. i, pp. 25, 27.
2. *Commentaries*, Book v.
3. Campano: *Vita Pii II.*
4. *Commentaries*, Book v.
5. Although he had been anxious to prevent her from coming, sending Cardinal Estouteville to Ostia in the hope of dissuading her. Pastor: *op. cit.*, p. 253.
6. The Cardinals were asked to supply a further 200 monthly. C. M. Ady: *op. cit.*, p. 310.
7. Thomas died 12th May 1465, his wife three years earlier. See Pastor: *op. cit.*, pp. 249–52.
8. The cope is fully described by G. B. Manucci: 'Il piviale di Pio II nel museo della cattedrale di Pienza' in the review, *Arte Cristiana*, July 1929. See also an article by May Morris in the *Burlington Magazine*, 1905.
9. He was the same Otto de Carretto who wrote such vivid descriptive letters to his master on other occasions. See Pastor: *op. cit.*, p. 250, n. *.
10. *Commentaries*, Book viii.
11. 11th April 1462. G. B. Manucci: *Pienza: arte e storia* (3rd edn., 1937), p. 46, says the date should be April 14 but as Easter Sunday fell on April 18 in 1462 the first date is obviously the right one. I am indebted to Canon Aldo Franci for pointing this out.
12. See Chapter heading.
13. *Commentaries*, Book viii. A tabernacle costing a hundred ducats was put in hand forthwith.
14. *Epistolario Santa Caterina con note di Niccolò Tommaseo*, Siena, 1913. There is a useful short biography of the saint by Can. D. Alfredo Silvestri: *S. Caterina, patrona primaria d'Italia, e Pio II*, Pistoja, 1940.

15. *The Life of St Catherine of Siena*, trans. by George Lamb; London, 1960, p. 357.
16. 29th June. See Carlo Baldini: *Pio II e la canonizzatione di S. Caterina*, Siena, 1958.
17. *Commentaries*, Book v.
18. The order was not confirmed until 1324; twenty years later it was further approved by Pope Clement V. See the study of Monte Oliveto by John Addington Symonds in *New Italian Sketches*, Leipzig, 1883, pp. 34–56.
19. *Commentaries*, Book x.

CHAPTER XVII

1. The date of laying the foundation stone is not certain: Biondo gives it as the Feast of S. Lorenzo (10th August), 1460. *Scritti inediti e rari di Biondo Flavio*, ed. B. Nogara, Rome, 1927, pp. clxx; 236.
2. *Op. cit.*, pp. 236–8.
3. *New Italian Sketches*, pp. 76–7.
4. *Commentaries*, Book ix.
5. The Piccolomini palace in Siena was built by Giacomo and other members of the family several years after the completion of Pienza; it is on similar lines though it lacks the prospect. The *Loggia del Papa* in Siena is one of the most graceful examples of Renaissance architecture; an inscription states that Pius dedicated the loggia to his family. The architect was Antonio Federighi.
6. Various portraits of the Pope exist; details and reproductions are given by Mons. G. B. Manucci in *Pienza: arte e storia* (3rd edn., 1937), pp. 1–10. The best likenesses are probably to be found in the medal by Andrea Guazzalotti of Prato (obverse) and the bust at S. Benedetto, for they both conform closely to Campano's description of the Pope's features.
7. *Commentaries*, Book ix. A full description of the palace and an even fuller one of the Cathedral are to be found in chapter xii of Dr Ady's *Pius II*.
8. Manucci: *op. cit.*, p. 68.
9. *Commentaries*, Book ix.
10. *Ibid*.
11. A. Bartacci: 'Il restauro del duomo di Pienza'; *La Diana* ix (1934), pp. 5–134.
12. Especially Sano di Pietro, Vecchietta, and above all Matteo di Giovanni. See the excellent article, with illustrations, by Manucci: *op. cit.*, pp. 115–121.
13. Especially that which commemorates the election of Pius II in 1458. (It belongs, however, to the year 1460.) See E. Carli: *La pittura senese*, Florence, 1935.
14. It is reproduced by Manucci: *op. cit.*, p. 7.
15. Eugenio Casanova: 'Un anno della vita privata di Pio II', *Bullettino Senese di Storia Patria*, new ser., anno II (1931), fasc. I, pp. 19–34.
16. *Commentaries*, Book ix.
17. *Commentaries*, Book ix.

18. The *palio* for a donkey was generally of linen or canvas. See Edward Armstrong: *Italian Studies*, London, 1934, p. 116. For a contemporary picture of a donkey race see the fresco in the Schifanoia Palace at Ferrara.

19. Cardinal Alessandro de Oliva. He is confused with the (unnamed) owner of the favourite in the first race in Armstrong: *op. cit.*, p. 117.

20. *Commentaries*, Book IX (end).

CHAPTER XVIII

1. Ed. Gaetano de Mincis & Marco Tabarrini, Florence, 1870.

2. *Commentaries*, Book IV.

3. *Ibid.* This was during Federigo of Urbino's campaign to recover the Sabina.

4. Pastor: *op. cit.*, p. 314.

5. The letter is in the Gonzaga archives at Mantua.

6. See the note on the *Commentaries* in Select Bibliography I.

7. Pastor: *op. cit.*, p. 318.

8. *Commentaries*, Book XII.

9. Excerpt by Pastor: *op. cit.*, p. 373.

10. Carvajal had at last succeeded (at Wiener-Neustadt, 24th July 1463) in engineering peace in Hungary, with the recognition of Matthias Corvinus as king for life. Pastor: *op. cit.*, p. 316.

11. *Commentaries*, Book XII.

12. *Ibid.*

13. Leonardo Benvoglienti. Quoted from the State Archives, Siena, by Pastor: *op. cit.*, p. 337.

14. *Ibid.*

15. Casanova: *op. cit.*, p. 26.

16. The last pages of his *Vita Pii Pont. Max.;* Muratori: *op. cit.* Also, see a long letter by Ammanati to Cardinal Francesco Piccolomini, *Epist. Card. Pap.*, no. XLI.

17. *Epistolae*, no. 41.

18. He did not reach Ancona until 25th July: see Pastor: *op. cit.*, p. 356.

19. In the State Archives at Siena.

20. Pastor: *op. cit.*, p. 358.

21. Campano: *op. cit.*

22. Given by Pastor: *op. cit.*, p. 372, n.

SELECT BIBLIOGRAPHIES

I. CHRONOLOGY OF THE CHIEF WORKS OF AENEAS SYLVIUS PICCOLOMINI

c. 1427   *Cinthia.* Printed by G. Cugnoni: *Atti Academia Lincei,* ser. iii, vol. VIII (1883), pp. 342–8

c. 1435   *Nymphilexis

1440   *Libellus dialogorum de Generalis Concilii authoritate et gestis Basiliensium*
Printed by A. F. Kollar: *Analecta monumentorum omnis aevi Vindobonensia,* vol. II, col. 691–790, Vienna, 1762.

1440   *De gestis Basiliensis Concilii*
Printed in the *Opera Omnia,* Basel, 1571, pp. 1–63.

1443   *Pentalogus*
Printed by B. Pez: *Thesaurus anecdotorum novissimus,* Vol. IV, part iii, pp. 736–44. Vienna, 1721–9.

3.7.1444   *Historia de Eurialo et Lucretia*
Printed by Wolkan: *op. cit.,* Ep. 152, also in the *Opera Omnia,* pp. 353–93. The best critical edition, ed. I. Devay, Budapest, 1904. German trans. Halle, 1914. Italian trans. Milan, 1936. *The Tale of the Two Lovers,* trans. Flora Grierson. London, 1929.

1444   *De natura et cura equorum*
Printed by Wolkan: *op. cit.,* part i, Ep. 154.

1444   *Epistola de curialium miseriis*
Printed by Wolkan: *op. cit.,* part i, Ep. 166, and in the *Opera Omnia,* pp. 720–36. Italian trans. by G. Paparelli, Lanciano, 1943. English version by W. P. Mustard, Baltimore, 1928.

1.10.1444   *Chrysis*
Ed. Ireneo Sanesi, Florence, 1941.
*English translation by Flora Grierson.

1446   *De ortu et authoritate Romani Imperii*
Printed by Wolkan: *op. cit.,* part ii, Ep. 3.
Text and translation (German) in G. Kallen: *Aeneas Silvius Piccolomini als Publizist,* Cologne, 1939.

1440–50   *De viris aetate sua claris*
Printed by J. D. Mansi: *Pii II Pont. Max. Orationes politicae et ecclesiasticae,* vol. III, pp. 144–213, Lucca, 1755–9.

1450   *De liberorum educatione*
Printed by Wolkan: *op. cit.,* part ii, Ep. 40: in the *Opera Omnia,*

pp. 963–92. Text and English trans. with introduction by J. S. Nelson, Washington, 1940. (See also Woodward: *op. cit.*, pp. 134–58.)

*A very beautiful MS. copy made for the sons of Francesco Sforza is in Milan, Bibl. Ambrosiana, Cod. T. 7. Supr.

1450   *De rebus Basileae gestis stante vel dissoluto concilio*
Printed by Wolkan: *op. cit.*, part ii, Ep. 44, also in C. Fea: *Pius II Pont. Max. a calumniis vindicatus*, pp. 31–115, Rome, 1823.

After 1450   *Dialogus de Somnio*
Printed at Rome, 11th September 1475, by Johann Schurener, also in the *Opera Omnia*.

1453   *Historia Gothorum*
R. Duellii: *Biga librorum rariorum*, Frankfurt, 1730.

1454   *Historia de Ratisponensi dieta*
Printed by Mansi: *Orationes*, vol. III, pp. 1–85.

1456   *Commentarii in libros Antonii Panormitae Poetae de dictis et factis Alphonsii Regis*
Printed in the *Opera Omnia*, pp. 472–99.

1456   *Artis retoricae praecepta*
Printed in the *Opera Omnia*, pp. 992–1034.

1457   *De ritu, situ, moribus et conditione Germaniae descriptio*
Printed in the *Opera Omnia*, pp. 1034–86.
Italian trans. *La Germania* by G. Paparelli, Florence, 1949.

Before 1458   *Historia Friderici Imperatoris*
Printed in the *Opera geographica et historica*, Helmstadt, 1699–1700. Also by Kollar: *op. cit.*, vol. II.

1458   *De Europa*
Printed in the *Opera Omnia*, pp. 387–471.

1458   *Historia Bohemica*
Printed in the *Opera Omnia*, pp. 81–143.

1460   *Lettera a Maometto II*, printed by G. Toffanin, Naples, 1952.

1461   *De Asia*
Printed in the *Opera Omnia*, pp. 281–386.

1463   *Supra Decades Blondi Epitome*
Printed in the *Opera Omnia*, pp. 144–281.

ORATIONS: These have been collected and published by J. D. Mansi: *Pii Pont. Max. Orationes politicae et ecclesiasticae*, 3 vols., Lucca, 1755–9 (and a later edition, 1842). Many were printed individually in the XVth century (*e.g. De captione urbis Constantinopolitanae* [n.d.] and *Oratio coram Calixto III de obedentia Friderici III* [n.d.], both by Stephan Plannck).

EPISTLES: Some of these have been printed individually or in small collections (*e.g. Epistolae in Cardinalatu editae* by Bartholomeus Guldinbeck, Stephan Plannck and others) but the main edition is that of

Rudolf Wolkan: *Der Briefwechsel des Aeneas Silvius P.* in *Fontes
Rerum Austriacarum*, ser. ii, vols. LXI; LXII; LXVII; LXVIII. Vienna,
1909–18. This covers the years from 1431–50. A. Weiss printed
149 letters in an appendix to his *Aeneas Silvius Piccolomini als
Papst Pius II*, Graz, 1897. See also G. Voigt: 'Die Briefe des
Aeneas Silvius vor seiner Erhebung auf den päpstlichen Stuhl',
Archiv für Kunde Österreichischer Geschichts-Quellen, XVI, pp.
321–424, Vienna, 1857. Forty-two letters concerning the war in
Naples were printed by Achille Ratti in *Archivio Storico Lombardo*,
ser. iii, vol. XIX (1903), pp. 263–93.

The *Opera Omnia*, pp. 500–962, contains the better known letters, but a number—mostly of minor importance—are still un-
printed. See the article by R. Wolkan: 'Die Briefe des Eneas Silvius vor seiner Erhebung auf den päpstlichen Stuhl' in *Archiv.
für österr. Geschichte*, Bd. XCIII, ii (Vienna, 1905), where he lists
and describes some of his sources (e.g. Cod. 1200 in the Bibl.
Univ. at Bologna).

* Unpublished letters, some of them autograph, are to be found
in the libraries of the British Museum, the Vatican, Siena (Archivio
di Stato), Florence (Bibl. Naz., Riccardiana, and Laurenziana:
esp. Cod. 90. 44), Milan (Bibl. Ambrosiana and Trivulziana),
also in Basel and at Prague†.

THE COMMENTARIES: The original MS., largely in Aeneas's own hand, was
given by him to Campano for revision, and his scribe Johannes Gobellinus of Lins was ordered to make a copy. This version
was signed by the scribe, when he completed it on 12th June
1464. It is now in the Vatican Library (Cod. Corsini 35 b.11).
When this manuscript came into the hands of Pius's kinsman Francesco Bandini Piccolomini, Archbishop of Siena, a century later, the
Archbishop edited it most stringently—actuated by the highest motives—cutting out all the more racy passages. He even withheld
Aeneas's name from the title page when he published the work
in 1584, and it is ascribed to the German Gobellinus who had written out the *Commentaries* so diligently and in so fair a hand. The
first twelve books were reprinted, together with the *Commentaries*
and *Epistles* of Jacopo Ammanati, at Frankfurt in 1614: this is
the best version and the one used throughout this work. The thirteenth book was published by Voigt: *op. cit.*, Bd. ii, pp. 359–77.

The original MS. in the Vatican, now Cod. Reginense 1995, was,
however, found and studied (on this point see Pastor: *op. cit.*,
vol. III: appendix 65). The omitted passages were published by

† I have only been able to consult those in the British Museum and a number
of others in Italian libraries. It does not seem likely that those remaining unpublished contain material of outstanding importance.

G. Cugnoni, keeper of the Chigi Library, from yet another MS. in 1883. See also G. Lesca: *I commentarii di Pio II*, Pisa, 1894. The *Commentarii* still await a complete and fully critical edition.

Two English translations have been made in this generation; one of them, by the Misses F. A. Gragg and L. C. Gabel in the U.S.A. (*Smith College Studies*, vols. XXII; XXV; XXX; XXXV and XLIII); also extracted passages under the title *Memoirs of a Renaissance Pope*, New York, 1959. The other was completed by °Miss Flora Grierson some years ago, after prolonged study of the Vatican and other MSS., but it has never been published. The typescript is deposited in four volumes in the Bodleian Library at Oxford, MSS. Eng. Hist. α 381–4; all the quotations in this book are taken from it. It has not been found practical to mark the passages from the original that are excluded from the Frankfurt 1614 edition, but Miss Grierson has indicated them clearly in her typescript.

Two extracts from the *Commentaries*, together with an Italian translation, are given by Eugenio Garin in his *Prosatori latini del quattrocento*, Milan/Naples, 1952, pp. 663–87. These concern (i) the Conclave of 1458 and (ii) the expedition to Tivoli.

II. AUTHORITIES

ADY, CECILIA M. *A History of Milan under the Sforza:* London, 1907.
Pius II, London, 1913.
'Pius II and his experiences of England, Scotland and the English', *English Miscellany,* vol. IX, Rome, 1950.

AMMANATI, JACOPO *Epistolae et commentarii Jacobi Piccolomini, Cardinalis Papiensis,* Milan, 1506. (Also in the Frankfurt 1614 edition of *Pii II Commentarii.*)

°ARETINO, FRANCESCO (ACCOLTI) Latin version of *Epistola Diogeni* with dedicatory letter to Pius II; Bologna, Bibl. Comunale, Cod. A. 914, 1–13.

ARMSTRONG, EDWARD *Italian Studies,* ed. C. M. Ady, London, 1934.

ATIYA, AZIZ SURYAL *The Crusade in the later Middle Ages,* London, 1938.

BABINGER, F. *Maometto il conquistatore e il suo tempo,* Turin, 1957.

BARBACCI, A. 'Il restauro del duomo di Pienza', in *La Diana* IX (1934).

BARON, HANS *The crisis of the early Italian Renaissance,* Princeton, 1955.

BATTAGLIA, FELICE *Enea Silvio Piccolomini e Francesco Patrizi: due politici senesi del quattrocento,* Siena, 1936.

BAYER, J. *Die 'Historia Friderici III' des E. S. Piccolomini,* Prague, 1872.

BEAUCOURT, DU FRESNE DE *Histoire de Charles VII,* Paris, 1890.

BECCADELLI, ANTONIO (PANORMITA) *De dictis et factis Alphonsi regis Aragonum libri IV.* (With the commentary of A. S. Piccolomini.) Florence, 1491.

BERTONI, G. *Poeti e poesie del medio evo e del rinascimento,* Modena, 1922.

BETT, H. *Nicholas of Cusa,* London, 1932.

BIRCK, M. 'Enea Silvio de Piccolomini als Geschichtsschreiber des Basler Konzils', in *Theol. Quartalschr. Jahrg. LXXVI* (1894).

BISTICCI, VESPASIANO DA *Vite di uomini illustri del secolo XV*, ed. E. Aeschlimann & P. d'Ancona, Milan, 1951.

BOULTING, W. *Aeneas Silvius*, London, 1908. (Uncritical praise of the subject. Should be read in conjunction with Voigt's indictment.)

BRINTON, SELWYN *The Gonzaga Lords of Mantua*, London, 1927.

BROWN, HORATIO F. *Venetian Studies*, London, 1887.

BROWN, RAWDON (Ed.) *Cal. State Papers in MSS . . . in Venice*, etc., vol. I, London, 1864.

BÜRCK, GERHART *Selbstdarstellung und Personenbildnis bei Enea Silvio Piccolomini*, Stuttgart, 1956.

BURCKHARDT, J. *Die Kultur der Renaissance in Italien*, trans. by S. G. C. Middlemore, London, 1929.

CALAMARI, GIUSEPPE *Il confidente di Pio II (Card. Iacopo Ammanati–Piccolomini) 1422–1479*, 2 vols., Rome–Milan, 1932.

CAMPANO, GIOVANNI ANTONIO *Vita Pii II Pont. Max.* in Muratori: *Rerum Ital. Scriptores*, III, part ii, Milan, 1734.

CAPUA, BLESSED RAYMOND OF *The Life of St Catherine of Siena*, trans. George Lamb, London, 1960.

CARLI, E. *La pittura senese*, Florence, 1955.

CASANOVA, EUGENIO 'Un anno della vita privata di Pio II', in *Bullettino Senese di Storia Patria*, 1931.

CASTIGLIONE, BALDASSARE *Il Cortegiano*, ed. V. Cain, Florence, 1908. (Eng. trans. by Sir Thomas Hoby: Everyman ed.)

CATERINA, SANTA *Epistolario Santa Caterina*, ed. Niccolò Tommaseo, Siena, 1913.

CHMEL, J. *Regesta Chronologico-Diplomatica Frederici III*, Vienna, 1840.

COGNASSO, F. *Amadeo VIII*, 2 vols., Turin, 1930.

*COTTA, GIOVANNI STEFANO *Epistolae*, Parma, R. Bibl. Palatina, Cod-Parm. 27, art. v.

CREIGHTON, MANDELL *History of the Papacy*, etc. (new edn.), London, 1897, vol. III. *Historical Essays and Reviews*, London, 1902.

DENNISTOUN, J. *Memoirs of the Dukes of Urbino*, 3 vols., London, 1852. (New edn. ed. E. Hutton, London, 1903.)

DOUGLAS, R. LANGTON *History of Siena*, London, 1902.

DUCHESNE, L. *De Codicibus MSS. Graecis Pii II in Bibliotheca Alexandrina-Vaticana*, Paris, 1880.

ENCYCLOPAEDIAS *Enciclopedia italianica* (new edn. 1949). *Dizionario enciclopedico italiano*, Rome, 1957.

EUBEL, C. *Hierarchia catholica medii aevi*, vol. II (2nd edn.), Münster, 1914.

FAZIO, BARTOLOMEO *De Viris Illustribus*, ed. L. Mehus, Florence, 1745.

FERMO *Cronache della città di Fermo*, ed. G. de Mincis & M. Tebarrini, Florence, 1870.

*FERRARIIS, GIOVANNI MATTEO DE *Comment. super Avicenna*, with dedication to Pius II, Oxford, Bodleian Library MS. Digby 135.

FERRI, F. *La giovinezza di un poeta*, Rimini, 1914.

FILELFO, FRANCESCO *Epistolae*, Venice, 1502.

FLAVIO, BIONDO, OFFORLÌ *Opera*, Basel, 1559 (for *Roma Triumphans*). *Scritti inediti e rari*, ed. B. Nogara, Rome, 1927.

FRATI, L., 'E.S.P. imitatore di Dante' in *Nuova Antologia* (1920), pp. 169–171.

FRITTELLI, UGO 'Le prediche volgari di San Bernardino da Siena', in *Bullettino Senese di Storia Patria*, 1931.

FRUGONI, A. 'E. S. Piccolomini e l'avventura senese di G. Schlik', in *Rinascita* (March 1941).

FUMI, L. 'Pio II e la pace di Orvieto', in *Studi e documenti di storia e diritto* (anno VI, fasc. IV), Rome, 1885.

FUMI, L., & LISINI, A. *L'incontro di Federico III imperatore con Eleanora di Portogallo . . . in Siena*, Siena, 1878.

GARIN, EUGENIO 'Ritratto di Enea Silvio Piccolomini', in *Bullettino Senese di Storia Patria*, ser. iii, anno XVII, Siena, 1958.

GILL, J. S. *The Council of Florence*, Cambridge, 1959.

GREGOROVIUS, F. *Geschichte der Stadt Rom im Mittelalter*, English trans. by Mrs A. Hamilton: *History of the City of Rome in the Middle Ages*, London, 1894–1902.

GRIERSON, FLORA 'Frank Confession', in *The London Magazine*, vol. I (1954); see also trans. of *Chrysis*, the *Commentaries*, etc.

HAY, DENYS *The Italian Renaissance in its Historical Background*, Cambridge, 1961.

HERVAL, RENÉ 'Euryale et Lucrèce (un roman d'amour siennois conté par un futur pape)', *Bullettino Senese di Storia Patria*, ser. iii, anno XVII, Siena, 1958.

HEYWOOD, WILLIAM *A Pictorial Chronicle of Siena*, Siena, 1902 (new edn. 1927). *Palio and ponte*, London, 1904. *History of Perugia*, London, 1910.

HINDS, A. B. (Ed.) *Cal. State Papers and MSS . . . in Milan*, vol. I, London 1912.

HUTTON, EDWARD *Sigismondo Pandolfo Malatesta, lord of Rimini*, London, 1906.

JACOB, E. F. (Ed.) *Italian Renaissance Studies*, London, 1960. (See also Peter Partner and others.)

KALLEN, G. *Aen. Silv. Piccolomini als Publizist*, Cologne, 1939.

KITCHIN, G. W. *Life of Pius II as illustrated by Pinturicchio's Frescoes*, London, 1881.

KRISTELLER, P. O. *The Classics and Renaissance Thought*, Cambridge (Mass.), 1955; *Studies in Renaissance Thought and Letters*, Rome, 1956.

LANE, F. C. *Venetian Ships and Shipbuilders of the Renaissance*, Baltimore, 1934.

LITTA, P. *Famiglie celebri italiane*, 11 vols., Milan & Turin, 1819–1899.

LUNGO, ISIDORO DEL *Umanista e pontefice*, Florence, 1905.

MALAVOLTI, ORLANDO *Historia de' fatti e guerre de' Senesi*, Venice, 1599.

MANUCCI, G. B. 'Il palazzo di Pio II ed i suoi restauri', in *Rassegna d'Arte Senese*, anno VII, Siena 1911. *Pienza: arte e storia* (3rd edn.), Pienza, 1937.

MARCOTTI, G. 'Il giubileo dell'anno 1450 secondo una relazione di Giovanni Rucellai', in *Arch. Soc. romana di Storia Patria*, IV (1881).

MAZZUCHELLI, C. *Gli scrittori d'Italia*, 2 vols., Brescia, 1753.

MILLER, W. *The Latins in the Levant*, London, 1908.

MITCHELL, R. J. *John Tiptoft*, London, 1938.

John Free. London, 1954.

'English Students in Early Renaissance Italy' in *Italian Studies*, vol. VIII (1952).

'Italian "Nobiltà" and the English Idea of the Gentleman in the XVth Century' in *English Miscellany*, vol. IX, Rome, 1958.

MORPURGO-CASTELNUOVO, M. 'Il cardinale Domenico Capranica' in *Arch. della Soc. romana di Storia Patria*, LII, Rome, 1929.

PACHT, OTTO *Italian illuminated manuscripts*, Oxford, 1948.

PAPARELLI, GIOACCHINO *Enea Silvio Piccolomini*, Bari, 1950.

'La Germania di E. S. Piccolomini' in *Italica*, vol. XXXV, no. 3, pp. 202–216 (1948).

PARDI, GIUSEPPE *Borso d'Este*, Pisa, 1906–7.

PAREDI, A. *La biblioteca del Pizzolpasso*, Milan, 1961†.

PARTNER, PETER 'Camera Papae: problems of papal finance in the later Middle Ages' in *Journal of Ecc. History*, IV (1953). *The Papal State under Martin V*, London, 1958. 'The "Budget" of the Roman Church in the Renaissance Period' in *Italian Renaissance Studies*, London, 1960.

PASCHINI, PIO *Roma nel rinascimento*, Bologna, 1940.

PASTOR, LUDWIG VON *Geschichte der Päpste*, Freiburg (new edn.), 1926. Eng. trans. by F. I. Antrobus: *History of the Popes*, London, 1898, vol. III.

PÉROUSE, G. *Le Cardinal Louis Aleman, président du concile de Bâle, et la fin du grand schisme*, Paris, 1905.

PICCOLOMINI, E. 'Alcuni documenti inediti intorno a Pio II e a Pio IV' in *Atti e mem. della sezione letteraria di Storia Patria*, new ser., vol. I, Siena, 1871.

PICOTTI, G. B. *La dieta di Mantova* (R. Dep. Ven. di Storia Patria Misc., ser. IV, vol. IV), Venice, 1912.

Di un manoscritto bolognese dei 'Commentarii' di Pio II ('Archiginnasio' ser. ii, no. VIII), Bologna, 1913.

'La pubblicazione e i primi effeti della "Execrabilis" di Pio II', in *Arch. della Soc. romana di Storia Patria*, XXXVII (1924).

PIERACCINI, G. *La stirpe de' Medici di Caffaggiolo*, 3 vols., Florence, 1924–1925.

PLATINA, BATTISTA *Vita Pii II*. (Prefixed to the 1571 edn. of A. S. Piccolomini, *Opera*.)

*PORCELLIO (GIANNANTONIO DE' PANDONI) *Carmina* dedicated to Pius II. Paris, Bibliothèque Nationale, MS. lat. 8384.

PRUNAI, GIULIO 'Lo studio senese dalla "migratio" bolognese alla fondazione

† This book did not come to hand in time for reference to be made to the useful information it contains concerning the young Aeneas. See especially pp. 234–7.

dalla "Domus Sapientiae" (1321–1408)' in *Bullettino Senese di Storia Patria*, ser. iii (1950).

RASHDALL, HASTINGS *Universities of Europe in the Middle Ages*, ed. F. M. Powicke & A. B. Emden, Oxford, 1936, 3 vols.

RICCI, CORRADO *Pinturicchio*, Perugia, 1912.

ROSMINI, C. *Vita di Francesco Filelfo*, Milan, 1808.

ROSS, JANET *Lives of the early Medici as told in their correspondence*, London, 1910.

ROSSI, VITTORIO 'Gli statuti di Pienza' in *Arte e storia*, Florence, 1910. *Storia letteraria d'Italia*, vol. i, Milan, 1945.

ROTH, CECIL *The History of the Jews in Italy*, Philadelphia, 1946.

ROTTA, P. *Il cardinale Niccolò di Cusa*, Milan, 1928.

SABBADINI, REMIGIO *Il metodo degli umanisti*, Florence, 1920.

SAITTA, GIUSEPPE *Il pensiero italiano nell'umanesimo e nel rinascimento* (vol. i), Bologna, 1949.

SANTORO, CATERINA *Codici miniati del rinascimento italiano*, Milan, 1952.

SCEVOLA, MARIOTTI 'Sul testo e le fonti comiche della *Chrysis* di E. S. Piccolomini' in *Annali* della Scuola Normale Superiore, classe di Lettere, ser. ii, vol. xv (1946).

SCHIVENOGLIA, A. *Cronaca di Mantova*, ed. Carlo d'Arco. In *Raccolta di . . . documenti storici lombardi inediti*, vol. ii, Milan, 1857.

SIENA *Bullettino della Società Senese degli Amici dei Monumenti nel quinto Centenario del Pontificato di Pio II° e della Canonizzazione di Santa Caterina*, Siena, 1958–9.

SILVESTRI, CAN. D. ALFREDO S. *Caterina, patrona primaria d'Italia e Pio II*, Pistoja, 1940.

SIZERANNE, ROBERT DE LA *Le Vertueux Condottière Federigo de Montefeltro duc d'Urbino*, Paris, 1927.

SOLDATI, B. *La poesia astrologica del 400*, Florence, 1906.

SORANZO, G. *Pio II e la politica italiana nella lutta contro i Malatesti* (1457–63), Padua, 1911. (Ed.) *Cronaca di un anonimo veronese* (1446–1488); *R. Dep. Ven. di Storia Patria–Monumenti*, ser. iii, vol. iv, Venice, 1915.

SORBELLI, ALBANO *Storia della università di Bologna*, Bologna, 1940.

SOUTHERN, R. W. *Western Views of Islam in the Middle Ages*, Cambridge, Mass., 1962.

SPADOLINI, E. *L'archivio storico comunale d'Ancona*, Ancona, n.d.

SYMONDS, JOHN ADDINGTON *The Renaissance in Italy* (new edn.), London, 1909, vol. i.

New Italian Sketches, Leipzig, 1884.

TAILETTI, ALBERTO 'Pio II e l'ospedale maggiore di Milano' in *Bullettino Senese di Storia Patria*, ser. iii, anno XVII, Siena, 1958.

TIRABOSCHI, G. *Storia della letteratura italiana*, vol. vi, Rome, 1783.

TOFFANIN, GIUSEPPE *Storia dell'umanesimo*, Naples, n.d.

TUCCIA, NICCOLA DELLA *Cronaca di Viterbo*, ed. I. Ciampi, Florence, 1872.

TWEMLOW, J. A. Ed. *Calendars of Papal Registers*, vol. XI (1455–1464), London, 1921.

VALLE, NICCOLÒ DE Translation of Hesiod, with *dedication* to Pius II, Rome; Sweynheym and Pannartz, 1471. (Proctor 3317.)

Epistola Constantinopolis ad Romam et Romae ad Constantinopole, printed (no date) by Stephan Plannck and by Johann Schurener.

VALTURIO, ROBERTO *De re militari*, Verona, 1472.

VAST, H. *Le Cardinal Bessarion* (1403–1472), Paris, 1878.

VERMIGLIOLI, G. B. *Di Bernardino Pinturicchio*, Perugia, 1837.

VOIGT, G. *Enea Silvio de' Piccolomini als Papst Pius II und sein Zeitalter*, 3 vols., Berlin, 1856–63 (new edn. Berlin, 1892).

WALEY, D. P. *Medieval Orvieto*, Cambridge, 1952.

The Papal State in the XIIIth Century, London, 1961.

WEISS, A. *Aeneas Silvius Piccolomini als Papst Pius II: sein Leben und Einfluss auf die literarische Kultur Deutschlands*, Graz, 1897.

WEISS, ROBERTO *Un umanista veneziano, Papa Paolo II*, Venice/Rome, 1958.

WIDMER, BERTHE *E. S. Piccolomini, Papst Pius II*, Basel/Stuttgart, 1960.

WOODWARD, W. H. *Vittorino da Feltre and other Humanist Educators*, Cambridge, 1897.

ZANNONI, G. 'Per la storia di due amanti' in *Atti della R. Accademia dei Lincei*, ser. IV, vol. VI, Rome, 1890.

ZDEKAUER, L. *Lo studio di Siena nel rinascimento*, Milan, 1894. 'Un consulto medico dato a Pio II' in *Bullettino Senese di Storia Patria*, vol. V (1898).

ZONTA, GASPARO 'Un conflitto tra la Repubblica Veneta e la Curia Romana per l'episcopato di Padova (1459–60)' in *Atti e Memorie della R. Accademia di Scienze, Lettere ed Arti in Padova*, vol. XL (1924).

INDEX

Date Due

R			

Demco 293-5